SUE MELLIS has worked in the theatre and for a small press which publishes plays. She combined her publishing experience with her interest in food by running Food & Futures Publishing, which involved publicity and promotion work for small food businesses, and a series of cookery books, including *The Wholefood Express*, which she co-wrote with Maggi Sikking. She is a keen organic gardener.

BARBARA DAVIDSON has run the kitchen in a wide assortment of catering establishments. She teaches wholefood cookery to retailers, caterers and at evening classes and helped set up East West Kitchen, a women's co-operative which supplies Asian food to retailers and hospitals, and Phoenix Foods, a new organic bakery. She is author of *Catering Without Meat*, and has contributed recipes to numerous publications, including *The Wholefood Express*.

THE ·BORN~AGAIN· CARNIVORE

THE REAL MEAT GUIDE

SUE MELLIS and BARBARA DAVIDSON

ILLUSTRATED BY CLARE PICKLES

An OPTIMA Book

© Sue Mellis and Barbara Davidson 1990

First published in 1990 by
Macdonald Optima, a division of
Macdonald & Co. (Publishers) Ltd

A member of Maxwell Macmillan Pergamon Publishing Corporation

All rights reserved

British Library Cataloguing in Publication Data

Mellis, Sue
Born again carnivore.
  1. Meat
  I. Title   II. Davidson, Barbara
  641.36

  ISBN 0-356-18793-4

Macdonald & Co. (Publishers) Ltd
Orbit House
1 New Fetter Lane
London
EC4A 1AR

Typeset in ITC Cheltenham by
Leaper & Gard Ltd, Bristol

Printed and bound in Great Britain
by The Guernsey Press Co. Ltd., Guernsey, Channel Islands.

CONTENTS

Dedication

For Rob, Jim, Thomas and Amy.

Acknowledgements

The authors would like to thank Stephen Greenwood (Master Butcher), Colin Blanchard, John Button, the Argent family, the Bullivant family and all those who gave their support and advice so generously in the making of this book; also Clare Pickles (our vegan friend!) for the illustrations.

INTRODUCTION

In recent years meat has received a lot of bad publicity and many people feel uncomfortable about eating it. Some have reluctantly given it up completely and become vegetarian, and probably many more feel that they should. The reasons for this unease are many and varied – concern for farm animals, concern about health, concern about the environment, or simply boredom with the blandness and poor quality of modern meat. Some farmers are responding to this anxiety, and good-quality humanely reared meat is thankfully becoming more freely available.

Doing justice to meat requires a different set of cooking techniques from those that serve for lentils and brown rice. We hope to reintroduce you to traditional meat cookery, often surprisingly simple and quick, so that you can really enjoy your meat. We have also given some background to farming, so that as a consumer you are better able to make your own judgements about what you eat and lend your support to those farmers trying to set new standards. Their efforts deserve encouragement – for the sake of our freedom of choice, the safety and quality of our food supply and the health of our environment.

Part 1
A BONE OF CONTENTION

WHAT SHALL WE EAT?

Since the late 1960s, people have started to take more notice of what they eat. Meat has, in many ways, become the most suspect and confusing part of our diet, and in some circles people no longer feel entirely comfortable admitting that they still eat it. Many have given it up, and many more of us do not enjoy it as we used to. Paradoxically, our anxieties don't seem to extend beyond our own kitchens, where we have most control. While sales of recognisable fresh meat are falling, sales of anonymous, nicely disguised meat products like pies and burgers are rising, and we are eating more meat prepared for us in restaurants.

The vegetarian cause has been one of the great success stories of the 1970s and 80s. The reasons for this are many and varied. Most people know something about conditions on factory farms, yet feel powerless to change them. We have become preoccupied with our own diet-related conditions such as cancer, heart disease and obesity. We have discovered that those with a sedentary lifestyle need less meat, and that eating plenty of fruit and vegetables gives us the fibre we need and helps keep our fat consumption down.

Then there are the health scares about salmonella, listeria and BSE – the list is seemingly endless. Add to all this the decline in the quality of meat, the blandness and lack of flavour, and the rise in price, particularly during the inflationary 1970s, and the waning of enthusiasm for fresh meat is understandable.

Far from dismissing vegetarians as cranky, many uneasy meat eaters now seem happy to concede the moral high ground to them. Coming up alongside the vegetarians, with an even more persuasive argument, are the vegans, people who don't eat any animal products at all. Their position is logical. For every female animal which provides vegetarians with eggs or milk, nature ensures a male counterpart. In the case of cattle they are fattened up, slaughtered and eaten, for what else is there to do with them? The male chicks whose sisters are destined for the battery have a more ignominious end – crushed or gassed in their thousands every day before they can demand to be fed. Why, say the vegans, should any animal be kept for the benefit of humans, especially when many argue that our digestive systems are designed only to take plant foods. So no more meat, no more milk, and no more cheese, eggs and honey; simply vegetables, nuts, cereals and fruit, and the choice between time-consuming, carefully balanced meals or a dependency on supplements to guard against the deficiencies which might arise from such a restricted diet. Not a welcome or practical prospect for most people.

HOW SHALL WE PRODUCE OUR FOOD?

Vegans are also offering the ultimate challenge to the farming community. There is no doubt that in order to feed a nation of vegans we would have to change the countryside beyond recognition. Lowland areas would be covered with intensive cereals and thousands of acres of glasshouses, all heavily dependent for the foreseeable future on chemical pesticides and artificial fertilisers. Without grazing animals to maintain them the hill pastures would be destroyed by the spread of nettles and scrub. The balance of nature, precarious even now, would be given a massive blow.

But there is a better way – the adoption of sustainable mixed agriculture, providing us with a wholefood diet in which meat plays a small but valuable part. This sort of rational farming has continued alongside conventional farming for years, but interest is mushrooming now that surpluses are being actively discouraged and farmers are seeking to diversify. For the foreseeable future livestock will play an essential part in a sustainable system – living outside for much of the year on grassland, in woodland and in the wild, converting food which we cannot eat into food for us. Arable and vegetable crops are fertilised by animal dung, and the soil is protected by it.

Farming in this way without the use of chemicals receives no subsidy, and is hard to practise in today's economic climate. The 'born-again carnivore' can play an active part in encouraging it by demanding and buying good healthy meat which is humanely produced. It is a form of support which is urgently needed, and it stops us over-indulging at the same time. When fewer animals are kept, in better conditions and with production governed by the seasons, meat reaches its true value and every part is put to good use in a spirit of thankfulness.

MEAT IN A WHOLEFOOD DIET

History alone should teach us that human beings are not herbivores or carnivores, but omnivores. It is not in our nature as animals to ignore a valuable source of nutrients – other animals – when they come our way. In the past, when meat was often hard to come by, it was usually prized above all other foods for its nutritive value as well as its flavour. In many parts of the world it still enjoys this status. When meat became cheaper and universally available, it was only to be expected that it would become the central part of nearly every meal. Although we now accept that it is not essential, it can play a part in a healthy diet – a valuable but occasional food to be eaten and relished.

Meat is an excellent source of protein which is easily assimilated into the body. It is also rich in vitamins and minerals, especially the offal or vital organs where the essential nutrients of the animal's food have been stored. (Though the toxins taken in by the animal are also stored there, as well as in the fat, which means that only the offal of animals which have been reared without chemicals should be eaten.)

There are other nutritional advantages in good meat, especially if the animal has been allowed plenty of exercise and a natural diet. There will be less fat from such a beast and it will not contain pesticide residues. Game, coming as it does from wild animals, has the least amount of fat and the smallest proportion of saturated fat. It is more than possible that the harmful effects of animal fats may be due in part to modern methods of rearing and cooking. If we follow the wholefood principle, instead of relying on a continuous supply of chicken drumsticks and steaks, we should learn again how to use all edible parts of the animal. This would give us a good balance of nutrients, and balance the rich and concentrated meat with the bulk of fresh vegetables, fruit and cereals. In this way we can make meat part of a healthy and enjoyable diet.

GETTING IN A STEW – CAUSES FOR CONCERN

THE RISE OF THE FACTORY FARM

Successive British governments have wanted to supply people with cheap food, and in pursuit of this aim they have subjected food and farming businesses to constantly changing economic pressures. Since its inception the Ministry of Agriculture, Food and Fisheries has had enormous influence over producers, encouraging them to take advantage of technological advances and new methods which have brought increased yields and profits. Thus, despite rises in labour and land costs, cheap food is still a reality, and one which we continue to cherish. We have reached a point where, although as a nation we are more prosperous than ever, we spend less and less of our disposable incomes on food, apparently unaware of the paradox of paying high prices for high quality clothes, cars and holidays, while at the same time complaining when the price of bread goes up by a few pence.

Whereas in the past most farms had a mixture of interdependent enterprises, modern farmers have had to specialise to provide us with this cornucopia. This is especially true of pig and poultry farming – the farmer doesn't need expensive land to accommodate the livestock and grow food for them or expensive workers to look after them. Pigs and poultry can live indoors, looked after semi-automatically and fed cereals which have been grown cheaply with chemicals by other specialist farmers. Similar systems are now being developed for sheep and cattle. In a competitive market the farmer is forced to choose the most economical methods to produce the cheapest product.

These short cuts, which enable us to eat pork chops or roast chicken every day of the week, might seem like a good thing, but they have been achieved at a price. Consumers are now beginning to realise that cheap meat usually means energy-hungry farming, inhumane conditions for animals and poor quality meat. It's an area of complicated issues where controversy burns brightly and vitriol flows, but despite the health warnings let's take a brief look at some of these causes for concern.

HUNGRY FARMS

In order to take advantage of new technology, farmers have been offered subsidies and encouraged to take on loans, just as other businesses do. Although some large farms have made huge profits under this system, smaller farmers have sometimes become imprisoned by financial constraints, and in many cases are permanently wedded to the new methods. These new methods are usually described as 'efficient', but their real cost is largely hidden. Not only have taxpayers had to fork out money for subsidies, but the farms themselves have guzzled resources with little choice but to spew them out again in the form of pollution. The success and power of the multinational agrochemical companies is telling evidence of the scale of farm inputs.

On an arable farm, fossil fuels are used to run farm machinery, and crops are grown with chemicals and artificial fertilisers which create pollution in their use *and* in their manufacture. On a livestock farm, where there was once a bucket to feed the animals from, there is now likely to be a computer controlling their diet. Animals are fed by automatic systems and permanently housed in buildings which have to be heated and lit. They eat massive amounts of cereals, grown here and in the Third World on land which could be used to grow food for people, and their effluence has become a major source of water pollution in this country.

Thus the real cost of cheap food produced by the farming industry remains largely hidden. The huge resources needed for its production come from chemical factories many miles away, and the resulting pollution adds to the anonymous burden of chemicals already borne by the air we breathe and the water we drink.

ANIMAL WELFARE

There are numerous laws, regulations and codes of welfare governing the keeping of farm animals, and the Ministry of Agriculture has the responsibility for administering these rules. Yet many of those concerned with animal welfare feel that the Ministry is far too lenient. Farms are unlikely to be checked without prior notice, and the policy of the Ministry is to try to persuade and guide the errant farmer to improve conditions, with prosecution a rarely-used last resort. It has been left to charities like the RSPCA to bring prosecutions against farmers. The Farm Animal Welfare Council, an independent advisory body set up by the Ministry, is continually reviewing methods of husbandry and making recommendations for improvements, but the Ministry is under no obligation to take them up. The Protection of Animals Act of 1911 forbids us all to allow our animals 'unnecessary suffering', but there now seems to be a tacit admission that to feed the nation with cheap factory-farmed produce the suffering of animals *is* necessary.

Confinement

Keeping animals for food will always involve a certain amount of unnatural confinement, but developments in factory farming have progressively robbed animals of every opportunity to express their normal behaviour. Many never see the light of day or breathe fresh, clean air, and they are penned in a minimum of space with little or no opportunity to form relationships with their companions. Indeed, in the case of pigs they may be permanently shackled to the floor to prevent them from fighting. Depriving an animal of exercise leads to poor muscle tone and circulation and a high level of fat in the meat. Eating such animals cannot be beneficial to our own health.

Breeding

As with confinement, the improvement of stock by controlled breeding has always been an intrinsic part of farming. Traditional agricultures have maintained a large diversity of strains and breeds to suit the local conditions. This provided a 'pool' of mixed genes, so that inbreeding was avoided and new characteristics could be developed when needed. Nowadays large-scale commercial breeders tend to concentrate on the reproduction of a few 'desirable' traits, often pushing them too far. The modern hybrid chicken and pig are the same all over the country, and don't have to suit different conditions. They have unnaturally heavy bodies to give the maximum amount of meat, but they also have congenitally weak legs. In the short term this doesn't matter because they aren't ever going to walk very far, they don't need to protect themselves from predators, and aren't able to reproduce.

But if the breeding stock all have identical characteristics this reduces the options and dilutes the gene pool. Farmers looking for animals which will produce good quality, flavoursome meat on free-range and a natural diet are grateful that the traditional and primitive breeds are still – just about – in existence, kept alive in many cases by enthusiasts.

Diet

Many farm animals, particularly those on factory farms, never eat anything other than a preformed capsule of reconstituted 'food' made from whatever raw material is most readily available on the market. It will be perfectly balanced to give them all their nutritional requirements, with lots of additives to make up for what is lacking in the raw materials but, especially in the case of food for ruminants, it is unlikely to have the roughage they need. This means that digestive disorders can easily arise, causing the animal obvious distress. Raw materials of dubious quality, such as slaughterhouse waste and recycled soiled litter, have already been blamed for outbreaks of food poisoning among consumers and the introduction of the brain disease BSE to the national herd. Animals should be able to stay in good health by eating a wide range of their fresh natural food as they browse, graze and peck at growing herbs and grasses.

Transport to market

As communications have improved, farm animals are being transported greater and greater distances to live-stock markets and eventually slaughterhouses. This is especially true of sheep and cattle, where many farmers specialise in one stage of the growth of the animals, then sell the animals on to other farmers. In this respect the large livestock businesses do have an advantage over the small farmer in that they tend to control the whole life cycle of the animals, so that they are not moved around so much.

Not for nothing do we still describe overcrowded, noisy and degrading conditions as being 'like a cattle market'. Markets are to a great extent an anachronism: frequent movements of animals around the country mean that disease and the illegal use of growth hormones are difficult to trace and control. But, like slaughterhouses, livestock markets have been moved to the outskirts of towns, away from the public gaze, perhaps because we don't like to be reminded of the 'unacceptable face of meat-eating'.

Increased export opportunities also mean that large numbers of animals from British farms are now being transported abroad, often still alive, because foreign buyers want the butchering done to their own standards. Under European Community rulings livestock are classed as agricultural products, not as sentient beings, and a lamb has no more legal protection than a cauliflower. This does nothing to minimise the stress which is the inevitable consequence of such a long journey.

Disease

Animal diseases are and always have been a problem for farmers. Current worries range from disorders related to breeding, like the broiler chicken's ulcerated legs which bear its overweight body, to bacterial and viral infections which can sweep through a group of animals kept in close confinement.

Some of these problems no longer affect the consumer because meat inspectors are well trained to detect signs of such conditions as parasites and TB in the carcass; contaminated meat is rejected. Invisible organisms like salmonella, which are present in the bodies of many animals and which thrive in intensive conditions, have recently become a more intractable problem. These types of bacteria go undetected by the meat inspection system, and as yet there seems to be no effective means of stopping infected meat arriving in the shop. When Edwina Currie MP, then at the Department of Health, stated that most egg production was infected with salmonella, the ensuing fracas led many to suspect that the problem is widespread. Eradicating these problems at source will be extremely difficult now that the meat industry is so large and unwieldy, and the individual consumer has little choice but to take extra care about cooking and hygiene.

The inadequacy of the present system has been shown up by the spread of bovine spongiform encephalopathy (BSE), a new incurable brain disease which started to show up in British cattle in the mid-1980s. Donald Thompson MP, then at MAFF, described it as the worst disaster to hit British agriculture since the War. There are several similar well-documented diseases in goats, deer, cats, dogs and humans, but BSE is believed to be directly related to scrapie, a disease of sheep which has become increasingly common since the 1950s. Its transmission to cattle is likely to have been through feedstuff containing sheep's offal in the form of bonemeal. Since the numbers of sheep have gone up sharply in the 1980s, bonemeal has been increasingly used in concentrates for intensive dairy and beef herds as a protein additive to replace more expensive soya and fish meal.

Afraid that people might start to contract the disease, the Government has gradually brought in controls such as the banning of the sale of milk from infected animals, and the banning of the use of brain and spinal chord tissue in food. These measures seem half-hearted and cosmetic when compared with the delays in making the disease notifiable and the inadequate compensation hitherto paid to farmers who presented an infected animal for slaughter. Even an ordinary milking cow is a valuable beast, and if a farmer suspected symptoms of the disease the temptation to offload it must have been enormous before 100 per cent compensation was paid.

Since the incubation period for this type of disease is several years, and as there is no reliable test, consumers are advised to be cautious. BSE is yet another reason for the consumer not to eat cheaper meat products, which often contain parts of carcasses made unrecognisable by processing (although children and hospital patients to whom they are often served have no choice). It is better not to eat any part of the head, the spinal column or the marrow of sheep or cattle. Meat from cattle and sheep which are grass-fed is safest, preferably from an enclosed herd.

Residues

The treatment of animal disease is the main reason why meat may contain chemical residues. Although modern drugs are expensive, they are usually the standard treatment if an animal is ill. This will not surprise any pet owner, who will know how heavily most vets use antibiotics as a precautionary measure. The pharmaceutical companies have also developed a vast range of medications – wormers, vaccinations, antibiotics and so on – which are administered routinely to healthy farm animals in order to prevent disease. There are recommended withdrawal periods from these treatments before the animal is slaughtered, but apart from spot checks at the abattoir or by the big supermarkets, policing is non-existent and consumers have no option but to trust the farmer. Factory-farmed animals may have particularly high levels of medication, because they are so susceptible to disease.

One of the possible consequences is that antibiotics may begin to lose their effectiveness as bacteria develop resistance to them. Many are drugs which are also used to treat human disease, and it may not please you to know that you might be getting a dose of medicine with your chop, or that when your child is ill the remedy might not be effective because the same medication has been over-used on the farm. But let us not lay all the blame at the vet's door – pet owners and farmers alike would probably balk at spending time nursing their animals to take them safely through the course of an illness, so drugs are demanded and delivered despite the possible consequences.

Growth promoters

Other residues in meat, usually concentrated in the vital organs, may come from various substances which are given to young animals to promote growth. These may be antibiotics, probiotics, steroids, heavy metals such as copper, and even tranquillisers and detergents! Every now and then a product is banned, but other products come thick and fast from the pharmaceutical industry to take their place. Synthetic hormones are now illegal, but when they were administered legitimately to beef cattle the slow-release hormone pellet was implanted in the animal's ear, which is discarded after slaughter. Following the ban in 1989 it was discovered that unscrupulous farmers had implanted hormones in the brisket where their presence would not be suspected, thus posing a severe threat to the health of anyone unlucky enough to eat the pellet. This aroused suspicions of a thriving black market in these substances, which the Government attempted to halt by making forty thousand random checks.

Pesticides

Since intensively kept farm animals eat a cereal-based diet, they inevitably consume a lot of the pesticides with which the crops have been treated. These will mostly be pesticides which are supposedly 'safe' for animal and human consumption, but they may also ingest what are by any standards extremely toxic pesticides from their bedding. Deep-litter wood shavings may have been treated with wood preservatives, and straw from conventional farms will have been sprayed with pesticides. The animals are also dipped and treated for their own insect parasites. Residues of all these pesticides will tend to accumulate in the fat and the vital organs of the animal.

SLAUGHTER

The one unavoidable fact about meat eating is that animals have to be killed, and it is surely our responsibility as meat eaters to ensure that their suffering is minimised. Unfortunately we have created a system that goes on largely behind closed doors, which we are thus able to ignore. The death of meat animals has become even more a subject of taboo than our own death, and most meat eaters prefer not to think about it.

Until fairly recently slaughtering was an unmechanised

craft-based operation, which happened once a week or so behind many a local butcher's shop. The conditions were basic by modern standards and there was not a lot of shiny equipment, but the small scale and the speed of the operation meant that the butcher had a chance to do the job properly, perhaps as the locals looked on. The meat trade's move into the supermarkets necessitated the establishment of large mechanised plants for the processing of the hundreds of thousands of animals destined for our tables each week. In 1977 new regulations were introduced, largely to control conditions in these new large plants, but the financial burden of making changes to premises and equipment led to the closing down of the vast majority of small abattoirs. A recent report revealed that even now very few of our thousand or so remaining abattoirs reach European Community hygiene standards, and are therefore not eligible for an export licence.

Although it is inevitably more difficult to maintain sanitary conditions in a large mechanised plant operating at full capacity, the regulations apply to everyone, and the cost of expensive updating will mean that it is the smaller plants which are most at risk of closure. Those small abattoirs that remain will still be under a different sort of threat, since we are unwilling to tolerate their presence in villages and towns near where we live, clamouring for their removal to the industrial part of town.

As consumers, humanity and hygiene are our legitimate concern. To maintain high standards in both these areas it is obvious that each process should be carried out as carefully as possible, with attention to detail. Unfortunately time is money, and management have to operate under the usual commercial pressures. Over and above this many slaughterhouse workers are still paid piece rates, which inevitably puts pressure on them to slaughter and process as many animals as they can in as short a time as possible. There is plenty of room for improvement in the system, but any changes will inevitably mean more expensive meat for the consumer.

Stunning and bleeding

Bacteria readily multiply in blood, so when an animal is killed to be eaten as much blood as possible has to be drained quickly from the carcass. This is why most animals are killed by being 'stuck', that is having their throats cut. It is believed that this enables the still-beating heart to pump blood out in the most efficient way. Recent research, however, has shown that blood loss is not adversely affected if the animal is killed and then bled. Bleeding is a slow death, so all animals, except for those exempted on religious grounds, have to be stunned to render them unconscious and insensible to pain before being slaughtered with a knife. Although stunning is humane if carried out properly, there are fears that too many things can go wrong, and that some animals and birds regain consciousness before they reach the knife.

Slaughter of red-meat animals

When the animals arrive at the abattoir they are kept in lairage – large pens which may be overcrowded and noisy. If this period can be kept to a minimum, or if (and ideally) they can go straight in to be slaughtered, stress can be greatly reduced. Not only is this better for the animal but it produces better meat. An animal which is stressed prior to slaughter will have less lactic acid in the muscles, producing 'dark-cutting' meat which tends to be tough, unattractive in texture and spoils more rapidly. When large numbers of animals are being processed this sort of individual attention is impossible. Many animals are also starved for a period of time before slaughter so that their digestive systems are cleaned out.

Traditionally even the toughest beef and mutton would be tenderised by the action of enzymes during lengthy hanging, a process which also greatly adds to the flavour. Nowadays it is not considered economical to store meat in this way, and most beef and lamb, which is young and therefore tender, goes straight through the system from farm to shop inside a week. Many people believe that the process of hanging contributes most to the quality of beef and game, and to a lesser extent lamb, and that lack of hanging time explains the blandness of modern meat.

Some older animals such as culled dairy cows may be subjected to alternative tenderising methods. The animal may be electrically stimulated after stunning but before bleeding, so that it is spared any suffering. Or it may be injected with papain enzyme, a derivative of papaya leaves, about twenty minutes before slaughter. This involves a massive injection into the jugular vein (administered not by a vet but by the slaughterman), so that the enzyme is distributed around the body giving a sort of internal 'marinade' to the meat. To a large animal this causes a great deal of pain and distress, but the Government has chosen to allow its continued use, until we are forced to come into line with the rest of the European Community, which has banned this practice.

Stunning

Cattle (and some sheep) are usually stunned with a captive bolt pistol which shoots a bolt into the animal's brain, rendering it instantly unconscious. Others are stunned with a concussion stunner which hits the skull but does not penetrate it. These methods are effective but not foolproof – if the animal moves or the bolt is not properly positioned it merely causes a wound and has to be done again. Most sheep and pigs and some calves are stunned with tongs held either side of the head, which pass an electric current through the brain. Depending on the voltage the tongs may have to be held in place for up to seven seconds in order to induce an electroplectic fit, but as the animal loses consciousness well before this and may slip to the floor, this can be difficult to administer. A sheep's woolly head provides some insulation and the stunning may not be completely effective. There are new methods which use an electric current passed from the back or the leg of the animal to the head, which are considered better. These necessitate extra equipment to restrain each animal to stop it struggling, falling away or escaping, and are more expensive.

After stunning the animal is hoisted up by a back leg, hanging head down. The throat is cut and the blood drains away. Obviously it is important that the cut is made properly so that brain death occurs in the shortest possible time. When the blood has drained the animal is then skinned and gutted – and problems of hygiene start to arise. The modern method of cleaning any spills of broken intestines and so on is to hose down the carcasses, but by making the meat wet it damages its keeping qualities and can spread bacteria.

Slaughter of venison

Although at present the majority of farmed deer are shot by a skilled marksman whilst grazing, it seems likely that pressure from the European Community to tighten up hygiene standards will eventually mean that they will have to be transported to abattoirs. Many would argue that rather than deer being subjected to the slaughter-house there is no real reason why the 'shot whilst grazing' principle could not be extended to cattle, sheep and pigs, especially when they are kept in small numbers.

Slaughter of poultry

The poultry industry does not give birds the status of individuals, and makes all calculations in terms of flock percentages. Unfortunately the manufacturers of auto-matic poultry slaughtering systems cannot, and do not, claim 100 per cent efficiency for them. The birds are shackled upside down onto a moving conveyor belt which moves over an electrified water bath: the idea is that their heads should go into the water, thus stunning them. However it is all too easy for them to flap and move, avoiding the water and arriving at the automatic knife fully conscious. The knife has to be set at the right place for the size of bird, so if this is not done properly, or if there are any variations in size, it may cut the neck too high or too low to be effective. Bleeding then takes place, but will be inadequate if the cut has gone wrong. This means that birds may end up being dropped alive into the scalding tank. Some processors have started to introduce higher voltages in the stunning baths to improve efficiency.

Every year, as well as the slaughter of spent laying hens and broilers, millions of unwanted day-old male chicks, whose sisters are destined for the battery, are drowned, gassed, suffocated or mashed to a pulp.

Ritual slaughter

Controversy has raged for some time now about Jewish and Islamic ritual slaughter, which allow the killing of animals without pre-stunning. Those outside the religions argue that instantaneous stunning is preferable to the slower loss of consciousness which results from bleeding to death. Jews and Muslims argue that their method is more certain, and that there is no danger of an animal regaining consciousness and falling from its shackle if not stunned properly.

The Jewish method of slaughter is known as *Shechita*, and involves a highly trained slaughterman making a single cut with a razor-sharp knife, severing the jugular veins and carotid arteries. Birds are held under the arm, but animals are turned upside down in a restraint with their throats stretched out to receive the cut. Fortunately the Government is soon to ban this practice, as it causes great distress to ruminant animals because of the suffocating weight of their innards. *Shechita* was originally introduced as a more humane and hygienic way of eating meat than the amputating of individual limbs, which is said to have been common practice in ancient times. Many Jews do not accept that modern methods are more efficient and humane, and therefore it is unlikely that significant change will come from within the Jewish community itself.

Halal, the Islamic method of slaughter, also involves the bleeding of animals, but because the Koran dictates that animals must be spared all unnecessary pain some Muslims are now accepting some methods of pre-stunning. The slaughterman pronounces the name of Allah over each animal to remind him that it is sacred, but the conveyor belt method of poultry slaughter is allowed under Islamic law with just one pronouncement for the whole batch.

While respecting different religions, many of the animal welfare organisations are concerned that efforts to improve standards of stunning will be hampered if ritual slaughter takes place in the same abattoir, and that the ever increasing market for *Halal* meat, especially for export, may lead to the exemption being exploited. Also, since Jews are only allowed to eat about one third of the carcass, the rest finds its way unmarked into the 'ordinary' meat supply, which means that it is eaten without knowledge of the method of slaughter.

MEAT PROCESSING

As sales of fresh meat decline and convenience foods become more popular, vast numbers of carcasses, mostly of the poorer quality, go straight from the slaughterhouse to the manufacturers. Here the meat is made into pies, sausages, burgers, nuggets, steakettes and other delights. Not only the meat is used – every last bit of the carcass which could be possibly considered edible, including rind, sinew, gristle and bone, is broken down, extracted, mechanically recovered and reconstituted, and called 'meat'.

Food technologists have devised numerous clever ways of emulsifying, extruding and flake-cutting these substances to look like meat, so that unsuspecting consumers could never guess what they are eating. During the manufacturing many additives are used, which apart from the necessary preservatives are purely

21

cosmetic. These include suspect dyes to 'improve' the appearance, and flavourings, flavour enhancers and emulsifiers to 'improve' the taste and texture. Unfortunately not all these ingredients have to be mentioned on the label – in fact, the labelling requirements are so incomplete that they could be considered almost pointless. A list of a few 'E' numbers might suggest that there is nothing extra added, and therefore be misleading. For a full and graphic description of the meat industry read *The Meat Machine* by Jan Walsh (Columbus Books).

FORCES FOR CHANGE

SUSTAINABLE FARMING

In the past agriculture was to a large extent sustainable; that is, provided the farmer cared for the soil and put back what was taken out, the system could continue with little or no help from outside. Most farms had a mixture of animals and crops. The farm grew all the feedstuffs for the animals, which in turn were the only source of fertiliser for the crops. Farms were more or less self sufficient, and simply sold their surplus. The drawback was that some years there wasn't a surplus, and people simply starved as a result. Nowadays this system is often described as low input, low output.

As the urban population grew the problem of feeding everybody was overcome, often at the expense of British farmers, by importing cheap food from abroad. We have continued importing ever since. But it is increasingly difficult to justify using vast amounts of energy to cart food across the globe to feed ourselves and our factory farm animals, and it is an unjust nonsense for people in the Third World to be turned off the land which has always fed them, so that it can be used to grow cash crops for export.

Obviously we can't just return to the old ways; we need to take the best that modern technology has to offer and use it to create a new efficient but sustainable agriculture. Research is needed into ways of improving the old methods so that they will feed large numbers of people reliably. At present this is being done on limited resources, mainly by the organic organisations and organic farmers themselves. Only a limited amount of help is likely to come from the agricultural industries as there are few profits to be made from low inputs, so government support is vital if we are to move towards a healthier agriculture and food supply.

During the Second World War British farmers provided enough food for the nation to live on, and studies have shown that it was a healthier, though more boring diet than we have today. Without the constrictions of war a moderate degree of self-sufficiency should be more than possible now, enabling us to live within our resources without plundering the rest of the world. At present the Government is seeking to control surpluses by allowing farmers to 'set-aside' land, to grow trees, or even sell land for building and leisure developments. We could keep far more options open if farmers were instead encouraged to grow a wider range of crops and keep a mixture of animals in small groups. We could also improve the nation's health by providing ourselves with nutritious fresh food.

Despite public unease, irradiation is soon to be allowed, apparently in the hope that it will help control mounting outbreaks of food poisoning by killing some of the bacteria which build up while the food lies around in shops and stores. Techniques like this, and preservative chemicals which are equally suspect, would not be needed if we grew and ate more fresh food. We could also improve and clean up our environment into the bargain.

What is sustainable farming?

Sustainable farming depends entirely on the creation and maintenance of healthy living soil, with plenty of humus and the right balance of minerals. This is a long-term process, during which everything that is taken out by the growing crops is put back as green manure (plants which are turned back into the soil), compost and animal manures. Some outside organic inputs such as lime are also needed, but the bulk of what is added can be recycled fertility from the farm itself. Straw burning would no longer be an economic necessity because the straw would be needed for animals' bedding. This means that as well as taking in the minimum of resources from outside, the farm would create little or no pollution.

In the same way there should be little need for bought-in pesticides and artificial fertilisers, which do nothing to help the soil, offering only a short-term benefit to the crop. All pests and diseases, whether of plants or animals, should be dealt with primarily through preventative husbandry, with crops and animals being rotated around the land so as to avoid a build-up of problems. None of the farm crops or animals should be forced to grow too fast, weakening their natural strength and immunity.

The role of animals in sustainable farming

A sustainable agriculture must take into account the natural conditions of the land and weather, and allow these conditions to dictate to a large extent what is grown. Although Britain has a kind climate, and in some areas and in some seasons a wide variety of plants can be grown, our most reliable crop is and always will be grass and the vitamin- and mineral-rich herbs which grow in grassland. The ruminant animals – cattle, sheep, deer and goats – are efficient converters of grass and herbs that we cannot eat into food that we can eat. They also utilise poor land, survive harsh conditions which will not support vegetable crops, and maintain the characteristic appearance of our countryside by keeping down the growth of scrub with their grazing and the trampling of their hooves.

Pigs and poultry too have their place in a sustainable system as scavengers and converters of surplus 'waste', though their numbers would be proportionately less than they are now. All farm animals, by providing fertiliser, play a vital part in the growing of good arable and vegetable crops. Kept as part of a sustainable system they will be healthier and probably more contented than they are in intensive systems, and provide healthier meat for us.

Having said all this, the total number of animals would have to be reduced. Animals farmed free-range without massive use of chemical wormers and constant use of drugs to fight disease must be kept at a low density. Consequently the price of meat would go up and our consumption would go down. Meat would again become more of a luxury, but probably one that we would appreciate more.

LOCAL IS BEAUTIFUL

Imported food has only a supporting role to play in an ecologically sound food supply. The chain of food supply from the farm to the consumer should ideally be kept as short as possible, with the general aim of local farms supplying local populations. Transport and storage time are kept to a minimum so that costs are reduced and food will be fresher. Local suppliers are accountable to the consumer if the food can be easily traced back to them. Small shop keepers are also better able to prevent food being illegally tampered with.

Unfortunately, as the system stands now the smaller shops and suppliers are at a great disadvantage compared with the big farmers and supermarkets. As more and more food passes into the supermarket system the Government has little choice but to bring in expensive and draconian regulations to keep up standards of food purity. This means that the small producer has to pay for tests which were designed for huge operations, when their own standards may be perfectly adequate.

A good example of this is raw, unpasteurised milk, which has been subject to stringent testing for years but which was nearly banned in 1989 following the adverse publicity surrounding listeria and salmonella. Since it can only be sold by doorstep delivery, unpasteurised milk is the freshest, least processed milk available today. Consumers and producers, confident about its quality, lobbied against the ban, and succeeded in gaining a reprieve. We can expect to have to fight similar battles in the future to keep other small-scale suppliers going.

LABELLING

Small producers are already finding that giving the maximum amount of information to the consumer is one means of persuading them to buy food which might be more expensive than the supermarket equivalent, and good labelling is one way to provide more information. The Government is unlikely to introduce legislation to improve labelling in the short term at least, but both Compassion in World Farming and the RSPCA are campaigning for producers and retailers to label humanely produced meat so that it can be clearly identified. A range of information could be given, from the method of slaughter to the breed of animal.

IMPROVEMENTS IN SLAUGHTERING

As you will see from our directory, most small producers try to take their animals to small abattoirs, as near as possible to the farm. This minimises stress, and means that farmers have more chance of seeing that the job is well done and that they are getting their own animals back. If small 'old-fashioned' abattoirs are forced out of business by the need to install improvements designed to improve hygiene in large plants, then the keeping of animals on small farms will be in great jeopardy.

The existing system is felt by many farmers to be an unsatisfactory end to the careful raising and rearing of animals. But there are alternatives – already island farming communities in this country use prefabricated slaughter units which can be moved on the back of a container lorry, and in the USA modern mobile slaughterhouses visit farms in vast outlying areas and slaughter in the field. Such systems could provide humane and hygienic facilities, benefiting the animals and the small farmer.

ALTERNATIVE MEDICINE FOR ANIMALS

Many people are using alternative medicine nowadays, and there is no reason why some practices cannot be used for animals as well. Herbalism and homeopathy in particular have some major advantages over conventional veterinary medicine, especially for more common ailments. They are safe, cheap, and most important of all to the consumer they leave no residues in the meat.

Although it might be difficult to make a hen drink a cup of herbal tea, when animals and birds are free ranging on good pasture they can get the beneficial effects of herbs through their diet. The plants, many of them deep-rooted, give the animals minerals and trace elements from a healthy soil, enabling the animal to build resistance to disease. Some farmers have observed that animals which are nearly always outside, living a semi-wild existence, instinctively search out the right herbs for themselves when illness threatens. For animals which are confined the farmer can provide fresh green food and such useful herbs as garlic, which helps the animal to resist parasitic infection.

Homeopathy is the medical practice of treating like with like. Symptoms are not seen as a part of the illness, as they are in conventional medicine, but as the body's effort to overcome it. Instead of giving drugs which suppress the symptoms, the homeopath gives remedies to stimulate them, thus helping the body's own natural healing process. Another important aspect is that each patient is seen as an individual – their temperament is studied and treatment is given accordingly. Since animals have bodies and different temperaments just as we do, this system of medicine is every bit as applicable to them as it is to us.

At present most farmers wanting to use homeopathy have to do it on a self-help basis, using advice from the Soil Association and other organisations. The number of practising homeopathic vets is very small, but a new qualification from the Faculty of Homeopathy – VetMFHom – bodes well for the future. Veterinary colleges are interested in the subject, and homeopathy is even appearing on the curriculum of some of them. It is also receiving more frequent mentions in the conventional farming press.

Although producers of humanely reared meat are all agreed that the routine use of drugs is dangerous and wrong, there are many shades of opinion about how far to go in giving up conventional drugs altogether. The Soil Association standards forbid their use except in life-threatening situations, but it is difficult for many to have faith in what may be a completely unfamiliar method when their livelihood and the welfare of the animal has to be considered. However homeopathy and herbal remedies have a growing part to play in reducing the vet's bills and helping to clean up meat for the consumer.

HOW TO BECOME A BORN-AGAIN CARNIVORE

- Buy good food, even though it may be more expensive. Good food costs money to provide and we should not resent paying for it, because it is the basis of our health and the health of future generations. Farmers deserve less criticism and more support – getting back a natural, uncontaminated food supply does not just involve farmers loosening their grip on their wallets. Modern farming techniques were developed to give the consumers what they wanted – cheap food. Better food will mean higher prices, but there will be other benefits too –

cleaner water, air and countryside; reduced costs of pollution control; better health and reduced costs of health care.

- Buy from small local producers. Actively searching out the best helps to ensure that supplies continue to be available. Giving your custom to the small local producer who has no transport or middle-man costs will help to keep prices down.

- Be prepared to cook food at home – this is the best way to eat fresh whole food. We know from our own experience that the odds seem to be stacked against feeding a family well, and we certainly aren't advocating a return to a life of drudgery, spending hours in the kitchen after a hard day's work. Aiming in the right direction is a start, with just one or two good sit-down meals a week if that is all that time will allow. Traditional meat recipes are useful here – they tend to be far less complicated than the exotic ones we have become used to, and can be left to cook by themselves.

- Grow some of your own food, including animals for meat. This could have other side benefits, like healthy exercise (as you chase them down the street), and can be done in conjunction with friends and neighbours.

- Join and support campaigning organisations.

- Write to your MP on every food, farming and animal welfare issue that concerns you.

- Eat well and have a happy life!

A BIRD IN THE HAND

Not so long ago keeping animals for meat was commonplace in the countryside, and indeed many households considered it essential. But since the last war it has become extremely rare, and all the accumulated knowledge of how to do it has disappeared. Today the vast majority of people would shrink from the suggestion, since their only contact with live animals is with their pets. But if you eat meat, and you are concerned about its quality, it makes sense to investigate the possibilities.

If you have a reasonable-sized garden, you might already be growing vegetables and perhaps keeping hens, and the next logical step is to provide your family with some of their meat as well. You might choose to eat your own limited supplies of meat only on special occasions, which is probably the dietary ideal. Another possibility is to start a joint enterprise with friends and neighbours, so that the chores and the costs can be shared. Either way, as with home-grown vegetables, you will get fresh, uncontaminated food with a much better flavour, and be in touch with the source of food which satisfies both soul and body.

Let's get down to the practicalities. It's no more difficult to keep animals for food than it is to keep them as pets, as long as you take the trouble to be well-prepared *before* you go and buy. If you are worried about your ability to manage livestock, remember that if you are sensible you can hardly provide worse conditions than those on factory farms, and can probably provide a higher standard of individual attention than most busy farmers. Even if your meat may not win prizes or save you much money, you have the confidence of knowing that it is fit to eat and that the animal has enjoyed a decent existence.

Start by reading up all you can on the subject. There are many books available, a lot of them published during the 1970s when self-sufficiency was fashionable. Get to know experienced local smallholders, so that you can ask for practical advice. The relevant animal society will be able to put you in touch with this sort of person in your locality, and will also provide much useful information (you can find addresses and much else besides in *Home Farm* magazine). At least one real-life advisor can be invaluable in a crisis – books can't answer questions in quite the same way.

Whatever animals or birds you decide to keep, the same basic rules apply for keeping them happy and healthy. They must be able to pursue their normal behaviour patterns as far as possible, be kept well-fed and clean, and given adequate shelter, space and companionship. Most of these points, except for the food, are covered by the type of housing and outside area that you give them. They won't be at all fussy about what this looks like and what state of repair it's in – sheds and fences can be made from waste materials costing little or nothing. Unless you have plenty of time, however, and are always on the premises to make minor repairs, it's a good idea not to cut costs in this way. It may be ecologically sound, but it's not psychologically sound. If you have a busy lifestyle, and want to do other things with your spare time, seriously consider buying new or nearly new purpose-built housing, and erecting the best fencing you can afford. This way maintenance is kept to a minimum, mucking out can be done easily, and you can go to work knowing that your animals are not coming to any harm, running amok around the neighbourhood.

For the same reasons don't overstock, or make the mistake of thinking that twelve hens are as easy to look after as six. They are, but only if they have twice as much space. The more animals you keep together the more attention they need to keep them happy and healthy. Find out the required area needed for each individual and then err on the side of generosity.

SLAUGHTER

Let's not beat about the bush – this is not going to be easy. Address the issue before you start, come to terms with it and make arrangements. Face the fact that you are a meat eater, and remember that keeping your own animals puts you in the privileged position among meat eaters of knowing that the animal you are eating has had a good life and a humane death.

Rabbits and poultry should be killed at home, but if you have never done the deed before you must get an experienced person to show you how. Larger animals for your own consumption may be killed at home, by stunning with a captive bolt pistol and bleeding, as long as it is done properly without causing the animal suffering. The Humane Slaughter Association are very willing to give advice, and their sister charity, the Universities' Federation for Animal Welfare, are shortly to publish a book covering the humane slaughter of all animals, which will be available from the HSA. Although if done properly this is the ideal from the animal's point of view, there are practical difficulties. Unless you are very resourceful, you will need a butcher to help bleed the animal and cut up the carcass into manageable pieces, avoiding any waste.

If there is a satisfactory abattoir in your area it may be a more practical alternative to take your animals there for slaughter. Make sure that you find a good abattoir that you can trust. Again the HSA will offer advice. Be aware that you could be given the wrong meat by an unscrupulous manager. Minimise the stress by taking the animal at a quiet time, and if you possibly can, go in with it.

It's probably a good idea not to give the animals names (other than Freezer or Pork Chop), and not to treat them as pets. This doesn't, however, mean that they should not be handled and to some extent tamed. Handling an animal regularly is the best way of checking its health and, if it trusts you, it will be less likely to feel distressed when loaded into the back of the car or picked up to have its neck wrung – even though *you* might feel like a traitor.

WHAT TO KEEP

If you don't have a freezer then keep the smaller beasts, such as poultry and rabbits, as they can be killed when needed. They also don't need much space, so they are the best choice for a garden enterprise. Chickens don't have to be free range – they are quite happy in a reasonable sized run if it is kept clean, with a good layer of litter to scratch in and plenty of greenstuff. It's best to have two runs, so that one can be rested while the other is in use so as to prevent the build-up of parasites.

Chickens

If you want to keep chickens for the table, it makes sense to keep them for eggs as well, and vice versa. Hens which have stopped laying will make a good meal, especially if fattened first for a couple of weeks, even if they have to be cooked carefully for a long time. If you keep a small flock of pure breed chickens with a cockerel you will have your own supply of male chicks to fatten, as well as the old hens. Alternatively you can buy in hybrid chicks or young birds for egg laying and for the table. Table chickens are just as easy to rear and look after as laying hens.

Take care what you feed them – there is no point in going to the trouble of rearing your own and then feeding them on an expensive proprietary mix full of additives bought in from the corn merchant. Let them free range if possible; if not, throw all your weeds and as much greengrocer's waste as you can find into the run. Mix all your kitchen scraps together every day, boil them into a porridge, and feed them warm to the chickens before they go in for the night. Explore other sources of waste products, such as chat potatoes and bread wastes from the bakers. Give the birds a daily supplement of a handful of mixed corn or wheat, thrown down for them to scratch for. Every garden should have some chickens – even just two birds will eat your waste food and weeds, provide valuable fertiliser for the garden, provide enough eggs for the small family, *and* an average of one meat meal a year!

Ducks and geese

Ducks and geese make excellent eating, but are only really suitable if you have a good area of grass which you don't mind being liberally spattered with wet droppings. Having said that, geese are a less troublesome alternative to sheep or goats if you need help to keep the grass short, although it will already need to be short when you put them on it as they will starve on long grass. With enough good grass they won't need extra feeding, so they are economical to keep. On the other hand, ducks eat a lot and will appreciate your scraps, waste potatoes and bread even more than chickens. If you have a pond or stream they will get some of their own food from it, but don't expect tadpoles and special pond plants to survive their dabblings. Although they won't damage the garden as much as chickens, it is a good idea to fence them away from the front of the house as they have a friendly habit of camping on the doorstep waiting for you to come home, depositing the day's droppings there for you to stand in.

Other poultry

If your enthusiasm grows, any sort of poultry – quails, guinea fowl, even turkeys – can be kept in the garden. They tend to be more difficult, so try hardy chickens first and avoid mistakes, costly for you and miserable for the birds.

Rabbits

Paradoxically, rabbits are both the easiest and the hardest animals for the non-farmer to keep for food. We are most familiar with them as pets, and they are too cuddly and easy to grow fond of for most people to contemplate killing them. This is a shame, because they are the ideal meat animal for the garden – backyard rabbit farming on a nationwide scale could feed us all. They are not smelly and messy, don't make any noise and are easy to look after, as many small children can testify. Neither do they need much space – a good sized hutch or ark, with a strong moveable run so that they can nibble the lawn in the summer months, will be close to their favoured habitat. Remember that in the wild they spend a lot of time in confined spaces underground. Their main virtue is that they can, at little or no cost, convert food which would otherwise go to waste – household scraps and green stuff from the garden or wayside – into flavoursome healthy food for you.

If you do keep rabbits, try to make full use of them by also tanning the skins. You will need to skin them before gutting them, which is the other way round from the routine for wild hunted rabbit. Look for instructions on how to do this in specialist books.

Sheep and cattle

If you have land, as opposed to a garden, it's possible to raise your own lamb or beef. As a beginner you are well advised to embark on your first enterprise in the spring, and buy in young animals to fatten them ready for slaughter before the bad weather sets in. Take advice about what and where to buy from an experienced smallholder. If you have enough grass and the animals stay healthy, they should be even less trouble than poultry. They won't need to be housed and fed, although you will need to have a good look at them daily. The major advantage if all goes well is that your one animal will provide a lot of meat. You *must* have good fencing, because if they get out both sheep and cattle can destroy gardens in seconds and be a positive danger on the roads. You must have the help and advice of an expert, not for crises so much as for continuous care and management to prevent disease and to help you through the mysteries of sheep dipping and so on. Although you must not hesitate to call the vet if necessary, the bills could easily make the whole venture very expensive.

Goats

Although it is probably not a good idea to embark on keeping goats just for meat, if you do have dairy goats and have always had the billy kids put down at birth, why not think about rearing them for meat? If you have the housing perhaps you could take other unwanted kids and rear them at the same time.

Pigs

> *Dearly beloved brethren*
> *Isn't it a sin*
> *When you peel potatoes,*
> *To throw away the skin?*
> *The skin will feed the pigs*
> *And the pigs will feed you,*
> *Dearly beloved brethren*
> *Isn't this true?*

Yorkshire skipping rhyme

In the past many cottagers kept a pig in a sty at the bottom of the garden, and its meat formed the basis of a healthy diet all year round. The animal would be fed garden waste and household scraps and killed in the autumn when it had had the warm summer months to grow. The 'sticking' of the pig – the killing and bleeding of it – was a terrifying and bloody business, vividly described in Thomas Hardy's novel *Jude the Obscure.* The family would eat the offal and some of the meat fresh, giving themselves a good nutritional boost for the coming winter, and salt down the rest of the meat as bacon. The lard was rendered down for use throughout the year, and sausages, brawn, and pork pies made from the poorer pieces. Everything was used (except, as they say, for the squeak) and the pig provided a great quantity and variety of food.

The pig-keeping habit remained with the working people as the industrial towns developed in the nineteenth century, and many pigs were kept on allotments and even in the cellar kitchens and back alleys of the slum tenements. A visitor to Leeds in the 1840s noted that pigs roaming the streets were more common in some parts of the city than cats and dogs. However all was not squalor, especially in Keighley which was famous as the birthplace of the Large White and Middle White breeds. They were developed by Joseph Tuley, a Yorkshire weaver, and Mrs Tuley his wife, who lavished such care on the animals that they were washed each week in the Saturday night bath water.

Today there are lots of regulations governing pigs, so the first thing to do is find out from your local council if you are allowed to keep them. Then make sure that you have first class accommodation and boundaries. An escaped pig is no joke – they are big, strong animals and can be aggressive. For the beginner, good solid walls are probably the best bet, as pigs can go under, over and through fences. Finally, although it makes ecological sense to feed them waste products rather than proprietary pig nuts, you must organise proper supplies first and not leave anything to chance. Pigs eat a lot, and will not do well if their diet is too haphazard. Also there are strict hygiene rules which state that no food wastes which might contain meat can be used unless processed first under licence. All in all, keeping a pig is for the dedicated!

Part 2

THE BARE BONES

THE PROPERTIES OF MEAT AS THEY AFFECT THE COOK

This chapter is designed to give new meat cooks, and those with a limited repertoire, a head start on the road to success. We have deliberately described only what you can see in front of you, and what you need to know to make the right cooking decisions. The biology lesson will be brief! But some technical knowledge will help to explain why it is possible to produce such different results, depending on the kind, cut and quality of the meat you have used and the way that you have cooked it. Everyday cooks with more experience will have learnt from others, or by trial and error; they will probably find that they knew it all along, but didn't realise why!

WHAT IS MEAT?

In the simplest sense meat is protein, fat and water. The protein is what we call the lean flesh, and consists of bundles of muscle fibres lying side by side, held together by membranes to form separate muscles. Connective tissue, as these membranes are called, joins and holds the flesh at each stage of its build-up. It varies in appearance and strength depending on its particular function, from the finest membrane between muscle fibres, the transparent one between flesh and skin or individual muscles, to tendons which anchor the muscles to the bone. Shin of beef, cut across the grain will clearly show the bands of bluish opaque connective tissue.

The proteins which make up connective tissue are insoluble – this is what the diner knows as gristle; you can chew until your jaw aches without rendering it fit to swallow. One type, however, called collagen, can be dissolved by moist heat which converts it to gelatin. This is what makes meat stock set like a jelly when cold.

Fat is deposited under the skin and around the internal organs, and throughout the flesh in streaks (where it is known as marbling). Fat is the body's store cupboard. Important reserves of energy, surplus to short-term requirements, are stored in this tissue. It also acts as insulation for the body and protects the internal organs.

Water is the most abundant component of organisms, and it provides the medium in which all the biochemical reactions of the body take place. The water content of animals varies from about two thirds in chicken to less than half in pork, with young animals containing more.

The proportion and nature of these three constituent parts determine the quality of the meat, and will also dictate the preparation and cooking method.

SUCCESSFUL COOKING

The essential qualities of a successful meat dish are tenderness, succulence and flavour. If you learn how to recognise the potential for these three qualities in the raw material, you will be able to choose the meat to fit your recipe or vice versa. You will also be able to discern between good and poor quality meat, irrespective of the cut or the cost. There are some general rules, but nothing is hard and fast. Opinions about recipes and techniques vary, and success comes from deciding what your own tastes and preferences are, and learning how to achieve the sort of dishes that suit you and those you cook for.

Tenderness and succulence

Meat varies in tenderness depending on the age and condition of the animal, where the cut is taken from and, to a certain extent on the hanging of the animal after slaughter. The most tender meat will have fine muscle fibres, some fat and not too much visible connective tissue.

Small-bodied and young animals tend to have finer fibres and therefore potentially more tender flesh than larger ones. But as growth simply increases the length and coarseness of the fibres rather than the number of them, there will be proportionally more connective tissue in a young animal. This is usually fine membrane, rather than the gristly kind, which is more easily broken down during cooking.

Young animals also have a higher water content than mature ones, but they are less rich in fat, particularly in the marbled fat which bastes the meat during cooking, lubricating the fibres and keeping them separate, plump and easier to chew. Therefore, while it may seem desirable to buy meat from a very young animal to ensure tenderness and succulence, you must take extra care to protect it while it cooks. Quick dry methods, such as roasting and grilling, will retain the meat's natural succulence. Marinading or adding extra fat will also help to stop it drying out and becoming stringy.

The flesh of older animals is coarser and potentially tougher, and there is usually more developed connective tissue of the gristly kind, especially in the poorer cuts. But on the plus side there is less water, which means less weight lost during cooking, and more fat, which holds more flavour compounds and keeps the meat succulent.

As a rule of thumb, the most tender meat comes from either side of the backbone, since in a grazing animal the back does the least work. These are the tenderloin and sirloin cuts. The further away from the backbone a cut comes, the more potential it has for toughness, although this can be overcome with long slow cooking. Shin of beef cooked in this way, for instance, will make a delicious meal.

Tenderness is also affected by the length of time that

the meat is hung after slaughter. The accumulation of naturally produced acid in the tissues after death causes a chain reaction which begins to break down the muscle fibres, making the meat more tender the longer it is hung.

Flavour

The food that an animal eats does more than just keep it alive. It is digested and transported to the cells for energy, body building and repair. Residues are then built up in the cells, particularly in the fat, and these compounds give the meat flavour. Consequently, the more active the body the more food it uses, and the stronger the flavour. This is why meat from a young animal, and cuts from the least active parts of the body, will be more delicately flavoured (or less tasty depending on your preference!).

Different feedstuffs affect the flavour of meat, often in quite subtle ways which are difficult to quantify. Very distinctive qualities of flavour, such as the tangy taste of lamb raised on a salt marsh, are well accepted in gourmet circles. So it is only reasonable to conclude that a good, fresh diet – pasture rich in herbs, good hay, root crops, etc. – will have a subtle and beneficial effect on the flavour, and make it preferable to that of animals reared on a diet of processed waste and cereals. Just as farm-bottled milk tastes different when the cows are turned out into the fields to graze in summer, the flavour of meat may vary from county to county, and even from farm to farm.

Flavour also varies with the breed of the animal, in the same way that it does with different varieties of vegetables and fruit. Modern farm animals are bred for fast growth and a lean carcass, often at the expense of flavour, and that is perhaps why older people often maintain that today's lean meat is tasteless. Farmers who don't mind waiting for results will often choose the traditional breeds which suit their particular conditions, or use them to cross with a leaner breed. As a general rule they grow at a natural, slower rate and have a distinctive flavour of their own.

Bad management at the slaughterhouse also affects the flavour. The stress of a long journey, overcrowding and fear cause the body to produce adrenalin which is said to taint the meat. After death the carcass needs to be hung for the correct time for chemical changes to strengthen the flavour. Unfortunately, the pressures of large-scale butchering mean that animals are slaughtered and processed far too quickly, producing bland, tasteless meat.

The sex of the animal will also change the flavour. Entire males when fully mature will have a stronger taste than a female, an immature male or a castrated male. In this country we have traditionally favoured castrated animals, and there is a common feeling that the meat of an entire male, especially that of a pig or goat, is tainted and unpleasant.

All the above suggests that the best quality meat comes from animals in their prime, humanely handled and carefully fed on a good fresh diet with plenty of roughage, with the freedom to exercise outside. In mainstream agriculture beef and lamb come nearest to this ideal, but pigs and poultry have disappeared inside the factory farm, and become a rare sight in the countryside.

How tenderness, succulence and flavour are affected by farming methods

Confined in the factory farm, in a constant temperature, animals are grown fast with carefully controlled amounts of nutrient-rich food and growth-promoting additives. Low-fat pigs, bred for a brief lifetime in these conditions, often have weak hearts and metabolisms which cannot supply enough oxygen to their huge muscles. This tends to produce poor-quality moist, sweaty meat with a special technical term to describe it – PSE (pale, soft, exudative). Increasingly cattle and sheep are being housed for fattening too, and they do not get the time or the space to develop their muscle, and to maintain a healthy balance of fat. Large-scale farmers and retailers often argue that the resulting cheap bland meat is what the public wants, and that free-range meat is tougher and more expensive.

Nobody could claim that farm animals that are left alone in the field to get on with it will automatically become good-quality meat. But the meat of a carefully reared animal, kept in natural conditions, will have a moderate amount of connective tissue and longer, firmer fibres which hold together well during cooking. Marbled fat which provides energy reserves, is only present in active muscle and when feeding is natural. It helps to lubricate the fibres during cooking, keeping them separate and therefore easier to chew. The juices are retained and the meat does not go to shreds. The free-range animal whose growth has not been forced will be older than its equivalent factory-farmed cousin, and will therefore have more flavour. However, economic pressures inevitably dictate that most farmers, including organic farmers, will slaughter animals at a younger age than was common in the past. Nor does natural rearing alone guarantee good meat – correct hanging and butchering and the breed of the animal still contribute a good deal.

STORAGE

STORING FRESH MEAT

There has recently been a great deal of publicity about food poisoning, and it has been suggested that we should improve our kitchen hygiene in order to protect ourselves. Although meat does have to be kept carefully it is not difficult to do, and there is no need to be anxious if you take simple precautions. There is less risk in fresh meat which is going to be cooked at home than in ready-prepared pre-processed foods.

Ideally meat should be cooked as soon as possible after purchase, but this isn't usually practical. The length of time you can safely store it depends on how fresh it is when you buy it, and whether you have the facilities to keep it clean and cold, protected from infecting agents (such as flies), harmful bacteria and toxins produced by those bacteria, and away from heat and light which would speed up the growth of bacteria already present in the meat.

To store meat for up to two or three days, first remove the wrappings and, if you think the meat may have been exposed to flies, wipe with a damp (cold) cloth, but do not wash. Remove any 'pipes' in back or loin cuts. Place the meat on a clean pot, glass or enamel plate or shallow dish, and cover it either with a bowl which does not touch the meat, or loosely with waxed paper or cellophane which does not cling to the meat and exclude air. If using a bowl I find that glass is best, because sometimes I forget that the meat is there if I can't see it. Keep the meat on the lowest shelf of the fridge, or in a cold dark larder (no warmer than 45°F). Large joints can be wrapped in butter muslin or coarse cloth and hung in a cold larder in a current of air, with the cut side uppermost.

Chops, steaks, diced and especially minced meat will

not keep as long as larger pieces or joints, because of the increased surface area exposed to contamination, so use smaller pieces within one or two days of purchase or freeze them. If you are going to mince or dice your own meat then do it just before you cook it. Offal should also be used as quickly as possible.

Pepper will to some extent slow the process of oxidation of fat. A large joint, or a bird which has been plucked before hanging, can be covered with ground pepper which will help to keep it. The spices in a dry marinade will also have the same effect. Marinading will also extend the keeping for a few days.

Boning joints

If you buy meat from a small farmer it may not be as expertly butchered as from a shop, and you probably won't get much choice of presentation. But if you want a piece of meat to go further, boning, stuffing and rolling is a good idea, especially for special occasion dishes. Boning is quite simple, although it may take a little practice to do a neat job. For individual joints from any animal the same principles apply as for poultry. With a very sharp knife start where the bone is visible and work the meat away carefully, keeping the knife close to the bone and cutting through the flesh as little as possible.

RESCUING TAINTED MEAT

However well your meat is kept, the naturally present enzymes and bacteria will continue to be active. In effect they 'digest' the meat. This in itself is not harmful, except that bacteria will multiply and eventually reach dangerous levels. Toxins are produced by the bacterial action and these are equally dangerous. If you are sensible, tainted meat can be rescued and eaten safely, but *never attempt a rescue operation on minced, thawed or cooked meat.*

If the meat has started to go off, the first sign is a

slightly slimy feel on the surface. A faint 'animal' smell may also be detectable. At this stage you can safely wash the whole thing with cold water, dry it with a clean cloth, cook it immediately or marinade it. Always cook it well.

The next stage is when the odour becomes readily discernible but not offensive, and a yellowish or greenish tinge appears on the surface. Cut off the discoloured bits, wash the meat quickly in vinegar and water (1 tablespoon of vinegar to 1 pint of water), dry it well and soak it in marinade or cook it immediately until well done.

Your eyes and nose will tell you when your meat has been left too long to be used safely. If this should happen wrap it up well and throw it away or burn it, and be thoroughly ashamed of yourself!

STORING CURED MEAT

Bacon and sliced cured meats should be wrapped in cellophane or waxed paper and stored in the fridge or the darkest part of a cold larder. Traditionally cured meat will keep longer than the factory cured kind because the concentration of salt is higher and the meat is dryer; traditionally cured whole hams can be hung in a dry, coolish dark place and will keep for up to a year. Mildly cured meat should be treated as fresh.

STORING VACUUM-PACKED MEAT

Vacuum packing is a method which is becoming popular for packaging meat, and if you buy meat by mail order it will probably be wrapped in this way. There is usually a minimum weight and carriage charges to pay on mail order meat, so you will probably need to be able to freeze most of your order as soon as it arrives or share it with friends. Otherwise vacuum-packed meat will keep for about a week in the fridge and will continue to mature in that time. Some butchers feel that the packing process draws some of the juices from the meat, that it may consequently be drier after cooking, and that the maturing process is not as satisfactory as when the meat is well ventilated. Because air is excluded from vacuum-packed meat it may have a slightly unnatural colour and smell when you unwrap it. This will disappear if it is left unwrapped in a cool place for about an hour before cooking.

STORING COOKED MEAT

Raw and cooked meat should never be stored together, as cross contamination can easily take place. Catering establishments have to have separate fridges for each, but at home you can take the simple precaution of storing cooked meat on a different shelf of the fridge, preferably above any raw meat, so that it will be safe from any drips of blood.

As well as being delicious, cold leftovers from a roast can be a valuable instant meal served with salad. If you take simple precautions you can keep the meat for a few days and preserve its nutritional value. Cool the meat quickly, remove from it any stock or gravy, and dry it well. Cut off any large areas of fat because fat goes off more rapidly than lean, and is not very palatable cold anyway. Since you have taken care in the buying and the cooking of this meat it is best not to risk the transference of chemicals or metals by wrapping it in clingfilm or aluminium foil! Keep the meat in the fridge, preferably on a plate covered with an upturned dish or bowl, or in a bowl covered with clingfilm or cellophane. The aim is to exclude air, which dries the meat out, carries bacteria and accelerates the inevitable process of fat oxidation. It is this which taints the flavour of the meat and affects its food value.

If you are going to serve leftover meat as a cold dish,

remove it from the fridge about ½–1 hour before serving or it will lack flavour, but don't keep it for long in the heat of the kitchen. Try to use cooked meat within three days, encouraging the family to make sandwiches for the following day's lunch for example but discouraging 'picking' every time the fridge door is opened! If you want to carve the leftovers for salad, or dice or mince them for cottage or shepherd's pie, then leave the carving or mincing until you are ready to use the meat because it will keep better in a large piece.

Rare cooked meat is dangerous to keep – the cooking may not have destroyed any harmful bacteria and may even have accelerated its growth by warming it. If you want to eat it cold serve it as soon as it has cooled down, and cook any leftovers as thoroughly and as soon as possible.

FREEZING

Frozen meat can never be as good as fresh in terms of texture, succulence and taste, but proper freezing techniques can make a lot of difference. The formation of ice crystals damages the structure of cells, so that when the meat thaws the juice runs out, taking with it proteins, vitamins and minerals. This thawing liquid must be thrown away – it also contains a lot of bacteria which multiply quickly in such a rich medium once the temperature is raised. Badly frozen meat will be dry and 'corky' when cooked and will lack flavour. Even well frozen meat will tend to be drier than fresh, so to help compensate for this the thawed meat may be marinaded before cooking.

Freezing does not prevent the oxidation of fat. As saturated fat is more stable than unsaturated fat, and will not denature as quickly, meat with a higher saturated fat content such as beef will keep better in the freezer than pork, which has more unsaturated fat. Salt also accelerates the process of oxidation. Ham, bacon, sausages and other prepared dishes containing salt will not keep as long in the freezer as unsalted meat.

Freezer burn is the result of freeze drying on the surface of the meat, and although it is not harmful it is unpleasant, so the affected parts should be cut off before cooking. The risk of freezer burn can be minimised by careful wrapping and ensuring that the meat is as dry as possible before freezing.

Buying frozen meat

As things stand at the moment born-again carnivores are usually going to have to use a freezer. Distribution is prohibitively expensive for many small producers, and anyway they cannot produce enough to have fresh meat available all the time. Neither can the average consumer travel miles every time they want some meat.

The cheapest way of buying meat is as a whole, half or quarter beast, and some producers only supply in this form. When buying in bulk check that the meat will be butchered first, unless you fancy trying this yourself! The selection of different cuts from a whole or half beast, including the offal, represents the basic principle of 'wholefood', and is the best way to get a good variety and balance of fat and lean. However you must be prepared to cook the joints which require more attention as well as the more easily cooked ones.

It is almost impossible to judge the quality of frozen meat, so when buying meat from a new supplier it is better to start with a small order if you can. Once you are sure of the quality, however, it's as well to buy ready frozen, because commercial freezers usually freeze better and quicker than domestic ones. Try to get the meat from shop to freezer in the shortest possible time. If possible take a specially made chill bag, or pack the meat in cardboard boxes with plenty of newspaper and some large plastic bottles which have been filled with water and frozen. Turn the setting on the freezer to fast freeze the night before, or at least before you set off, and follow the manufacturer's instructions for maximum loads. If the meat has begun to thaw when you get home then you should thaw it completely and cook it before refreezing.

Freezing fresh meat

If you want to freeze fresh meat, check with the butcher or producer that it has not already been frozen. On no account must raw meat be refrozen, but it can be cooked first then frozen. All fresh meat, poultry and game should be properly hung before freezing – never try to hang it after thawing.

Fast freezing is absolutely essential – if the process is too slow the ice crystals forming inside the meat will be larger and therefore do more damage to the structure, causing excessive loss of juices when the meat is thawed. When you buy fresh meat for freezing in bulk, make sure the freezer is prepared before you bring the meat home, with enough space to accommodate it, and the fast freeze turned on in advance. Freeze the meat in batches: the rule of thumb is no more than 4lb of meat per cubic foot of freezer space. Plan if possible to have an empty fridge too; this way you can chill the meat before freezing it so that the temperature in the freezer does not rise too much, and you can keep your stock cold while it waits.

Preparing fresh meat for freezing
Remember that defrosted meat will not keep as well as fresh meat, and should be used within twenty-four hours, so it is vital to divide meat into meal-sized portions. Stewing cuts can be diced, and steaks, chops and so on interleaved with greaseproof or cellophane to make separation easier. Made up dishes such as meat loaf, meat balls and burgers should be prepared quickly, then be thoroughly chilled before freezing. To save space, joints can be boned and rolled (but *not* stuffed) before freezing, although they will lose some of their succulence in cooking without the bone in. Raw bones can be frozen for stock.

Any protruding bones should be covered with an extra twist of paper to prevent them tearing the wrapping. Wrapping should be strong enough not to tear and should be water impermeable. Aluminium foil or strong brown paper are good, but wrap the meat in paper or a freezer bag first. The meat should be wrapped closely and air excluded before sealing to prevent freezer burn. Chill the meat if possible before freezing. Place the packs against the floor or walls of the cabinet and try to avoid them touching other packs of frozen food while they freeze. Fast freeze should be left on for up to 24 hours for large joints or several packages.

Freezing poultry, game birds, rabbits and hares

Young poultry and game freeze well, either whole or jointed. Older game meat tends to be very dry after freezing, and is better made up into casseroles or pies and then frozen. Try to remove any shot in game before freezing, but if it is badly damaged, then cook the meat and freeze it as a prepared dish.

Poultry and game should be hung to the required state before freezing, as they will decompose very quickly after thawing. It is probably better to pluck or skin and clean before freezing, because although it can be done after thawing the skin and entrails are more likely to tear and drawing can be unpleasant. If you pluck a bird using hot water, avoid scalding it as it increases the risk of freezer burn. If, in an emergency, you have to freeze with skin or feathers on, ensure that the animal or bird is well wrapped. Giblets and any blood which is going to be saved for cooking should be frozen separately. Small birds which you may want to eat with the entrails in can be frozen whole.

Thawing raw meat

Simple precautions should be taken when thawing meat, as it is important to remember that it will go off much faster than fresh meat. Store thawed meat in the fridge and try to use it within twenty-four hours of defrosting.

The thawing liquid should be discarded and the meat should not stand in it for too long.

Thaw large joints and whole birds and game for approximately 5 hours per lb in the fridge, 2 hours per lb at room temperature. Poultry and pork should be thawed completely, but small pieces of other meats – mince, cubes, sausages, steaks and chops – can be cooked from frozen, although they are likely to be less succulent and tasty. If you do roast a small joint from frozen, use a meat thermometer to check that the meat is thoroughly cooked. Frozen meat balls and burgers are best cooked from frozen, otherwise they may break up.

Freezing times for raw meat	
Sliced bacon and ham, sausages, burgers and stuffings containing raw meat	1 month
Cubed and minced meat, offal	2 months
Whole ham and bacon	3 months
Pork	6 months
Game birds, wildfowl, goose, duck	6 months
Lamb	9 months
Goat	9 months
Beef	12 months
Prime venison	9 months
Chicken, turkey, guinea fowl (except giblets)	12 months

Freezing cooked meat

Always cool and freeze cooked meat as quickly as possible, and aim to use it within two months. Frozen meat can be reheated from frozen or thawed – do it thoroughly but gently as it will get tough if heated quickly.

Sauces and gravies made with wheat flour may curdle on reheating from frozen, so either reheat gently, stirring occasionally, preferably in a double boiler; or use corn-flour, or leave out the thickening until the sauce is thawed and thicken with *beurre manié*. If cooking casseroles, especially for freezing, undercook root vegetables such as carrots but leave potatoes, rice and pasta to be added later.

Excess fat and jelly must be removed from pâtés and terrines if they are to be frozen for more than a few days, and they should not be kept for more than one month. Wrap them carefully as these dishes are usually highly flavoured and may taint other foods which come into contact with them. Strong flavourings like garlic and spices sometimes develop odd tastes if frozen too long, and herbs may lose their flavour. Dishes with these ingredients should be used quickly or the seasonings left out until they are reheated.

Pastry can be frozen successfully, raw or part cooked. Line a pie dish with shortcrust pastry, brush it with melted fat to prevent it from going soggy, fill it with *cold*, cooked filling, cover it with pastry, chill and freeze. Or you can cook the pie (but do not brown the pastry), cool it completely then freeze it. Thaw and finish cooking in a moderate oven for thirty minutes, or cover and reheat from frozen in a slow to moderate oven for approximately one hour. Hot-water crust will not freeze successfully, but a steamed suet pudding can be frozen cooked, and resteamed thoroughly.

It is useful to have a supply of stock in the freezer. Strain off the solid ingredients, skim and reduce by boiling to half the quantity so that it takes up less space. Stock can be frozen in bags or in ice cube trays, then turned out and packed into bags so that the cubes can be taken out as needed.

Freezing leftovers

It can be very useful to freeze the remains of a roast if it is not going to be used up cold, but it shouldn't be kept too long in the freezer as it could go rancid because of the fat content. Large pieces of roast meat tend to be very dry if frozen in the piece, so carve the meat thickly, removing as much fat as possible. Separate the slices with paper or cellophane and wrap very closely. When thawed the meat will tend to be wet, so it is best heated gently but thoroughly in a gravy or sauce, or you can freeze the slices in gravy or sauce.

When freezing leftover casseroles, soups and stews, if possible remove well cooked vegetables and any potatoes, rice or pasta because they will go soggy.

MARINADES

Marinades originated as a means of preserving meat, and as the name suggests, involved the use of salt or brine. In the past, journeys could take months, so travellers became adept at keeping whatever meat they had: salt beef was eaten by sailors, and marinading in wine probably began when meat in danger of rotting was thrown into wine barrels. A wine marinade was also found to help to tenderise tough meat, and add flavour.

Today we use marinades to prepare meat for cooking, turning the meat in well-flavoured liquid or dry ingredients for anything from an hour to a few days. Marinades can be used for meat which is going to be roasted, braised, casseroled, fried, grilled, stir-fried or made into pâtés and terrines. It's a useful technique which can give very different flavours to the same cut of meat, and can enhance the natural flavour if it is too bland or too strong. It also helps to keep the meat and tenderise it.

Keeping

Marinading in a cool place will help to keep fresh or defrosted meat for a few days. This can be very useful on those occasions when your guests don't turn up, or for whatever reason you can't cook the expensive joint you have ready. It works better with larger pieces, but you must take care to turn the joint regularly in the marinade. If there is any danger of the marinade fermenting, for safety's sake you will have to boil it every day and cool it before you replace the meat.

Tenderising

Meat which is potentially tough can be effectively tenderised with a liquid marinade containing acidic ingredients. Vinegar, wine, fruit juice or tomato juice will begin to break down the fibres of the meat, so that it will be more tender when cooked. Quite often a lack of fat goes with toughness, so some oil in the marinade will help counteract any dryness.

Flavour and variety

Free-range or organic meat should have more flavour than its intensively reared counterpart (although it may be just as tough, gristly or fatty, depending on the age, feeding or breed of the animal). The simplicity of a well-roasted piece of flavoursome meat in its own gravy, with vegetables, cannot be beaten. For festive occasions, especially when the meat is going to be served cold, the extra flavour from a marinade will add something special, and the richness will make the meat go further! Stews and casseroles can also be made extra special if the meat is marinaded first, and the marinade can be cooked with the dish.

Dry marinade

A combination of salt and freshly ground spices are the usual ingredients for a dry marinade. Dry ingredients take longer to permeate the meat than liquids, so this means using strong flavours and taking extra care to see that the meat does not go off. This does not necessarily mean keeping it in the fridge, because the colder the temperature the longer the process will take. The best place for all marinading is a cool, darkish, well ventilated space like a cellar.

Spiced beef is the best known dry marinaded dish. Recipes vary, but the beef can either be rubbed with salt for a day to get the moisture out, dried and rubbed with spices and a little saltpetre if the piece is big; or the beef can first be rubbed with sugar to tenderise it, then rubbed with a mixture of salt and spices. When the beef has finished marinading, the joint is pot roasted very slowly in water or stock under a tight fitting lid. When completely cold it is pressed by placing a bowl over it, and weighting it down with something heavy.

Liquid marinade

Marinades usually have liquid ingredients, and the acid and/or alcohol in them helps to keep the meat. Use an earthenware, glass or enamelled vessel. Plastic can be used but definitely not aluminium – the acids may react with it and discolour the food, spoil the flavour and possibly leach aluminium into the food. Make sure that the meat, and any fruit or vegetables, are as dry as possible so the marinade is not diluted, mix all the chosen ingredients together and put in the meat. If the meat has been frozen make sure it is thoroughly defrosted, and that any juices which have come out are discarded.

Turn the meat from time to time, if possible every two hours and at least twice a day, so that every part of it gets some marinade. When the marinading is complete, remove the meat and pick off all the bits clinging to the surface. Strain the marinade liquid and use it for cooking the meat in if you want to, with fresh herbs, vegetables and spices.

Small pieces of meat like steaks, chops and meat for stir fries can be marinaded for a very short time before cooking, to add flavour and to help baste them if they are very lean. This sort of marinade needs to be strongly flavoured – a few spoonsful of sherry or oil and lemon juice or vinegar, herbs, spices, tamari and soya sauce, tomato paste and mustard. Yoghurt is also good for a quick marinade. Turn the meat from time to time, and incorporate the marinade in any sauce that you make.

Slices of cold roast meat, fresh or frozen, can also be marinaded before reheating in a mixture containing oil. This will help reduce any dryness and add flavour which will inevitably have been lost in freezing. Add the marinade to the sauce that you reheat the meat in.

Marinades are usually uncooked, but if you are going to marinade a large piece of meat it's a good idea to cook any vegetables and spices to extract the flavours. Cool the marinade before use. If the weather is hot or the meat is to be soaked for a few days, take the meat out every day, reboil the marinade for a couple of minutes, and allow it to go cold before replacing the meat.

Suggested ingredients

Liquids
Spirits, fortified wine, wine, cider, beer, fruit juice or vinegar. Oil can also be added to help baste the meat if it is very lean. You can also add oil on its own with other flavourings, sauces like barbecue and mushroom catsup, tamari and soya sauce, mustard, tinned or ripe fresh tomatoes or tomato purée.

Spices and herbs
Spices should always be whole or coarsely ground, but not powdered – try peppercorns, coriander, juniper berries, fenugreek, cumin seeds, cardomom pods, cinnamon stick and root ginger. The common kitchen herbs are also good – bay leaves, parsley, thyme, rosemary, dill and sage.

Vegetables and fruit
Carrot, onion, shallots, celery and garlic (either in the marinade or slit the meat and push the garlic slivers into

it). Fruit also adds interest and flavour, especially to game – hard apples, citrus fruit pieces or peel, dried fruits, pineapple, firm pears. Small amounts of preserved fruits such as plums, cherries, etc., with their liquor; red-currant, crab apple, rowan jelly, etc.; pickled fruit and vegetables.

PICKLED GARLIC BEEF

We used pickled garlic in this marinade because we had some, but it is a good example of how to experiment with unusual flavours. It can be used for prime roasting cuts, just for the flavour, but it is also suitable for cuts which are on the tough side for roasting, such as topside, silverside, brisket, or roasting cuts from an older beast. You could also marinade braising or stewing steak for a few hours in this mixture to tenderise and add flavour, and use the strained marinade as part of the cooking liquid.

For a piece of beef weighing about 4lbs we used pickled garlic and 3tbsp of its vinegar (you could use fresh garlic and wine or cider vinegar), 2tsp whole spice berries – a mixture of black pepper, coriander, fennel, cumin, black, white, green mustard seed, black or green cardomom (pickling spice is fine, but you may need to add more peppercorns), fresh or dried chillies, two bay leaves, a bunch of fresh herbs, and some red wine.

Choose a glass or earthenware container into which the joint just fits, so that the marinade will be as deep as possible. Wipe the meat, then take a sharp, long, narrow-bladed knife and make incisions at regular spacings lengthwise through it. Insert slivers of garlic as deeply as possible, filling the cuts. Place the meat in the container, rinse and dry the spice berries and add with all the other ingredients – the liquid should come halfway up the side of the meat. Cover loosely to protect from dust and flies and leave in a cool place, preferably not the fridge, for one to four days, turning as often as you remember but at least twice a day.

Remove the meat and scrape off any bits sticking to it. Place in a baking pan, strain the marinade over it. Add a fresh bunch of herbs to the marinade and, if you want to, a few stock vegetables and/or a few pickled capers and a couple of anchovies. If the meat is very lean cover with a piece of suet or smear a little dripping or a couple of tablespoons of oil over it to help baste it. Cook in a fairly hot oven for about twenty minutes until the meat is browned on top. Lower the heat to a slow oven and cook until tender, about three and a half hours, basting or turning occasionally.

If you want to serve it hot, plan to have the meat cooked about twenty minutes before serving. Remove the meat and allow it to rest for easier carving, strain the stock and skim off excess fat, and use it to make gravy. To serve cold, remove the meat from the oven, cover and weight (a plate and a bag of flour does very well) in the stock until completely cold. Strain and skim the stock and reduce it to a syrupy consistency, taking care it does not burn, and either use this to glaze the meat before serving or turn it into a kind of relish by adding chopped herbs, chopped capers, mashed anchovies, or whatever takes your fancy to fit in with the theme of 'pickled beef'. Carve the meat very thinly and serve at room temperature with a selection of salads.

A DEVIL OR SWEET AND SOUR MARINADE SAUCE FOR ANY MEAT

This should be a thickish paste which will cling to the meat. Use sweet and sour ingredients with hot spices. Select from honey, sugar, fruit juice, tomato paste, sweet chutneys; vinegar, lemon juice, ketchups, pickles (onions, green peppercorns) and chutneys; Worcestershire sauce, mustard, garlic, pepper, ginger, tamari. Include some oil for lean meats and some strongly flavoured herbs such as bay leaf, tarragon, thyme. Add pot herbs such as celery, if you are marinading for a longer time. Soak steaks, chicken portions, etc., for barbecuing and grilling, or make incisions in larger joints and press the marinade in.

SALTING

Salting, curing, pickling – call it what you will – can easily be done at home. If you buy good meat in bulk, or rear your own, it is an excellent way of preserving some of it, and at the same time enhancing and changing the flavour. By contrast freezing only preserves the meat and often diminishes the flavour. As long as you are careful and pay attention to detail and cleanliness, it is really quite simple to salt joints of meat and, when you have had some practice, to make your own bacon and hams. If you have made wine and beer successfully at home, you should find salting no trouble.

Just about any meat can be salted, but the cheaper cuts are better than the leaner prime cuts. Brisket of beef can be used to make corned beef, and lamb and duck will also salt well, and of course pork. If the meat is usually hung this should be done before salting begins.

Start with small pieces to gain experience before you attempt a whole ham! The cure can be as weak or as strong as you like (this depending on the time it takes), but in general it is only worthwhile to make it strong if you want to keep the meat for a long time. Although excess salt can easily be removed by soaking and boiling in clean water, there is no point in doing this as soon as the cure is finished, especially as you risk losing flavour as well as salt. Many roasting joints are improved if salted for 24 hours before cooking, which enhances the flavour rather than changing it, and seasons the meat.

The following guidelines are only meant to give an idea of how simple salting is, but before starting consult a book such as *The Self Sufficient Larder* by Mike Foxwell (Optima) for comprehensive up-to-date instructions. If you get enthusiastic there are many different ingredients to try. It would also be interesting to track down local recipes and techniques. Older people often have rich resources of knowledge which they are willing to pass on, and their methods may have variations which suit the local conditions or particular breeds of animal.

What you need

The only equipment needed is a container deep enough to immerse the meat in completely for wet salting, although a shallow container will do for dry salting. The container may be earthenware if it's in good condition, or the more easily obtainable food-grade plastic – a brewing bucket is good. The only other necessary item is salt – rock salt or good quality sea salt; ordinary table salt will not do.

The other main ingredients are all optional; saltpetre, ascorbic acid, sugar and herbs and spices. Saltpetre (sodium nitrate) and ascorbic acid (vitamin C) are extra preservatives to help the salt, and they create the 'right' pink colour, especially saltpetre. Without either bacon and ham will be fine, although some people think that the taste is not so good, and the meat will certainly be greyer. If you want to use saltpetre you only need a very little, much less than in many traditional recipes. Some form of sugar, muscovado, treacle or honey (honey is particularly good as it is said to accelerate the curing process) is useful for flavour and for counteracting the toughening effect of the salt on the meat. Fresh herbs and whole spices such as juniper berries, nutmeg, peppercorns, cloves, thyme and bay leaves, also add flavour and interest, but shouldn't be overdone. Beer and vinegar are also used in some cures.

You must have somewhere cold to do the salting as a warm atmosphere might spoil the meat, wasting it or posing a health risk. A refrigerator would control temperatures best, and in a modern house may be the only alternative, but of course there will not be much room for anything else in it while the meat is curing. If you live in an old house and are lucky enough to have a cold larder or cellar it may well still have the stone slabs built in specifically for the curing of meat. As long as there is reasonable ventilation, this may well be the ideal environment. If you cannot guarantee that the temperature will remain consistently cold, save salting for the winter and use the garden shed or an unheated room.

Dry method

Dry curing is the quickest method. The required amounts of salt and other ingredients are mixed together and rubbed into the meat carefully every day until the salt has been absorbed and the cure is complete. The salt draws moisture out of the meat as it sinks in. Traditionally the meat was often stood on sticks or straw in a shallow bowl, or on a shelf on which it could drain, but you can stand the meat on the salt in a bucket. Very large pieces for wet salting are sometimes dry cured for a couple of days first so that the moisture can be drawn out and discarded, so saving the brine from dilution.

Wet method

Wet curing takes a little longer and involves mixing the salt and other ingredients with water to make a brine, immersing the meat completely in it until the cure is complete. Every three or four days the brine has to be checked and more salt added if necessary, since the salt is being absorbed into the meat and weakening the solution. If this is not done then moulds appear on the surface of the liquid and the brine becomes viscous, which will mean that it must be discarded and a new brine started to save the meat. At home a new solution is recommended for each salting, but traditional bacon manufacturers often kept the same solution going in vats for years. The development of friendly bacteria helped the quality of the cure in the same way the bacteria in the air and walls of an old cheese store often contain the 'secret ingredient' which gives the cheese its flavour.

Drying

When salting is finished the meat is washed in cold water to remove any surface salt which may draw moisture from the atmosphere, wiped dry, and hung up in a warm, airy place like the kitchen. This is to allow the meat to dry out thoroughly. Some surface bloom or mould will grown on the outside and this is a good sign. When it is completely dry, which may take days or weeks depending on the size and type of meat, the cure is finished and the meat will keep for many months as long as it is cool and free from flies. There are specific insects which like salted meat, and the traditional method of protecting a ham from contamination was to encase it in a muslin bag and paint it with limewash. However it is much easier to bury it in a box or bucket of bran which has been baked in the oven to kill any creatures which might be in it. You can cut pieces off a large joint and, as long as air is excluded, return it to storage with no ill effects. Remember that the salt is preserving the meat, and therefore that it is unnecessary, in fact positively harmful, to store it in the fridge.

BOILED BEEF AND CARROTS

Silverside and brisket were the usual cuts of beef used for salting. Salted beef can become dry if kept too long, so it is usually salted just for the taste and cooked soon after coming out of the brine. Wash off the cure, cover with fresh water and bring gently just to boiling point without allowing the water to boil. Remove the scum, and simmer *very* gently for ten minutes. Taste the liquid and, if very salt, drain and repeat the process. Cover and continue to cook very gently for about one hour to the pound, adding bay leaves, peppercorns and pot herbs if wished. When the beef is cooked, remove it from the pan. If you want to serve it cold, allow it to cool completely and weight it so that it carves easily. Strain the stock and use for soup. To serve it hot, remove the meat to a warm place, strain the stock, add fresh carrots and bring to the boil. Add dumplings, cover and simmer until the dumplings and carrots are cooked, about twenty to twenty-five minutes.

SMOKING

In the past when meat had been salted and needed to be hung in a warm airy place to dry out, the logical place was in the chimney, out of the way and free from flies. It was discovered that as well as adding flavour, smoking added to the preservative qualities of the salt – tarry deposits in the smoke settle on the food and inhibit the growth of harmful bacteria.

If you have successfully mastered the art of salting then smoking is the next step in meat preservation. But it is more complicated than salting, so home smoking should really be seen as a hobby which is enjoyed for its own sake. Chimneys are not recommended because there are far too many things which can go wrong, so some investment in equipment is necessary, although it need not be too expensive. You also need a good book on smoking. If you can cope with salting but can't face smoking, then search around for a small smoking business that may do it for you.

Equipment

Cold smoking simply adds flavour and preserves the meat without cooking it. Temperatures must be kept low, and a solid kiln is needed to keep the temperature stable. If money is no object then there are small versions of commercial smoking kilns available, but if you are keen on the idea of smoking you will probably be the sort of person who enjoys improvising, and a perfectly satisfactory kiln can be made from suitable new or recycled materials. A disused outside toilet is the right shape and size, or a kiln can be constructed inside an old shed or outbuilding. They have been made out of old refrigerators! Then you need a smoke producing unit, for which a dustbin incinerator is ideal, and a source of heat, like a calor gas ring. The fuel is usually oak, but can be more or less any hardwood, and sawdust, chippings or logs can be used, although sawdust is easiest to control. You also need racks or rods on which to suspend the meat.

Hot smoking actually cooks the food, and is a good method for tougher meats. They usually have to be cold smoked for a period of time first to give the flavour. Game and poultry are particularly suitable for hot smoking. Hot smokers are easy to build as they are more or less temporary ovens, with higher temperatures needed over a shorter period of time. They can easily be converted from metal dustbins or old oil drums, and need a drip tray to catch the fat as it runs out to prevent it going on the flames.

COOKING TECHNIQUES

The following cooking techniques are all you will ever need for cooking meat, especially for traditional dishes. Once you have mastered them, then if you use recipes at all it will probably only be for ideas. Remember to look carefully at your piece of meat first and try to judge what technique is needed to make it tender, succulent and tasty.

ROASTING/BAKING

Roasting is a simple method of cooking meat which uses dry heat. Many people find that roasting is their favourite way of doing justice to a piece of good meat, and the traditional Sunday lunch is still a good way of getting a busy family to sit down and eat together.

The most suitable cuts are the prime tender joints, and if the joint is on the bone it will be extra juicy. A good covering of fat, and some fat marbled through the lean, are desirable for a roast because it bastes the meat, helping to keep it tender and succulent and giving it more flavour. If the meat is roasted well the fat should be crisp and tasty, and a small portion should always be served with the lean. Immature meat such as lamb, kid and pork should always be cooked medium to well done.

When roasting less tender meat with coarser fibres, for example from a part of the animal which has highly developed muscle or from an older animal or cuts with little fat such as fillet, marinade first with oil for two to four hours or longer before cooking, and/or baste with fat or the marinade during cooking.

Cuts suitable for roasting

Beef Sirloin, round, forerib, wing-rib, fillet, aitch-bone, topside.

Venison Loin, haunch (roast farmed venison as for beef). Baste game venison well during cooking or marinade it first; if age is in doubt, pot roast or braise.

Pork All larger joints can be roasted – leg, loin, belly, shoulder, spare rib.

Lamb, kid and young goat (chevon) All cuts except middle and end of neck. Loin cuts are best roast in whole joints rather than individual chops. The meat from older sheep and goats can also be roasted, but marinading will reduce the risk of toughness.

Poultry and game birds Young birds are the best for roasting; baste well or bard the breast. Older birds may be 'steamed', then roasted or pot roasted.

Rabbit and hare Young animals can be roasted, but they must be well basted.

Preparing meat for roasting

Truss poultry or boned meat. Wipe the meat with a slightly damp cloth and trim off excess fat, sinew or pipes. If the meat is very lean add extra fat by:

- Covering with the caul, which is the 'lacy' piece of skin which holds the fat around the internal organs.

- Barding the meat – covering it with rashers of fat bacon. This is usually only for poultry and game.

- Larding the meat – inserting matchstick-size strips of pork fat into the meat just below the surface. This is usually done with a special larding needle, but with patience it is possible to make do with a sharp, thin-bladed knife.

- Soaking in a marinade containing oil.

- Smearing or brushing with dripping, butter or lard, and basting regularly during cooking (butter will burn at very high temperatures).

- Stuffing the meat, if appropriate, with a stuffing enriched with fat. Butter and oil can be used, but tend to run out quickly. Suet melts more slowly but may spoil the flavour of delicate meats.

Season with herbs, spices or pepper before cooking. You can salt meat which has a good covering of fat, which will enhance the flavour and make it more palatable, but don't salt lean meat because it draws out moisture from the surface and makes a hard crust on the meat. Alternatively you can dredge the meat with a mixture of salt and flour about fifteen minutes before the meat is ready, then baste it with the hot pan juices. This process is known as frothing; it gives a crisp and tasty coating to the fat, and is also used for crisping the skin of poultry and game birds.

Method

The meat can be placed on a rack over a baking tin to allow the drippings to run into the tin to roast the potatoes underneath. Always begin roasting meat with the surface fat uppermost to start the basting. If you want you can turn the meat while it is cooking to get an evenly cooked surface, but don't pierce the surface of the meat or you will lose some of the juices into the pan. This will enrich the gravy but make the meat less juicy. For the same reason, unless your oven burns hot and the meat is in danger of turning into a charred log, try

71

not to poke with a fork or skewer to test whether the meat is done until the end of the cooking time.

The meat is best left uncovered so that it roasts properly in the dry heat, but you do need to take care to see that it doesn't dry out. If you want to cover the joint with foil or greased paper for most of the cooking time, uncover it again half an hour before the end of cooking to brown and crisp the surface.

As the cooking times given can only be approximate until you have got used to roasting, using a meat thermometer will be the only way that you can be sure that your joint is properly cooked. They usually have a table to indicate the right temperature for different meats, and take out all the guesswork. Stick the spike into the joint as near the centre of the meat as possible, or right down to the bone if there is one. When the temperature reading reaches the required level the meat is cooked.

Remove the meat from the oven at the prescribed time, and if possible plan this to be at least half an hour before you serve the meal. This will give time for the meat to 'rest'. This makes it easier to carve because the juices settle and don't run out so much, and the meat contracts and becomes firmer. The colour of any juices which do come out while the meat is resting will indicate how well the meat is cooked, and they should be added to the gravy.

Dripping can be used to roast potatoes or other roots, or to cook a Yorkshire pudding, or saved for spreading, cooking or baking. Leftover fat or trimmings can be further rendered down in a slow oven and added to the dripping pot.

Quick roasting

This method is only suitable for tender, less gristly, younger meat, or meat which has been well hung. It does give a very juicy result, and is good for meat which is to be served rare, and smaller joints, but be careful not to overcook as the meat will dry out and shrink very rapidly.

Quick roasting times

Beef   220°C 425°F gas 7

On the bone or fillet	20 mins per lb + 20 mins
Rare	15 mins per lb + 15 mins
Boned and rolled	25 mins per lb + 25 mins
Stuffed (weigh after stuffing)	30 mins per lb + 30 mins

Pork   200°C 400°F gas 6

On the bone or tenderloin	30 mins per lb + 30 mins
Boned and rolled	35 mins per lb + 35 mins
Stuffed	40–45 mins per lb + 40 mins

Lamb   220°C 425°F gas 7

On the bone, medium done	20 mins per lb + 20 mins
Well done	25 mins per lb + 25 mins
Boned and rolled, and stuffed	30 mins per lb + 30 mins

Turkey
200°C 400°F gas 6   20 mins per lb + 20 mins

Chicken and duck
200°C 400°F gas 6   25 mins per lb + 25 mins

Goose
200°C 400°F gas 6   25 mins per lb + 25 mins

Game birds   15 mins to 1 hour depending on size.

Rabbit and hare   *15 mins to 1 hour depending on size.*

Slow roasting

This is an 'easier' method in that there is less likelihood of spoiling the meat by burning it, and it is easier to get an even result. It is the best way to cook very large, or more fatty joints.

Put into a pre-heated oven, gas mark 4, 350°F, 180°C. Add 10 minutes per lb to the quick roasting times.

Very slow roasting

This is suitable for very fat cuts of pork and lamb, or when you want to baste the meat, say with a marinade. The meat is cooked in a very slow oven for a long time and is ready when almost falling apart. Much of the fat will render out of the meat leaving the rest crisp and delicious. Very slow roasting is used in Mediterranean and African countries by wanderers, who leave their meat to cook on the fire all day, quite often wrapped or covered. It's also good for meats which may be tough, such as game, older meat, etc., but be careful not to let it dry out.

Put into a cold oven, turn oven to gas mark 2 or 3, 325–350°F, 160–180°C, and roast for 50–60 minutes per lb.

Gravy

When you have removed the meat from the roasting tin use the juices and some of the fat to make the gravy. Game, poultry and leaner meats, or meat from old animals, will give less pan juices than fat meats, so a stock made with trimmings, bones, giblets and a few pot herbs is especially useful.

To make thickened gravy, spoon off excessive fat, leaving about a couple of tablespoonsful per pint of gravy with the juices. If you want browner gravy, brown the deposits in the pan or add a little onion or tomato and fry for a while. Sprinkle in an ounce of flour per pint, stir and cook over a medium heat for a few minutes, scraping up the pan juices and deposits. Remove from the heat and whisk in hot stock or vegetable cooking water and any marinade, return to the heat and stir until the flour is cooked through. The quickest way to get the fat and juice to separate is to tilt the pan and let it settle for a few seconds, or you can use a special bulb baster or gravy separator, or pour the fat and juice into a jug or tumbler and leave it in a cool place.

To make thin gravy, again you will need to remove most of the fat, leaving the deposits and juices. Add hot stock or vegetable water and any blood which has come out of the meat while it has been standing. Cook gently for five minutes, but don't let it boil if it has much blood in it. You can strain the gravy before serving it.

Carving

If you are a bit nervous about carving it's best done in the kitchen, where you will be able to make mistakes and test the meat to see if it is done! You must have a very sharp, fine bladed knife for neat carving; if you hack at meat with a blunt thick knife you will tear the fibres and a lot of juices will be lost. A long blade is good for big cuts on the bone, but a shorter blade will do for poultry and rolled joints. A carving fork is useful because it has a finger guard and the long prongs will hold the meat steady. Make sure the platter you are carving on is big enough and that it is hot.

A boned, rolled, stuffed joint is the easiest to carve, and can be simply cut into slices of the required thickness. Poultry can be jointed and each joint served with a slice of breast meat: cut off the wings and the legs close to the body, dividing the legs into thigh and drumstick. The legs of bigger birds can be carved into slices. Very small birds are either served whole or cut in half lengthways.

Joints on the bone are more difficult – the only way to do it neatly is to know where the bones are. This will only come with practice. To begin with it's probably easier to cut chunks of meat rather than slices from smaller joints such as shoulder and leg of lamb or pork, and to slice larger joints until you get near the bone. Very tender meats are traditionally carved with the grain and less tender ones across the grain.

A rib or loin joint which is made up of chops is easier to carve if the butcher has 'chined' the bones (cut part way through them) so that they can be separated.

If you have cooked a roast which is going to be served cold, don't be tempted to carve into it before it has cooled completely.

How to rescue a roast

If things go wrong there are remedies to save the day. If the meat is too rare, carve it quite thickly and make the gravy. Lay the slices of meat in it and leave the pan on a low heat uncovered for two or three minutes until the meat loses its underdone appearance. In poultry the part where the leg joins the body may be underdone, especially if the bird has been trussed too tightly, so joint the bird and place the underdone parts well into the gravy to cook through.

If the meat has dried out, make a thick gravy and whisk in a couple of nuts of butter. Carve the meat, lay the slices in the gravy and heat over a very low heat, turning once or twice, until it becomes softer.

LEFTOVERS

Roast, pot roast or braised meat is delicious served cold so long as it is not very fatty, with a selection of salads and pickles. You need imagination and a certain amount of skill to turn leftover cooked meat into a hot gourmet dish, but with only a little care you can make it into a tasty and nourishing family meal. You need to know one or two things about the nature of the meat you want to re-hash, then the rest is up to your own ingenuity and whatever other ingredients you can muster. My family often remarks that the meals that I make at the end of the month when money and food stocks are low are often the most delicious.

The secret of success is in the way you reheat. Dry cooked meat will tend to become tough if subjected to fierce heat for any length of time, and may also be rather tasteless since it will have lost most of its juices when it was initially carved. Make the heat source fierce but quick, so that the meat just reaches boiling point, and try to include some fat to prevent dryness. You can also protect the meat by coating it in batter or crumbs. To compensate for lack of flavour make your reheating sauces tasty, using good stock, leftover gravy, relishes, tomato purée, herbs and spices, tasty vegetables, citrus juice or rind, pickled capers or gherkins, or small amounts of ham or bacon.

Here are a few alternatives to try:

- Put the meat into a hot sauce, gravy or stew then turn down the heat and allow the meat to heat through gently but thoroughly without boiling.

- Mince the meat and add to a sauce or gravy, then cover with a layer of creamed potatoes (such as cottage pie) thick sauce (such as moussaka) or pastry. Or mix with a thick sauce or gravy and turn into individual or large part-cooked pastry cases and finish in a hot oven.

Stews and casseroles are often tastier after reheating, and some recipes will recommend making these dishes in advance to let the flavours develop. Care is needed in reheating and steady gentle heat is best.

What to do with smaller quantities

- Heat them up on their own or with added small ingredients to make a tasty filling for a baked potato or a pancake.

- Add to a stew of beans or pulses or vegetables.

- Thin down and use as the basis of a soup.

- Make into a pie with pastry or cover with mashed potatoes or other roots.

- Mince with extra onion, herbs and breadcrumbs and use to stuff vegetables such as marrow, aubergines or peppers for baking.

Shepherd's/cottage pie

Shepherd's pie is made with minced lamb and cottage pie with minced beef. It can be made with fresh meat but works well with leftovers. Add freshly minced cooked lamb or beef to a tasty thickened sauce or gravy containing any onions or fresh vegetables which you want to add. Turn into a pie dish, cover with light creamed potatoes, dot with butter and heat through in a fairly hot oven until browned. You can make a small amount of meat go a long way by adding fresh vegetables, lentils or beans so long as the base sauce is tasty.

Potted meat

Leftover roast meat can be blended or shredded with softened butter and herbs to make a delicious spread for sandwiches. Put in a mould and cover with melted butter to help it keep for a few days.

Croquettes, rissoles or meat patties or cakes

Almost any leftover meat mixed with a starchy ingredient – potatoes, thick white sauce, breadcrumbs, rice or flaked grains – and moistened with milk, sauce or egg can be formed into shapes, left to rest, then deep or shallow fried.

Croquettes
A true croquette is very crisp on the outside and creamy inside. Mix ½ pint of seasoned thick white sauce with

¾–1lb chopped or minced cooked meat, 4oz finely chopped spring onions and mushrooms, finely chopped fresh herbs and 2 egg yolks. Allow to go completely cold and set. Take a tablespoonful at a time (wet the spoon to make it easier), drop into breadcrumbs, then into beaten egg, then crumbs again. Leave to rest for at least half an hour before frying. A rissole is a croquette (without egg and with other ingredients such as vegetables) in a pastry case, which is then fried.

GRILLING AND BARBECUING

Grilling and barbecuing both use dry heat. Choose fairly thin slices of prime cuts which are tender and have a fair amount of fat, like chops and steaks, bacon and gammon. Other cuts can be marinaded. You can also use the method for sausages, kidneys, burgers and joints of poultry.

Slices and smaller pieces are best because the heat source is so fierce the meat has to cook through quickly before it burns on the outside. Larger pieces or joints can be spit roasted or barbecued, but you will need to baste them during cooking to prevent them burning and drying out. Choose meat with some marbled fat in it so that it will keep juicy.

Take care when you are grilling – the fat may ignite as it runs out of the meat. It is best to use a grill pan with a grid, or a tray with holes in it, to allow the fat to drain away underneath.

Preparing meat for grilling

1. Wipe the meat with a clean damp cloth, don't wash it. If you have marinaded it, dry the surface.
WHY? If the meat is wet it will begin to cook in steam, and not form the brown surface characteristic of dry cooked meat.

2. If the meat has a layer of fat around the edge try to

cut it into portions which each have a rim of fat. Slash the fat around the rim.

WHY? The fat around the rim helps to prevent burning at the edges and to a certain extent prevents shrinkage. If the fat is not cut it may curl and prevent the meat from cooking evenly.

3.   If your piece of meat is thick or you think it may not be very tender you can marinade it for an hour or so beforehand.

WHY? To begin to break down the fibres.

4.   If the meat is too thick or not very tender you can beat it with a special meat mallet or even a rolling pin.

WHY? To make it thinner and break down some of the fibres. This will help to make it more tender and cook more quickly.

5.   Leave the skin on chicken, or coat delicate meats with egg and breadcrumbs and brush with fat before cooking.

WHY? To protect the meat from fierce heat and allow the fat under the skin to baste it.

6.   Season the meat and brush it on both sides with fat or oil and grease the rack.

WHY? To prevent the meat from charring or sticking before its own fat melts and begins to baste the meat.

7.   Preheat the grill.

WHY? So that the meat sears quickly and forms a crust.

8.   Place the meat on the tray ensuring that the pieces are not touching and that every piece will be directly under or over the heat.

WHY? To ensure even cooking.

9.   Cook thick pieces of meat further away from the heat source than thin ones, perhaps 2–3 inches away up to 1½ inches thick; 5 inches away over 1½ inches thick depending on the temperature and whether you want your meat rare or well done.

Method 1

Cook for half the recommended time, then turn to cook the other side.

WHY? Gives a dark crust to the meat and a more intense flavour, but more care is needed to prevent burning. I think this method is best for rare to just done meat, because the contrast in flavour and texture is better.

Method 2

Turn the meat every two minutes or so until cooked.

WHY? It's easier to regulate cooking, and better if you don't want burnt-tasting meat or if you like your meat very well done.

Well grilled meat should be plump and slightly puffy and springy to the touch, which indicates that the meat has not dried out inside its crust.

Grilling times

These are only a guide, since times will vary depending on the temperature, the thickness of the cut and how well done you like your meat.

Beef steaks (medium rare – shorten or lengthen times for rare or well done)

¼–½ inch	4 to 6 mins
¾ inch	8 to 10 mins
1 inch	10 to 15 mins
1½ inches	15 to 18 mins

Veal chops

1 inch	15 to 18 mins

Lamb and pork (well cooked)

Chops and steaks cut from the fillet or leg.

¾–1 inch	8 to 12 mins
1½–2 inches	20 to 25 mins

Bacon

Cook to taste, either lightly done or crisp.

Gammon

Cook over more moderate heat than other meats, since the saltiness becomes rather unpalatable if the meat is overbrowned.

¼ inch	10 mins
½–¾ inch	15 to 20 mins
1 inch	20 to 25 mins

Game

Grouse	25 to 30 mins
Partridge	20 to 25 mins
Baby pheasant	40 to 50 mins
Pigeon	30 to 40 mins
Quail	10 to 12 mins
Duck (rare)	15 to 20 mins
(well done)	25 to 30 mins
Woodcock	15 to 20 mins

Poultry   20–35 mins

Unskinned, jointed, halved or split and flattened. Do not grill a bird weighing more than about 2lbs. Cook mostly on the flesh side, basting if possible as the skin chars easily.

STEWING AND CASSEROLING

For our purposes we'll call this technique stewing, although stewing and casseroling are in fact the same method, stewing on top of the stove and casseroling in the oven. Stewing is possibly the most economical, easy and appetising method of cooking meat. A small amount of meat can be made to stretch a long way by the addition of vegetables, pulses or dumplings, and these can be so varied that tedium never sets in. It's a long slow method, using less liquid than boiling and more than braising, and is particularly suitable for tougher cuts of meat. 'Prime' tenderer cuts can be used, but don't overcook them or they will disintegrate into shreds. Very fatty meat is not so good in a stew unless you trim the meat first, or cook the dish and allow it to settle so that the melted fat can be skimmed off the top before serving.

There are two kinds of stews: brown stews and white stews. A brown stew is richer and darker and the meat is browned before going into the stewing liquid (liver and bacon casserole, *boeuf en daube*, goulash). A white stew is lighter and milder – the meat is simply layered raw with the other ingredients into the casserole dish (Irish stew, Lancashire hot pot). Sometimes choice cuts are cooked in this way and the stock is used to make a creamy sauce (chicken supreme).

The basic method of making any stew or casserole is the same. If you master the technique you can dispense with recipes and use what you have in the cupboard.

Meat suitable for stews

Beef Cheek, chuck, shin, flank, neck, brisket.

Lamb Lean breast, flank, loin, neck, shank, shoulder.

Pork Spare ribs, shoulder, hand and spring, trotters, lower leg.

Goat Breast, neck chops, loin, cushion, ribs, scrag end and best end of neck, shoulder, small leg bone as far as the knuckle.

Venison All parts of wild venison, forequarter cuts of farmed venison.

Poultry and game Especially older birds and animals.

Method

Trim off excess fat and melt down for dripping. Cut the meat into suitable size portions for the recipe – dice, slices, chunks, or whole in the case of chops or joints. In general make the meat pieces correspond in size to the vegetables that are going in with it. If the meat is likely to be very tough or if you want to add extra flavour, marinade it first for a couple of hours.

BROWN STEW

1. Decide whether you want to thicken the stew with flour, and when you want to do it. For very tough meat it is better to thicken near the end of cooking. Other

methods of thickening include adding pulses, rice, barley, potatoes, or pasta part way through the cooking, or extra blood as in jugged hare.

2. If you decide to thicken at the beginning, coat the meat in seasoned flour, approximately 1 level tbsp for each pint of liquid.

3. Heat fat to very hot in a heavy pan and brown the meat quickly, turning until evenly brown all over. Drain and remove. Sauté one medium onion for every pound of meat in the remaining fat until browned to taste. Add crushed or sliced garlic when the onions are nearly done. If you are using spices such as chilli powder, sprinkle them in now and stir for a few seconds. Remove the onions and put with the meat.

4. Add your chosen cooking liquid – stock, cider, wine, beer, marinade, fruit juice, tomatoes/juice or water, or any combination which takes your fancy. Bring to the boil and scrape up all the deposits from the bottom of the pan. Season lightly with salt and pepper and herbs. Combine the meat, onions and liquid in the stew pan or casserole dish. Add the root vegetables – carrots, parsnips, turnips, whole potatoes and any pulses or grains (kidney beans should be boiled rapidly for ten minutes to destroy the toxins in the skins before being added to the stew). Make sure that everything is well covered by adding more liquid if necessary.

5. Cover closely and cook gently until the meat and vegetables are tender. The lower the temperature the longer the cooking.

6. Tender vegetables such as peas, green beans, mushrooms, courgettes, baby carrots and new potatoes, and pasta, should be added towards the end of cooking, so that they just cook through.

7. If, when it is cooked, you want the stew to be thicker there are several alternatives. Take the lid off and cook a little longer so that some of the moisture is

evaporated; or mix a little cornflour, potato or rice flour with water, add to the pan, stir and allow to cook a few minutes longer; or add *beurre manié* – equal quantities of flour and butter worked to a paste with the fingers and added in little lumps, each one being stirred until it's dissolved before you add the next one. Allow to cook for five to ten minutes until the taste of raw flour has disappeared.

The best accompaniments to a hearty brown stew are baked potatoes, rice, noodles, or crusty bread and a green vegetable or side salad.

WHITE STEW

1. Simply layer the meat alternately with sliced root vegetables and onions to fill the pan, finishing with a layer of potatoes. Cover with stock or water and add seasoning to taste. Bring to the boil, skim if necessary, cover closely, and cook gently until all is tender. Remove the lid for the last half hour of cooking to brown the potatoes on the top. Serve from the pot.

2. If you are going to finish a dish with a white sauce made from the stock, as in chicken supreme, cook the meat and vegetables with stock or water in a closed pan very gently on top of the stove. To keep the meat white you may soak it overnight in water with added lemon juice or vinegar and salt. When the meat is tender remove and keep warm, strain and skim the stock. Make a light roux with butter and flour (1oz to 1oz per pint), add the stock and cook through. Adjust the seasoning and add any other ingredients such as egg yolk, cream, capers, mushrooms, parsley or lemon juice. Serve the meat with the sauce poured over.

BRAISING AND POT ROASTING

These two techniques are really the same – cooking in a sealed pot with a little liquid (rather than a lot, as in a stew), so that the food is partly steamed and partly stewed. Pot roasting is the term normally used when cooking larger joints, and braising for smaller pieces. Almost any meat can be braised, but it would be a waste of the more expensive prime joints, such as rib or sirloin of beef, or spring lamb, which may even go stringy. Use this method for cooking less tender or gristly meat. The longer, slower cooking and the moist heat will make it more tender and digestible, but you can still give the appearance and taste of a roast to larger joints.

Braising can be done on top of the stove or in the oven. Use a heavy casserole dish or pan with a well-fitting lid, so that the food cooks evenly. When pot roasting a joint, half an hour before the end of cooking take the lid off, drain off the stock to make the gravy, and put the dish in the oven to brown the meat. Meat for braising and pot roasting can be marinaded first. If the meat is cooked in a marinade it is, strictly speaking, braised and not roasted, even if cooked without a lid.

Method

1. If the meat is very lean, lard with pork fat or fat bacon. This is usually done with a special larding needle, but if you have the patience it can be done with a sharp, thin knife with a long blade. Push the needle or knife into the joint and insert the fat into the slits. Alternatively introduce some fat into the cooking liquid, or stuff the meat with a fat-enriched stuffing and tie it together. *WHY? To help baste the meat and make it tender.*

2. If you like garlic insert it into the meat using a sharp

87

knife. Brown the meat all over in hot fat or in a hot oven, and remove it from the pan. Cut a selection of onions, root vegetables and celery into medium sized pieces and gently sauté them in the same fat, with some garlic and bacon if you like, for about ten minutes. Add the stock, strained marinade or water to just cover the vegetables.
WHY?   To improve the flavour and appearance of the meat and stock.

3.   Place the meat on the vegetables and cover with a heavy, well-fitting lid. A sheet of greaseproof paper between the lid and the pan will give a better seal. Cook in a slow oven gas mark 2–3, 325°F, 160°C. Baste or turn the meat once or twice (optional) during cooking, and add more liquid if any is lost.
WHY?   To prevent the steam escaping during cooking, so that the flavour of the vegetables is kept in and the meat doesn't dry out.

4.   If you are cooking a joint, when it is almost ready remove the lid, baste the meat, then turn the oven up to gas mark 7, 425°F, 220°C, and allow the meat to brown for about twenty minutes. To make carving easier allow the joint to rest a while before serving, which will also give you time to skim and prepare the stock for gravy.

To serve
Serve braised meat dishes as you would a casserole. Pot roasts can be served with the vegetables and the skimmed stock as gravy. If you are serving it with Yorkshire pudding or mashed potatoes and want a thick gravy which won't soak in too much, thicken with a little *beurre manié* or cornflour. If you don't want gravy, skim the stock, reduce it to a syrupy consistency and use it to glaze the meat. Serve with another sauce and vegetables.

This glaze is also good for a cold dish. Paint the meat with the glaze about half hour before serving, carve and serve at room temperature.

STEAMING

Steaming was once a favourite method of cooking meat and other foods for children, invalids, or for those with a delicate digestion. It was used for cooking even the most choice cuts such as fillet steak or chops, as well as beef for making beef tea. Steaming is the only way to cook a traditional suet pudding, such as steak and kidney.

Steaming has some distinct advantages – it conserves the soluble nutrients, helps tenderise the meat, and prevents any shrinkage due to evaporation of the natural juices. Although not suitable for very large coarse-textured cuts, it is a good way of cooking less tender cuts and joints, especially if you are on a low-fat diet and cannot eat fatty meat. A boiling fowl such as an old laying hen can be successfully steamed, then finished in the oven to make a 'roast'. Or it can be jointed and steamed.

Steaming can also be very economical – with a little planning a whole meal can be cooked in the same pan. This is invaluable when cooking for one, and saves on fuel. If you steam in a pressure cooker you will save time as well.

There are two ways of steaming. For small pieces of meat such as chicken joints the food can be cooked in its own steam, for example between two plates over a pan of boiling water which may be cooking vegetables for the same meal. You can also use a tightly-lidded baking dish in the oven, but it may be necessary to grease the dish first. In the second method the food is placed on a rack or trivet and cooked directly by the steam from the boiling water in the pan:

1. Wipe the meat and truss large or boned joints or poultry.
WHY? To prevent the meat going out of shape.

2. Bring water to the boil in a covered saucepan (a tight-fitting lid is absolutely vital if your whole house is

not to fill up with steam). Place the meat on a rack or trivet with legs long enough to keep it above the water, or in a covered basin with the boiling water coming half way up the sides of the basin, or use a pressure cooker.

3. Cover small pieces of skinned meat with greased paper.
WHY? To prevent the meat becoming sodden with condensed steam dripping from the lid.

4. Replenish the cooking water with boiling water as required.
WHY? Using cold water would check the process of cooking and may cause steamed puddings to sink.

Cooking times
Cook small pieces of meat, and any size of poultry, until tender. For larger pieces, cook beef for twenty-five minutes per pound plus twenty-five minutes, mutton for thirty minutes per pound plus thirty minutes, and pork for thirty-five to forty minutes per pound plus forty minutes. Steamed puddings, such as steak and kidney, will cook faster if the basin is stood in the boiling water with the level coming halfway up the side of the basin, but they can be cooked in steam on a rack if preferred. Immersed in boiling water, a one-pint basin will take one-and-a-half hours and a two-pint basin two-and-a-half hours. Add an extra half hour for steaming on a rack.

BOILING

It would be more correct to call this method simmering, as *boiling* the meat is exactly what you must not do. A rapid boil would be too hot, and simply make the meat tough. Once boiling point has been reached the meat should be simmered gently in a tightly sealed pot.

Boiled meat is somewhat out of fashion as nowadays we try to conserve the nutrients in food. However this method is useful for those on a low-fat diet or who do not like rich food, and for cooking salted and pickled meat. There is the added bonus of a tasty stock to make the basis of many soups and stews. It is also possible to use this method to get a decent looking and tasting roast from even the toughest joint or bird, browning it in a hot oven after long slow simmering to tenderise it.

The pieces most suitable for boiling are the larger joints which you might otherwise pot-roast or braise. These joints would become hard if cooked by a dry heat method such as roasting, either because of the age of the animal or bird or because they contain a lot of gristle, but don't boil meat which is very old or gristly – this is always better cut up and stewed.

Cuts suitable for boiling

Beef Thick rib, topside, silverside, aitchbone, brisket, and salted beef. Cook for 15 minutes per lb + 15 minutes.

Lamb and mutton (very young lamb is not suitable) Breast, leg and shoulder. Cook for 20 minutes per lb + 20 minutes

Pork Belly, shoulder, spring, hand, cheek, head and leg. Cook for 25 minutes per lb + 25 minutes.

Bacon and ham Soak overnight in cold water to cover, or longer with a change of water, if likely to be very salty. Cook for 25–30 minutes per lb, depending on size (less for larger joints).

Poultry Cook anything from 1–4 hours depending on age.

Method

1. Choose a pan large enough to contain the meat and enough water to cover it.
WHY? So that the meat cooks evenly.

2. Wipe the meat and weigh it, so that you can gauge the cooking time. Tie poultry or boned or large joints firmly with trussing string.
WHY? To hold the meat in shape.

3. Plunge *fresh* meat into boiling water, and return to the boil.
WHY? So that a crust forms on the meat.

4. Cover *salt* meats with cold water, and bring to the boil. If they are likely to be very salty, drain and repeat the operation.
WHY? To remove some of the salt.

5. Skim and lower the heat to simmer. Add the stock vegetables, seasonings, herbs and spices of your choice at this stage. Cover tightly and replenish the cooking liquid with boiling water as necessary.

For a complete meal from one pan remove the meat when cooked to rest it and add extra vegetables and dumplings to boil in the liquid for about twenty-five minutes before serving. Boiled joints are also good served with a creamy sauce.

FRYING

Frying is suitable for thin cuts of very tender meat: fillet and rump steak, lamb chops and cutlets, pork chops and steaks, bacon and gammon rashers, liver, sweetbreads, poultry joints, sausages, fritters, rissoles and croquettes.

Shallow-fat frying

Lard, clarified dripping or oil are usually used. You can use butter, bacon fat or dripping from any meat for shallow frying, but if they are not clarified solid particles will burn at high temperatures and spoil the appearance if not the taste of the dish. Butter can be mixed with oil to reduce this risk if you want the taste of butter (some people like chicken, steak or gammon rashers cooked in butter).

Only the barest covering of fat is needed in the pan to cook thin slices of meat and sausages. Use more for thicker cuts, chops or small joints of chicken. For rissoles or croquettes have the fat come halfway up the sides of the food, but don't fill the pan more than one-third full. Bacon needs no extra fat unless it is very lean, but begin cooking over a low light to allow its own fat to melt.

Deep-fat frying

Raw meat to be deep fried must be lean and tender and needs a protective coating such as egg and crumbs or batter. Deep frying is a good way of serving leftover meat, in the form of croquettes and rissoles. Use clarified fat, beef dripping, lard or vegetable oil. Cold pressed oils such as olive oil aren't suitable because they burn at these temperatures.

Food	Temperature
Frozen food	180°C, 350–60°F (depending on size)
Uncooked food	190°C, 360–80°F (depending on size)
Cooked mixtures	195°C, 375–85°F (depending on size)

Method

1. For shallow frying use a heavy frying pan with an even base.
WHY?   To ensure evenness of cooking.

For deep frying use a pan large enough to take the required amount of fat without filling more than one-third full.

2. Heat to the required temperature before you put in the food. For most shallow fats this will be when the fat becomes still and the faintest haze can be seen on the surface. For butter wait until any foam subsides. For deep fats the temperature can be quite critical, so a

thermometer is recommended for good results.
WHY? To stop the food absorbing a lot of fat and becoming soggy.

3.   Make sure the food is dry before putting it into the pan.
WHY?   Any liquid will boil on contact with the hot fat and this will cause it to splash.

4.   Do not overload the pan.
WHY?   It will cool the fat, making the food greasy and soggy. Turning the food will also be difficult.

5.   For thin pieces, or if you want the meat rare, have the fat hot and cook for half the time on one side, then turn and cook the other side. For meat which is thicker or if you want it well done, have the fat very hot, brown on one side and then the other; then lower the heat, and continue turning occasionally as it cooks, according to your preference.
WHY?   The high heat sears the meat and prevents the juices running out and causing the fat to burn.

6.   Turn the meat carefully to avoid piercing it, which will allow the juices to escape. Try to skim off any particles of food which float off into the fat during cooking.
WHY?   These will quickly burn and spoil the food.

7.   Drain fried food on absorbent cloth or paper.
WHY?   To remove the excess fat.

Part 3
GOING THE WHOLE HOG

GOING THE WHOLE HOG

'Please study the matter, for if you eat meat you should face honestly the fact that it is animal, and should know the basic facts of its preparation before letting it be used for human food.'

Dorothy Hartley
Food in England

In the following sections of the book we have attempted to follow the passage of individual animals through their lives and deaths to our tables. We believe that if we are going to eat meat, it is only by increasing our knowledge that we can come to respect and do justice to animals in their lives, and their meat when we come to prepare it.

Britain is an urban society, and we are so far removed from our sources of food that our understanding of farming is not very great. Perhaps this is why advertisers and food manufacturers can so easily sell their products using images of a countryside which has long since disappeared, if indeed it ever existed. We have tried to give an impression of what happens in farming today, although much of it has had to be simplified. Farming nowadays is an alarmingly complex subject even for those who use more natural methods. Changes in techniques occur all the time – they may be for economic reasons, the price of land, labour and bought in feed-stuffs, or they may be brought about by technological advances or by changing fashions, farmers being human like the rest of us!

A note on recipes

The recipes are mostly for simple meals of the sort that are not made so often nowadays, but which lend themselves to the better flavour of good meat. The basic recipes can be adapted easily with a little practice and imagination. Most of them use quite modest amounts of meat, so they are both economical and healthy. We have also included some special recipes, again simple and easy, for those festive occasions when you will want to make the most of a large piece of meat.

How much meat?

Four ounces of uncooked weight off the bone will provide a satisfying portion of meat for most adults if it is served as part of a meal with vegetables and some starchy food like potatoes or rice. However, we don't actually need that much meat – dishes containing much less can be just as satisfying if the meat is used as a concentrated flavouring, combined with other protein foods such as pulses and grains, or cooked imaginatively with vegetables. Cooks from many cultures have found ways to make meat go further by serving it with beans, potatoes, rice, dumplings, pastry and stuffings. Grilled or roasted on its own, a little meat provides the perfect foil for large dishes of cooked vegetables. Why stop at 'meat and *two* veg'? Cold roast meat is also perfect with large mixed salads. One word of caution: too much smoked, salted or barbecued meat might be harmful to health, so moderation is called for.

BEEF

Domestic cattle are hardy ruminants with a natural life-span of about twenty years. Their digestive system enables them to eat bulky, rough grasses consisting mostly of cellulose, which most other animals, including humans, find inedible. Once they are weaned their stomachs develop four separate but connected compartments. Food passes first into the rumen, which is the largest part of the stomach. Here it absorbs water and starts to be broken down by a delicate balance of bacteria. Lumps of partially digested food are passed back up the gullet into the mouth to be chewed and swallowed again. This is known as chewing the cud, or ruminating. The food is then gradually dried out and digested completely as it passes through the other compartments of the stomach.

If kept on a natural diet, the ruminant's digestive system provides the animal with body heat from within, which is one of the reasons why sheep and cattle are so hardy. Cattle can spend up to a third of their lives chewing the cud, and they need to feel secure while they are doing it. They like to live in herds, so that those who are busy ruminating can be watched over by others.

As everyone who has ever walked in the country knows, the cow's fibrous diet produces copious amounts of dung which are deposited frequently and haphazardly as the animal grazes. This manure fertilises the land but also contains the eggs of many parasites. In the wild, the herd will keep down its burden of parasites by wandering over vast areas. On a farm they can be controlled by having a low stocking density and by regular movement of the cattle onto clean pasture. Chemical wormers called anthelmintics are also used, and their use has to be routine in intensive systems.

THE MOST IMPORTANT ANIMAL IN BRITISH FARMING

Beef cattle are well suited to the British land and climate. They can survive even on poor grazing but grow fast on rich pasture, both of which Britain has in abundance. Their size and their digestive systems equip them to withstand cold winters. They also produce large amounts of manure, which was once the main source of farm fertiliser and still is on many organic farms.

Traditionally beef cattle were slaughtered as well-grown mature animals, often (but not always) very fat by modern standards. The carcass was then hung for at least two weeks. The strong flavour and robust texture of this beef made it a national favourite and the pride of our cuisine. Nowadays beef cattle are slaughtered at a much younger age and with a leaner carcass, and may be rushed from farm to shop counter in less than a week. Consequently the quality of beef has declined, and delicacies like dripping have disappeared from our kitchens.

HOW BEEF CATTLE ARE RAISED

There are three main methods of raising beef – intensive, semi-intensive and traditional – with many variations in between.

The intensive system

Calves are artificially reared on powdered milk and fed large amounts of carefully controlled concentrates, so that growth is fast and constant. This unnatural diet can cause problems in the digestive system. They are housed all their lives, sometimes on straw but often with no bedding on a floor of concrete slats. Slaughtered at no more than twelve months and often younger, they produce a lean carcass for the supermarket. Management, as in other intensive farming systems, has to be strictly monitored, as the threat of disease is ever present. This system was popular in the 1960s when the price of cereals for the concentrates was low and the product was known as 'barley beef'. Other cheap feeds, such as vegetable and animal wastes, are also used in intensive systems.

A similar intensive system, called the 'feedlot', is much used in the USA for hamburger beef, and it has started to appear in this country. The animals, sometimes tens of thousands at a time in the USA, are kept crammed together outside in pens or pits which, in our climate, are permanently in a quagmire.

Semi-intensive-system

This is probably the commonest type of system presently used in Britain. The semi-intensive calf has a similar start to the intensive calf, but is kept longer, averaging about eighteen months depending on what time of the year it is born. The animal will spend some of its life out on the summer grass, and in winter will be housed in yards eating bulky, good-quality silage, fodder or concentrates.

Traditional

Calves are raised on their own mother's milk or that of a suckler cow, often on the hilly pastures of the North and West. At eighteen months to two years old they are either finished on the better pastures of the farm, or sold through livestock markets to lowland farms to be finished in yards or on lush grass. In the past this method would involve a 'store' period when little or no growth took place, but today the farmer tries to keep the animal growing all the time to get an earlier return on the investment.

Castration and dehorning

By tradition British farmers have castrated bull calves, so that the resulting steer, being more docile and slower growing than a complete bull, can take full advantage of the open grassland. Bull beef must be raised intensively indoors on high-quality feed to avoid the meat becoming too lean and rangy.

Calves of the horned breeds are sometimes disbudded for the safety of other animals and farm workers. This is done either by chemical cauterising or with hot irons and an anaesthetic. Some farmers prefer to use the polled breeds, which do not have horns.

BREEDS

Different systems demand different characteristics, and because of this the variety of cattle breeds has been more or less maintained. Modern beef farmers nearly always cross breed their animals to produce a calf suited to their particular conditions, though as we can see by looking at the animals in the fields this does not lead to a ragbag of mongrel cattle. The appearance of the animal will be affected by their dominant genes, with such characteristics as a black coat, a single coloured coat, a polled head, and the white Hereford head usually predominating. Although sophisticated new breeding techniques will doubtless have profound effects on the present system, the pedigree beef bull still has a tremendous importance in agriculture, demonstrated by the spectacular prices which they command.

Some small farmers prefer the native breeds; they value their ability to thrive and grow on home-grown food without the necessity for expensive imported feeds, from often dubious sources. The hill breeds are extremely hardy and 'thrifty' and can convert to good beef on the highest, coldest, poorest quality land. A rich diet of concentrates would be wasted on them as they will only put on fat before they have achieved a good body size. The Galloways (small cattle, all black or black with a wide white 'belt'), the Welsh Black (another small black beast) and the shaggy, long-horned brown Highland cattle are all typical. Also hardy and bred to do well on marginal land are the Aberdeen Angus, a very stocky, all-black animal with a reputation for producing the finest beef, and the Hereford, the main British beef breed, which is brown and white with the characteristic curly 'top knot'.

In recent years several continental beef breeds have been introduced to this country, such as the cream coloured Charolais, the brown and white Simmental and the rich reddish-brown Limousin. They are large animals, generally with a good 'conformation' – that is, they produce a lean carcass with a large back-end which makes up the prime cuts for the butcher. They need good feeding to do their best.

Controversy rages in the farming press about the virtues and vices of these breeds. Their meat, although lean, is often thought to be coarse grained and tasteless. More serious for their smaller dairy breed mates is the suffering that can be caused in giving birth to their calves. They often have to be delivered by caesarian section, and can be difficult to rear.

Veal

Veal is the meat of the four to six months old calf. It is tender and pale, and the flavour is often described as either delicate or bland, according to your prejudices. The traditional ways of rearing calves for veal have long been notorious for their cruelty. Although they are being phased out in this country, they are still in common use on the continent. Gourmet standards dictate that the meat has to be as tender as possible, so young animals are confined in chains or crates from birth to restrict their movements. The whiter the meat the better, so they are kept in total darkness and fed a milk diet deficient in iron. The result is an inherently unhealthy animal which would be unlikely to survive even if it were spared the slaughterhouse.

Veal has never been a popular meat in Britain, although probably not because of any objections to the system. In dairying areas there would always have been some veal, but farmers with beef cattle would consider it wasteful to slaughter a valuable meat animal when there was plenty of grazing to rear it. In Europe veal has always been prized more than beef, and veal production still flourishes on a massive scale, underpinned by the huge surpluses of milk in the European Community.

People are now prepared to accept a slightly darker meat, so more humane systems of raising veal have been developed. In simple terms this merely means the earlier slaughter of a beef calf still on a predominantly milk diet.

BEEF AS A BY-PRODUCT OF THE DAIRY INDUSTRY

In general cattle are bred either for beef or for milk. One dual-purpose breed, however, the familiar black and white Friesian dominates the national herd. The Friesian is unusual in that it gives a copious amount of milk and grows quickly to produce a lean beef carcass. Most home-produced beef comes from Friesians, either pure bred or crossed with a beef breed. The involvement of the dairy herd in beef production is likely to grow with the development of the technique of embryo transfer. Pure-bred beef animals at the embryo stage can be implanted into the wombs of dairy cows, reducing the need to keep expensive beef animals.

The dairy industry also helps to satisfy the demand for cheap meat from manufacturers and caterers who make ready-prepared meals, burgers, pies and meat products. Dairy cows are culled from about four years of age, and sold on to be fattened intensively before slaughter. This rather wastes their talents, because they can go on lactating for many more years. It also means that regular customers of canteens in schools, hospitals and factories consume this poorer quality meat, which is likely to contain more chemical residues since dairy cattle are usually kept fairly intensively.

BEEF YOU CAN TRUST

The most humane systems are those in which the natural behaviour of the animal is accommodated as far as possible. The ideal is probably the self-contained herd where the whole life cycle is completed on the same farm. The cattle can live in family groups, and don't have to endure the stress and suffering which are undoubtedly caused by travelling and handling in the livestock markets. It also removes the risks of diseases being introduced by bought-in animals, and gives the farmer the confidence of having known the animals since birth.

HANGING

Whatever the system of husbandry or the breed of cattle, many farmers, butchers and experienced cooks think that the main reason that today's beef is no longer as tasty or as tender as it used to be is because it has not been properly hung. Correct hanging is more important for beef than for any other meat, so when buying you should ask how and for how long this has been carried out. Most experienced butchers and farmers now hang beef for ten days to two weeks, although some hang for three weeks, and each individual will no doubt have a different opinion. A measure of the effect of hanging is this recommendation from *The Complete Illustrated Cookery Book* of 1934 – '(for roasting) the buttock is excellent and very economical ... but it should be hung for some time until quite tender.'

The maturing of beef is usually done in two stages. First it is hung for about ten days, and then the forequarter is butchered into stewing cuts. The hindquarters, which are the roasting cuts, are then hung for up to a further eleven days. Only then is the meat ready for the jointing, trimming, boning and rolling process which gives us the finished product ready to cook.

FAT

Although customers are nowadays demanding, and getting, lean beef, many farmers are of the opinion that a good proportion of fat on the beast is necessary if the meat is to be tender, tasty and succulent, and that excess can be trimmed off by the butcher. Butchers, however, find this uneconomical since their customers will not accept the fat with the lean.

Of course huge quantities of fat are wasteful for the cook and unpalatable as well as unhealthy for the diner. But good beef fat eaten in moderation with the right accompaniments is tasty and nutritious. Any excess poured from the roasting pan or trimmed off before cooking and rendered down, as housewives learned to do during the War, is useful to enrich your non-meat meals. For many Northern cooks, myself included, there is no substitute for clarified beef dripping for making chips (after the first frying which produces pale inedible results which have to be thrown away).

AVAILABILITY

The availability of beef is not seasonal, but traditionally it is at its best in the winter, because then the animal is in its prime, having been fed on the best of the summer grass.

WHAT TO LOOK FOR WHEN BUYING BEEF

Fresh beef
As with all fresh meat, beef should be firm to the touch and should not retain the impression of fingers as it is handled. It should not smell strongly. Clammy or wet meat which exudes moisture may mean that it is old or that it has been frozen. Ox beef, from the male animal, should be a good red colour, be fairly fine grained depending on the cut, and be intermingled with grains of fat. Heifer beef, from the female, is paler and closer grained.

The fat and the suet should also be firm, but the colour may vary from white through cream to yellow depending on age, breed, feed and sex. Grass-fed animals will have a more yellow fat. Whatever the colour it should be even, look neither dried out, wet nor tired, and should not be too copious. Very lean beef is potentially tougher than any other meat, and lack of fat must be compensated for during cooking. If the beef is for roasting ask the butcher for a piece of fat or suet (sometimes called the caul) to lay over the meat in the oven.

Frozen beef
It is almost impossible to judge the quality of any frozen and packaged food. For basic guidelines see the section on freezing in the storage chapter.

CUTS OF BEEF AND HOW TO COOK THEM

The butcher cuts the beast in two down the backbone, and then separates the fore from the hindquarters. The choicest, tenderest cuts come from the hindquarters, because most of the flesh is there; also in a grazing beast most of the work is done by the front of the body, which toughens up the muscles; the back end just follows on behind!

Starting with a hindquarter, the big wedge of fat known as suet (inside which the kidneys are found) is cut out from the body cavity. Then the flank is cut off – a thin flap covering the belly which has lots of fat and long-fibred muscle without much gristle. The leanest parts of the flank are sold as skirt for stewing, and the rest is used for rough mince and sausages. Skirt is perfect for pies, meat puddings and stews. It is quite tough, so long slow cooking is needed, but care must be taken not to overcook it, since the lack of connective tissue combined with the long fibres can cause those fibres to break apart and the meat to disintegrate into the gravy.

Cuts of beef

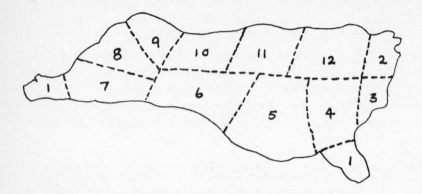

1. shin
2. head/neck
3. clod
4. fore-rib/thick flat rib
5. brisket
6. thin flank } skirt
7. thick flank
8. topside/silverside
9. rump
10. sirloin with fillet underneath
11. wing-rib
12. shoulder

Then the sirloin is cut off. When sold with the bone in, it is known as the wing rib (a roasting joint). When boned out it simply becomes sirloin, and is sold as roasting joints or grilling steaks. Sirloin is the prime roasting joint, said to have been knighted by Henry VIII as a mark of his appreciation, although the word may be derived from the French *sur loigne*. Roast meat tends to retain its succulence when the bone is left in, although this makes carving more difficult. Sirloin steaks can be grilled or fried.

Then the rump is cut off, which makes rump steak and chump steak (sometimes known as aitchbone). These are frying steaks and sometimes a larger cut is taken from the chump end for roasting.

Sirloin

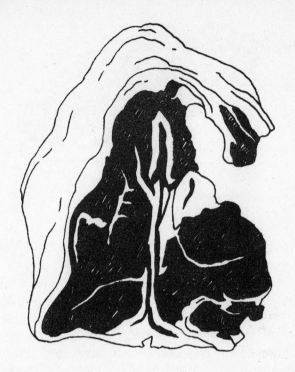

Wing rib

Rump steak

Running underneath the sirloin and the rump is the fillet, also known as undercut. This is the leanest, tenderest and most expensive cut of beef. The whole or part fillet can be made to serve more people by roasting and carving thinly, carefully braising with vegetables, or smothering with sautéed mushrooms and baking in a pastry crust. The fillet steaks are small and thick, and are also known as *tournedos*, *filets mignons*, *medallions* or *chateaubriand* according to the size and thickness of the cut. They are usually grilled and served with a little pat of herb butter, and may be marinaded in oil for an hour or so to help keep them juicy. If fried they are best done in beef dripping.

Then the buttock or top is cut away from the shin. This makes four cuts, which may be rolled – two topside cuts from the inside leg, and two silverside cuts (sometimes known as salmon cuts) from the outer part. Topside is cheaper than the more traditional roasting cuts and is very tasty. If you have a piece which is gristly then pot roasting will do it justice. It can also be slowly roasted if it has been properly hung, or if it is from a young beast, or if it has been marinaded first. Silverside is usually braised or pot roasted. Old recipes for salted, boiled and pickled beef usually call for silverside.

110

Whole fillet and fillet steak

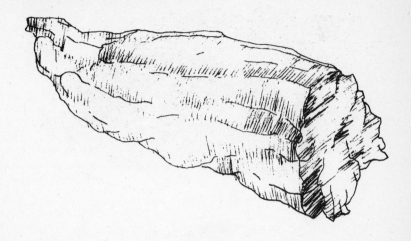

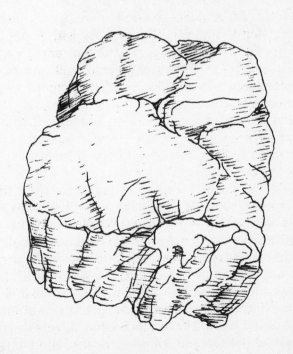

Topside and rolled silverside

The shin, which is the lower part of the leg down to above the hoof, is the most gristly cut, tasty but suitable only for stewing. It's a good cut for leaving in a slow cooker all day without it reducing to shreds, the gristle slowly dissolving into the gravy and giving it body and flavour. A dish of this kind is welcome summer and winter alike and goes equally well with crusty bread and a side salad or baked potatoes and vegetables.

Starting the forequarter, the butcher cuts out the skirt which is the diaphragm muscle separating the thorax

Shin

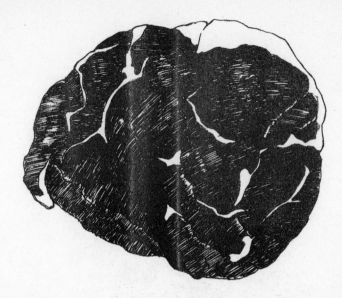

from the abdomen. The forequarter is then cut in half along the length of the beast, from the crop to the middle of the back.

The top half gives fore-ribs, or crop, to roast, shoulder steak (also known as chuck steak) for braising, and neck end or gravy beef for stewing and mince. Fore-rib is a good slow roasting joint, fattier and cheaper than sirloin and wing rib, which can be bought either bone-in or boned and rolled. Chuck steak or braising steak almost always has a good marbling of fat. It is good braised, in slices or serving-sized chunks on a bed of vegetables with very little liquid, or used for beef olives. The neck end (or gravy beef) is tougher, good for stews, soups or pies.

The lower half of the forequarter is sometimes called the gate or breast side. The loose flesh of the throat, known as clod or sticking (because that is where the animal is bled), is cut off and used for stewing or mince. This leaves the shoulder and leg joints and the front flank. The meat over the shoulder joint is known as thick

Fore-rib

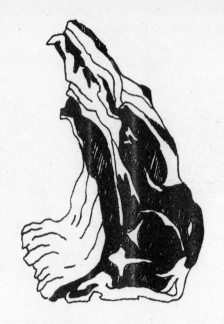

Shoulder

flat rib, or rand, and is for braising or pot roasting, marinaded well and basted with the marinade and extra fat if lean. Cooked this way, it can rival a roast for taste and succulence.

Thick flat rib

All the rest of the leg at the front is known as shin. The front flank is called brisket, and can be divided into two sections; the meat from the front to the end of the sternum is leaner and thicker, and that which covers the last four ribs is thinner and fattier, and is sometimes known as the heart spoon. These cuts are boned and rolled for braising or pot roasting.

Brisket

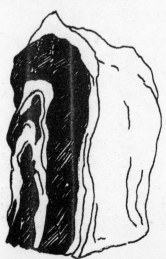

Rolled brisket

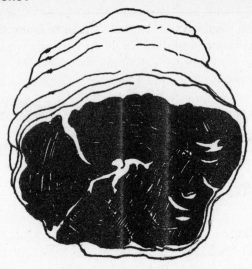

TO SUM UP

Hindquarters Top part – prime roasting, grilling, frying cuts, most expensive. Lower part – ranging from braising cuts down to stewing cuts.

Forequarters Top part – roasting, pot roasting, braising cuts. Lower part – braising and stewing cuts.

Prime cuts have a plump fine close grain with a marbling of fat, and can be cooked by a quick dry method or carefully by a moist method to avoid breaking up the meat. If there is little or no fat, add some during cooking to keep the meat juicy. If you decide you have a roasting cut but it looks gristly, roast it more slowly, or marinade or pot roast it to soften the gristle. If the texture is open and the fibres coarse, then slower cooking in some liquid is called for.

ROAST BEEF

In recent years roast beef has fallen from its revered position as the culinary high spot of the family week. Post-war generations are likely to regard it as 'over the top' – too much protein, too much saturated fat and too expensive. What's more it doesn't even taste the way it used to. But a joint of well reared and hung beef doesn't have to be expensive or unhealthy: just a couple of slices from a succulent roast, with its own gravy and plenty of roast potatoes, onions, parsnips, steamed greens and carrots is a well balanced meal. The left-over meat will provide delicious sandwiches and convenient cold cuts to serve another day with generous helpings of mixed salad.

A roast beef dinner is easy and convenient to prepare: it's no more trouble than putting a ready-cooked meal in the oven and infinitely easier than struggling with a complicated dish. You can roast beef in two ways.

Fast method
This is best for lean cuts or if you prefer your meat rare. There is not as much margin for error as there is with the slow method, so beginners will need to concentrate. But success will reward you with a dark, appetising, thinly crusted joint which carves neatly, and a moist tender inside perfectly cooked to your taste.

Heat the oven to gas mark 6, 400°F, 200°C. If the beef is very lean lard it with pork fat, dripping or beef suet and baste once or twice during cooking. Season with garlic, herbs or ground spices if you wish, and roast uncovered and unsalted for fifteen minutes per pound and fifteen minutes over, to twenty-five minutes per pound and twenty-five minutes over, depending on how well done you like it. These times are approximate and you will probably want to test the meat. Stick a fine skewer right to the centre of the joint or to the bone, *after* the prescribed cooking time. If blood runs out the meat is rare, if clear juice runs out it is well done.

Slow method

This is good for larger cuts, or rolled and stuffed cuts. Although slow cooking is less risky than fast, there is a potentially greater loss of moisture, so make sure that the meat has a good cover of fat, or that you baste the meat with a marinade. If you use a marinade baste the meat every fifteen to twenty minutes, turning it over every now and then. Prepare as for the fast method and roast at gas mark 4, 350°F, 180°C for twenty to twenty-five minutes per pound and twenty minutes over.

You can use lower temperatures and progressively longer cooking times to suit your own convenience. Phil Haughton of Real Food Supplies in Bristol recommends roasting a 4–5lb joint for as long as twelve hours at the same temperature you would eat it, having given it a blast of heat for twenty-five minutes first.

Gravy

For ease of carving, let the meat rest in a warm place for up to half an hour while you make the gravy. A traditional roast beef gravy is easy to make – simply skim off the fat from the roasting tin, deglaze the juices with stock, adding any blood which you have saved from before cooking or which runs out of the joint while it rests, and reduce it to a rich, syrupy consistency. The problem is that this method doesn't produce much gravy, and although it will be delicious, it is inclined to soak into the Yorkshire pudding and disappear. A thickened gravy won't do this so much. To make a thickened gravy sprinkle a little flour into the pan juices, stir and cook for one minute, add stock and blood and simmer until the flour is cooked.

Accompaniments

The traditional companions to roast beef are Yorkshire pudding, potatoes and roots, steamed greens and horse-radish sauce, but for a change try a vegetable casserole, or tartare or redcurrant sauce. With cold roast beef serve pickles and chutneys, salads with mayonnaise, or cream dressings and crispy potatoes like game chips.

BEEF PARCELS

This dish makes a pleasant change from the more usual method of cooking tougher meat diced in a stew or casserole. The flattening process helps to break down the fibres and gristle and makes the meat go a long way.

For each person you need a ¼ inch-thick slice of braising steak cut across the grain and weighing about 3oz. Spread the slices flat on a board, cover with greaseproof paper or a piece of plastic bag, and beat with a rolling pin until very thin, taking care not make any holes. Trim off any ragged bits and cut into fairly even sized pieces. For approximately four servings sauté three shallots in a little fat until just beginning to soften, and mix with 8oz fresh breadcrumbs, 8oz finely chopped flat mushrooms, one finely chopped green or red pepper, a good handful of fresh herbs or 1tsp dried herbs, one crushed clove of garlic, flour and salt and pepper.

Divide the stuffing between the slices of beef, then roll the meat up round the stuffing, tucking in any edges. Secure with wooden cocktail sticks or string. Gently brown the parcels in a little fat over moderate heat. Arrange just touching in one layer in a shallow casserole dish, making sure not to pack the parcels too closely together or they won't cook properly.

Back to the frying pan – turn the heat up to high to brown all the juices left in the pan. Sprinkle in about ½oz flour and brown. Remove from the heat, gradually add one pint liquid (stock, or a combination of water and wine, beer, cider, tomato juice, Worcestershire sauce or soya sauce). Stirring continuously, return to the heat and bring to the boil. Adjust seasoning (remembering the seasoning in the stuffing) and pour the liquid over the meat so that it comes about halfway up the parcels.

Cover and cook in a slow to medium oven for approximately one and a half hours until tender. Gentle cooking will help to prevent the stuffing bubbling out, although some of it is bound to. At the end of this time the sauce should be fairly thick; if not remove the lid and allow to reduce. Serve with a green vegetable and potatoes. You can also use thinly sliced left-over roast beef for this dish – simply fry the parcels gently or casserole them, but not both.

STEAK PUDDING

A steamed suet pudding does take a long time to cook, but is simple and quick to prepare and gratifyingly comforting on a cold winter's day. The suet gives the pastry just the right savoury taste – grate your own humanely reared suet! Use 4oz suet for 8oz self-raising flour, and mix the pastry a little wetter than shortcrust. Roll out three-quarters of it and line a one-and-a-half-pint greased pudding basin, leaving half an inch or so standing up all round. Cut about 1lb beef skirt into bite-sized chunks, roll in a little seasoned flour, and layer into the basin with one large chopped onion and a crushed clove of garlic until it is almost full. You can add mushrooms, kidneys, carrots, etc., as well.

Fill the basin about three-quarters full with stock or wine – not too much or it will burst out into the steaming water. Roll out the remaining pastry for the lid and put it over the pudding, having wet the edges with water; then pinch the edges together and seal it. Cover with pleated greaseproof paper to allow for expansion, then foil or a cloth, and tie tightly round the top of the basin with string. Place in a large pan of boiling water, so the water comes about halfway up the sides of the basin. A safe way to do this is to use an old handkerchief as a sling to lower the basin into the water. Cover and simmer for about three hours, being careful not to let the pan boil dry – add boiling water as necessary. Serve with a selection of vegetables, and potatoes as well so that the meat and pastry goes further and the meal will not be too heavy – you may like to serve extra gravy.

BRAISED STEAK

Jennifer Warner of Brentlands Beef sent us this simple, hearty recipe. Coat 2lb chuck or blade steak, cut into eight pieces, with seasoned flour and brown evenly in hot fat. Gently brown two large onions and four medium carrots, or any other vegetables of your choice. Place the meat on top of the vegetables in a large shallow casserole with a very small quantity of stock and tomato purée. Add herbs and seasonings. Cover with a tight-fitting lid or foil, and cook in the centre of the oven (gas mark 3, 325°F, 160°C) until tender (two to three hours).

BEEF IN ALE PIE

Beer is a useful substitute for stock and makes a rich hearty stew in which the taste of the beer is hard to detect. Add roots as well if you like, and red kidney beans (soaked and boiled for ten minutes first) or brown lentils. Cut 1lb shin beef into 2oz pieces, coat in seasoned flour, fry until quite brown and remove to a casserole. Sauté onion rings and crushed garlic briefly and add to the meat. Turn up the heat to brown the residues, add some stout or beer, and bubble, scraping the pan. Add a bay leaf and pour over the meat to just cover it (allowing more liquid if you are using half-cooked beans or pulses). Cook slowly, tightly covered, for one to two hours or longer. Turn into a pie dish and cover with a thick lid of shortcrust pastry made with lard or suet. Bake in a moderate oven until the pastry is cooked. You can easily make the filling one or two days in advance – in fact it will probably improve with a little keeping.

FILLET STEAK IN MUSHROOMS AND GARLIC

If you ever buy two fillet steaks for a candlelit dinner for two and your entire extended family arrives, this recipe will enable you to feed them all. You can also cook other tender cuts in the same way, for instance tenderloin of pork, chicken breast and fillet of lamb.

Cut the meat into fine slivers and marinade it if you want to. Sauté in hot fat or oil for approximately thirty seconds, remove with a slotted spoon and keep warm. Throw plenty of mushrooms, sliced or whole, in the pan with garlic to taste, and stir and fry again for about thirty seconds. Replace the beef, add soya sauce or tamari or Worcestershire sauce to taste. Allow to heat through and bubble for a minute, and serve immediately with rice or noodles.

LAMB

Sheep have been kept for thousands of years for their wool, their milk and their meat. Wool is relatively less important now than in the past, when it formed the basis of a major industry in Britain. Flocks of milking sheep are being developed but are still uncommon here. Today sheep are raised primarily for their lambs, and the majority are slaughtered young. Mutton, the meat of the older animal traditionally killed at about four years of age, has more or less disappeared. Breeding ewes are culled when they are at least six years old, and the meat goes to meat processors and the rapidly expanding Halal market.

Sheep, like cattle, are hardy ruminants, and are able to convert poor-quality grass to meat. They make useful scavengers and good grassland 'managers'. They can share pasture with cattle because they graze in a different way – cattle preferring the longer grass which they can tear with their tongues, sheep nibbling the short grass which is left. Mountain sheep can survive on the coarse grasses and heathers which cattle will not eat. Because sheep are cheap to buy, feed and house they have kept their place in British agriculture despite the fact that they only produce one, two or at the most three lambs a year. Sheep farmers have also received various subsidies to help what can be an uneconomic enterprise.

SHEEP MANAGEMENT

Sheep do not easily do well under intensive conditions; they are nervous, prone to parasitic infection and a host of diseases – hence the farmer's favourite saying: 'A sheep's worst enemy is another sheep.' Consequently they are the most free-ranging farm animal in Britain, and their diet is still primarily grass.

Systems of management vary more or less according to conditions. The farmer's main aim is to ensure that every year each ewe gives birth to and rears the maximum number of lambs. This is done by careful management and breeding, and making sure that the ewes are well fed before mating. The lambs must grow fast with no checks, be healthy and have a good conformation for the butcher – not too fat or too bony.

Many lambs are still born outside, although increasingly large flocks of ewes are housed in sheds for lambing. The vast majority of lambs are raised naturally on their mother's milk. They need to suckle often, so rather than feed artificially the farmer will try to get other ewes to foster orphan lambs. Mothers and babies then graze outside making the most of the spring and summer grass, and weaning is gradual. Prime fat lambs may be ready for slaughter from about three and a half months, but if they are not ready at the end of the summer they may be kept or sold as store or house lambs to be fattened over the autumn and winter.

Sheep of all ages are bought and sold for breeding, fattening and bringing flocks up to strength, through the long-established system of livestock markets and sales. Not many sheep escape at least one journey to market, as well as the final one to the abattoir. There are some self-contained flocks, which have the advantage for the farmer of keeping out diseases which may be introduced by bought-in stock.

Castration, tail docking and dipping

In many parts of the country male lambs are routinely castrated, usually with a rubber ring which cuts off the blood supply to the testicles. A similar device is sometimes used to dock their tails if the farmer believes that fly strike may be a problem. Blow flies can lay their eggs in the soiled area around the animal's backside – the maggots burrow into the skin of the animal, which dies in a few days if not treated.

Sheep have to undergo compulsory dipping twice a year, to help eradicate parasites such as those which cause sheep scab and fly strike. Organo-phosphorus insecticides are normally used. They are extremely toxic, leaving residues and sometimes cause health problems for people handling the sheep. Dipping can be a problem for the organic farmer – truly organic lamb must either be dipped with a pyrethroid dip, which is not as effective, or slaughtered before dipping time comes round.

BREEDS

About fifty breeds, and many more cross breeds, are still in common use, and there is a breed or a cross breed to match every local condition. Most sheep have been bred to have white or black wool, or a combination, because brown and grey wools are resistant to dyes and therefore not as useful.

Mountain and moorland sheep live a semi-wild existence. They must be able to look after themselves, surviving the rockiest terrain and bad weather conditions, although the hill farmer will bring food to the ewes on the hillside in the bleakest weather. They will usually only bear one lamb each year, but their meat will be low in fat and have a good flavour from the constant activity and the diet of heather and herbs. Mountain sheep tend to have long, shaggy coats of coarse wool. Among them are the Scottish Blackface, the Cheviot, the Herdwick and the Swaledale. Some of these upland breeds, like the Cheviots, are also suitable for crossing with the big longwool breeds to produce prime lambs for fattening in the lowlands. Another cross breeding type is the roman-nosed Bluefaced Leicester.

Down breeds are the prime meat sheep. They are typically stocky animals with a thick, short fleece. The rams are kept to sire prime lambs which grow fast.

Primitive breeds are 'unimproved' and can be difficult to contain, but they do have advantages. They are small, hardy and thrifty, and therefore able to do well on poor quality land. They also have a very lean, finely flavoured carcass. Typical are the brown Soay sheep, descended from the feral sheep of the St Kilda islands, and the black Hebridean.

THE FUTURE

At the moment the sheep is a fortunate farm animal, able to live a comparatively natural life, especially in a self-contained flock. Unfortunately this situation is not likely to continue. The European market for lamb will increase the possible returns from investment in production. This will inevitably mean that sheep become candidates for intensification, and more sheep will probably be kept indoors in large flocks under artificial light. Techniques for increasing and controlling fertility are already in use which make human fertility clinics seem positively unsophisticated. The genetic engineers have a large gene pool of different breeds at their disposal with which to produce a more prolific ewe and a lamb that grows fast on concentrates.

The same gene pool could be used to benefit farmers who want a better sheep for more humane systems, but unfortunately they don't tend to have the same economic clout. At the moment some farmers are finding virtues in the smaller and primitive breeds, which can utilise heather and herb pastures and produce a lean, delicately flavoured carcass. They also produce smaller joints for today's smaller families.

HANGING

Recommended times for hanging lamb vary from a few days for young lamb to three weeks for older lamb and mutton; some say that the forequarter should not be hung but the hindquarters may. The taste becomes quite gamey after long hanging and the meat is more palatable roasted than stewed or casseroled. It is often said that since lamb is an immature animal it must be used as freshly as possible and be well cooked. Personally I find a small joint from a very young animal is usually rubbery whatever I do with it. Unless I can rely on it having been properly hung, I leave it in the fridge for a few days.

FAT

Lamb tends to have more fat both around the joints and within the muscle than beef. For this reason, and because lamb is young, all lamb cuts, with the exception of the middle and scrag end of neck, can be successfully roasted. Slow roasting is best for very fatty cuts – much of the fat renders out, leaving a thin coating of fat which is crisp on the outside and buttery on the inside. If you are making a lamb stew trim off the excess fat, and render it down for dripping. Always serve lamb on hot plates because the fat congeals very quickly, and is cloying when eaten cold.

Spring lamb is less fatty and should be cooked quickly. If roasted, it should be basted or cooked with a fat enriched stuffing. Spring lamb casserole is a classic dish using young lamb and tiny new vegetables; the best results are obtained by using a joint or chops on the bone rather than boned, diced lamb.

AVAILABILITY

Young spring lamb is available from June, older store or house lamb from December.

MUTTON

As we have said, mutton is very hard to get these days and many older people are thankful, remembering the unpalatable layers of fatty boiled mutton and the whole house reeking of the smell. In countries where sheep and goat meat is all that is available, cooks cope better with the large amounts of fat and stronger flavour. They incorporate beans and other starchy foods to soak up the fat, thus making a little meat go a long way, or they cook the meat with acid foods such as tomatoes and fruit to cut the richness.

If you want to try the stronger taste of mutton, it's worth asking a small producer who takes orders in advance if they might keep an animal for you.

WHAT TO LOOK FOR WHEN BUYING FRESH LAMB

Lamb should be plump and not flabby or shrunken. The lean is paler than beef, and a more orangey-red – a brown tinge indicates older meat. The fat is hard, white and slightly waxy. You will need to buy more lamb per serving than leaner meats; it will shrink somewhat during cooking as the fat renders out and, because young animals have a high water content, weight will be lost due to evaporation.

CUTS OF LAMB AND HOW TO COOK THEM

The butcher cuts the lamb in half down the backbone. The leg is cut off at the pelvic girdle. Leg of lamb is a prime joint, the top being the most tender and succulent. When butchering a large lamb the leg is usually cut to make two joints, the shank and the upper leg, known as the fillet. Both are roasting joints, but the fillet is often sliced and sold as steaks for frying or grilling. The leg of a smaller breed or younger animal is often left whole, equivalent to the French *gigot* joint, and some say this improves the flavour. A good way of making a full leg feed more people is to remove the aitchbone and fill the pocket with stuffing, which will also make carving easier. Leg of lamb can be boiled and served with the traditional accompaniment of caper sauce.

Cuts of lamb

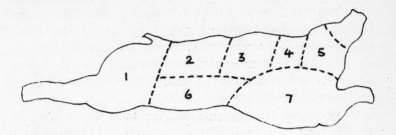

1. leg
2. loin
3. best
4. middle } end of neck
5. scrag)
6. breast
7. shoulder

The back is cut from the fore-leg and shoulder behind the (shoulder) blade bone, and then cut along the length of the beast, separating the breast from the back. A good way of cooking the breast which helps make the fat more edible is to braise it over vegetables until tender, then slide out the bones. The meat is then covered with breadcrumbs and roasted in a hot oven, or pressed between two plates after boning until it has gone cold, then sliced, egged and crumbed, then fried or grilled. Serve with a sharp sauce such as barbecue sauce.

The back gives the chops, which can be cut and cooked in many ways. Starting from the rear there are four chump chops, then the loin or middle back chops, then the cutlets or best end of neck. Divided into individual chops, the chump, loin and best end of neck cutlets are grilled or fried. The loin can be bought as a row of several chops from one side of the back bone and roasted as it is, or it may be boned out, rolled and tied (with or without stuffing). Rather confusingly, loin can also be called fillet. The saddle is a joint consisting of all

Whole leg, shank and fillet

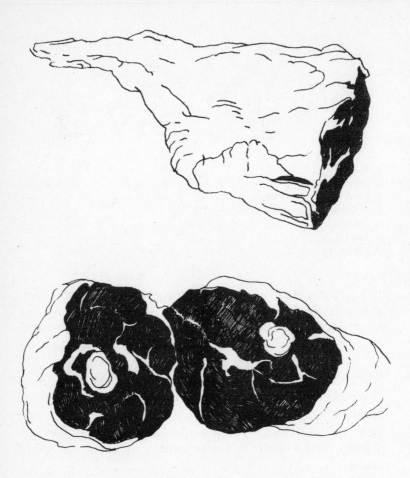

the loin chops from both sides of the back bone. The best end cutlets are used for crown roast, and when boned and rolled become a rack. Cutlets, individually boned, curled round and tied are called noisettes.

The rest of the neck chops, middle neck and scrag end of neck, are stewing cuts. These are cut away leaving the shoulder. The shoulder can be bought whole or halved, boned out and rolled with or without stuffing for roasting or braising, or diced for casseroles and kebabs.

Breast

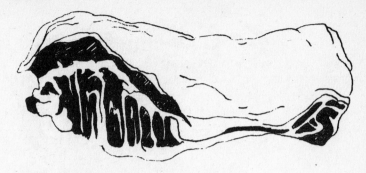

Cutlet

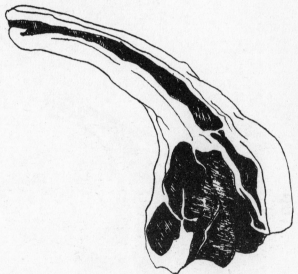

Chump chop

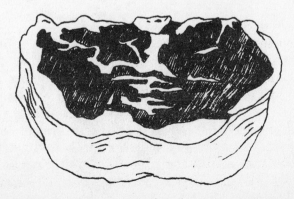

Loin chop

Best end

Scrag end

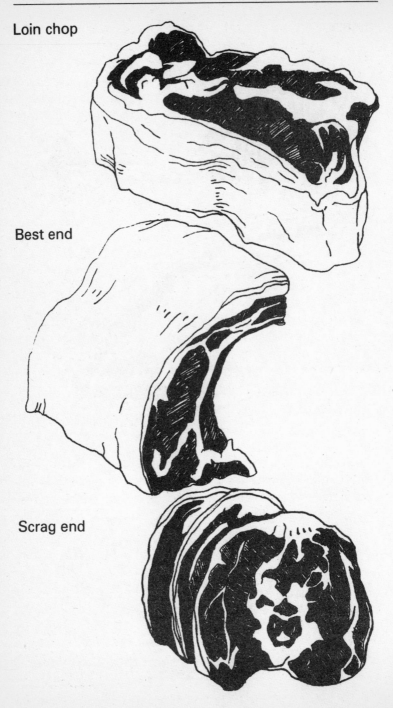

Blade end

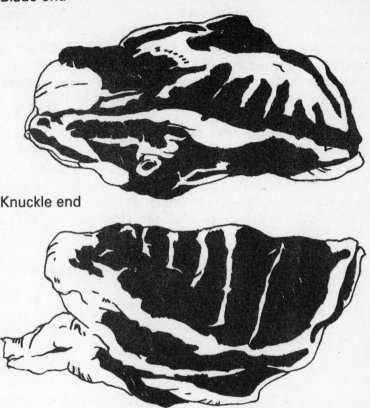

Knuckle end

The lower half is less gristly, and the blade (upper) side is sometimes called casserole lamb. Fores of lamb is the complete shoulder and best end of neck, and is sometimes sold whole for roasting.

ROAST LAMB

Most joints of lamb can be roasted using either a fast or a slow method, but in general young lamb is best done quickly and older lamb slowly. Try to find out how long the meat has been hung for, especially if it is young and lean, and keep it for two or three days to mature if necessary.

Lamb can be roasted just as it is, uncovered, with a sprinkling of salt, on a rack if you want the fat to run away. Or you can insert or tuck underneath sprigs of herbs such as thyme or rosemary, slivered cloves of garlic, or sprinkle the meat with dried herbs. You can 'froth' the joint: half an hour before the end of cooking baste, sprinkle with flour and return to the oven so that it gets a crispy coating.

When cooking a fatty cut such as breast or shoulder by the fast method, bone and stuff the cavity, or bone, stuff and roll the meat – the stuffing helps to absorb the fat. Lean cuts such as leg, loin and rack can also be boned and stuffed to make the meat go further.

You can cook fatty cuts by the slow method, which renders out most of the fat and leaves what remains crisp and more palatable. Try cutting the meat into large chunks so that a lot more surface area is exposed to the heat and more fat comes out. The fatty cuts are not very appetising cold, so leftovers need to be reheated.

Accompaniments

Traditional accompaniments are mint sauce or mint, redcurrant, apple or rowan jelly, roast or new potatoes and caper or onion sauce. Spring lamb is often served with baby vegetables, such as carrots and garden peas. For a change try a sharp tomato and vegetable casserole or mushrooms in tomato. Serve cold lean lamb with pickles and minty potato salad or fresh herb salad and tartare sauce.

Stuffings

For the base use breadcrumbs, flaked grains such as wheat or oats or just-cooked rice. Add herbs such as rosemary, tarragon and thyme or spices such as cinnamon, nutmeg and pepper. Grated or chopped fresh or dried fruit, or piquant ingredients such as capers, pickled walnuts, chopped spinach and tomato purée are also good with lamb.

CASSEROLING LAMB

Fattier cuts such as shoulder can be skimmed very thoroughly after being stewed or casseroled, cooked with other ingredients such as beans to absorb some of the fat, or with sharp ingredients such as tomatoes or spinach to cut the richness. Recipes for lamb are usually suitable for pork as well.

LAMB WITH TOMATOES

Brown cubes of lamb with very little fat in a saucepan. Drain off the excess fat and add sufficient chopped tinned tomatoes or very ripe fresh tomatoes to cover the meat. Add a little hot water and chopped garlic (but not onions), season with salt and pepper and a bay leaf, a piece of cinnamon stick or bouquet garni. Bring to the boil and allow to simmer very gently until the lamb is tender and the sauce is thick, rich and concentrated. Serve smallish helpings with rice, potatoes, pasta or crusty bread. For a change, add stick beans or chopped spinach with the tomatoes, or partly cooked haricot beans and extra water.

SPRING LAMB CASSEROLE

This one-pot dish is a good way to use lean lamb like neck, or lean shoulder of young lamb. Brown the meat in a little fat, then remove it and brown some chopped onions in the same fat. Sprinkle in a little flour, stir, add stock or water, and season with salt, pepper and herbs. Return the meat to the pan, cook gently for about half an hour, and skim off the fat. Add spring vegetables, whole if possible, all one kind or a mixture. Add roots first and finish with shredded greens and young peas which only take a short time to cook. The gravy shouldn't be thick.

GOAT

In world terms the goat is an extremely important farm animal, and it is thought that more people eat goat meat than any other meat. It can survive even in near desert conditions, and in hot dry areas it is *the* major meat animal. Despite a traditional British prejudice against it, our ethnic communities have retained their liking for goat meat, and have always sought it out wherever available. Milk-fed kids for roasting are favoured by Greeks, Spaniards and Italians, while Asians and Afro-Caribbeans tend to favour older animals with a stronger taste, particularly good in curries.

The goat is a ruminant animal and likes to browse for its food, taking leaves and branches of trees and shrubs in preference to grass, although as it needs a high level of minerals in its diet it also eats deep-rooted herbs and grasses. It is an efficient dairy animal – a well-fed nanny can produce her own weight of milk in two weeks. Consequently in gentler climates where the herbage is good, goat's milk is more important than the meat. In Europe it is used to make cheese, and forms the basis of an important industry. In France alone there are more than a million goats. In Britain we have no such tradition, probably because we have too much rain for goats, who hate getting wet and need shelter all year round. But things are changing. In the 1970s an expanding market for quality goat's cheese (which can still be made from unpasteurised milk), coupled with comparatively low set-up costs, created a flurry of interest in commercial goat's milk production. At present there are about 100,000 dairy goats in Britain, and the number looks set to increase. The 1980s saw a similar growth in Angora and Cashmere goats, which are kept for their valuable wool.

Meat should be the obvious and inevitable side-product of these two enterprises. At present, however, many billy kids are put down at birth, and this situation is likely to continue unless the ethnic market can profitably be tapped and goat's meat becomes more popular. One major problem is that although goats compare reasonably well with lambs in their feed conversion and growth rates, it can be too expensive to have them slaughtered because of the low value of the skin. Whereas the value of a sheep's skin will more than pay for the cost of its slaughter, a goat farmer may have to actually pay the slaughter house an extra £2–3 per animal. To be commercially viable there must be sufficient demand to justify the investment needed to overcome these problems and to set up a marketing system.

If we were to overcome our prejudice against goat meat, this waste would be avoided. Unfortunately many people dismiss it as being smelly and tough, even though they've probably never eaten it. Kid meat is often compared to lamb, and studies have shown that there is little difference between the two meats under the age of eighteen months. The older meat is compared to venison, as the flavour becomes stronger and more gamey. Goat's meat tends to be very lean – it has less subcutaneous fat than lamb, and what little fat there is is stored around the abdominal organs. This can be an advantage from the point of view of healthy eating, though it needs cooking methods which will make the most of its leanness.

BREEDS

There are four main types of British goat, all of them open breeds. This means that they have been upgraded by crossing with other breeds. Perhaps the most popular is the British Saanen, a placid white animal with the heaviest milk yield. The brown and white British Toggenburg is the best grazer of grass, and the black and white British Alpine the hardiest and best forager; these two breeds are the best suited to free-range and extensive

systems. The Saanen, Toggenburg and Alpine all originated in Switzerland. The Anglo-Nubian, with its distinctive Roman nose and floppy ears, gives the creamiest
milk, and was derived by crossing native stock with
goats from the East. Many commercial herds are likely
to be crosses, and the farmer will breed to get a strain
which suits the particular conditions of the chosen system.

Of the common breeds, the Anglo-Nubian currently
has the best reputation for meat. Breeding trials have
begun in Britain using the South African Boer goat, a
stocky well-muscled meat animal.

SYSTEMS

Commercial goat dairying is now well established in
Britain, although the number of herds is still not large.
Goats are kept under similar conditions to dairy cattle.
The system of management tends to be quite intensive,
as goats from Saanen and Anglo-Nubian stock do better
when permanently housed. Some dairy farmers fatten
and sell billy kids as a sideline, although it is hard to
make it a successful enterprise. Goats have also
remained popular with smallholders and backyarders,
and there are thousands of them kept in twos and threes
all over the country, often in very humane conditions. If
you live near an enthusiast you may well be able to
persuade them to keep and fatten a kid which they may
otherwise have had put down. In major cities goat meat
can be bought at ethnic butchers. Young kid meat is
sometimes marketed as 'chevon'.

COOKING GOAT'S MEAT

Cook young goat meat like lamb, but take care to see
that it doesn't dry out as there is less fat on the surface.
Older meat may be cooked in the same way as venison.
Mediterranean and Asian recipe books are a good
source of recipes and ideas.

BETTY LOCKE'S ROAST LEG OF KID

Lard the meat with garlic and fat bacon if you wish. Dot with lard or butter and sprinkle with pepper. Put the meat in a roasting tin with ½ pint of stock and a teaspoon of salt and cook for twenty minutes per pound in a moderate oven. Remove the joint and rest it. For the gravy add a little stock if necessary to the pan juices, heat through and strain.

LEG OF KID COOKED IN HAY

Place the leg in a large casserole on top of a layer of hay (organic, of course) mixed with thyme and bay leaves. Season the meat with salt and pepper, cover with more hay and moisten it with 7tbsp of water. Cover tightly and cook for forty minutes in a pre-heated fairly hot oven. Bring to the table in the casserole and serve with herby gravy and vegetable purées.

PORK

Pigs are intelligent, inquisitive and naturally clean animals. In some ways they resemble human beings more than cattle and sheep. Not only are they naked, disliking extremes of heat and cold; they also have a simple digestive system like we do, and need more concentrated food than ruminants. They are practically omnivorous and will eat waste and farm by-products such as whey and cereal stubbles. They can also clear, cultivate and fertilise land if their noses are not ringed, and they don't share the same parasites and diseases as other farm animals. All in all, pigs fit in very well on a mixed farm.

Few of these virtues, however, are allowed to shine in the modern intensive pig unit. Pork and bacon have become increasingly popular foods as their price has come down and red meat has begun to fall from favour. Today the pig's only commercial asset is that she breeds prolifically, producing large litters twice a year. Pig meat is versatile because it can be eaten fresh or made into bacon, although different strains of pig are often used for each product, and a heavier type is used for meat for manufacturing.

Intensively kept pigs live all their lives on concrete or slatted floors, never getting the opportunity to root for food and keep themselves fit with exercise. To control the aggression which often erupts in confined spaces they may be isolated in individual stalls, or tethered to the ground. They are fed rations controlled by computer, and are routinely dosed with medications in an effort to control the spiral of ill health which such cramped conditions induce. Chronic disease sometimes reaches such a peak that a unit has to be completely cleared out and restocked.

FARROWING

The breeding sow probably gets the worst deal in the unit. While she is dry she may be permanently tethered in a stall, and when the time comes to give birth she will be confined in a concrete and metal cage called a farrowing crate so she does not crush or eat her piglets. To add insult to injury there is now a machine on the market which blows cold air at the sow every time an electronic eye detects her attempt to lie down, making her stand up again. When pigs are given the privacy and space they need, they make nests to farrow in. In natural conditions they are good mothers and can rear their litters with little interference.

Teeth removal, tail docking and castration
Young piglets sometimes have their sharp eye teeth removed to avoid damage to the sow's teats. In intensive units they may also have their tails cut off so that they cannot be bitten in fights. In this country there is a long-standing tradition of castration, to avoid 'boar taint' in the meat, but when animals are slaughtered at a young age the necessity for this is removed.

HUMANE SYSTEMS

Pigs can be kept free-range, especially where the climate is mild and the land is light enough not to be damaged by their enthusiastic attentions. They need shelter from sun, rain and wind, but this can easily be provided with simple, moveable arks. They can also be kept on deep litter in covered yards and runs, where they can indulge their urge to root and dig in the straw. A combination of indoor and outdoor accommodation is common.

BREEDS

Since the late 1950s the breeding of pigs has passed

largely into the hands of large commercial firms who use the Large White and the Landrace to form the basis of most of their pork, bacon and heavy pig strains. They also use imported breeds such as the Hampshire, the Pietrain and the Duroc. These crosses and hybrids are bred for specific feeds and management systems. They tend to have a high proportion of muscle (lean meat) to bones and vital organs, and lack of exercise aggravates the weakness of their metabolism. The result is the bland, lean meat which has become the norm.

To a great extent the traditional breeds have passed into the rare breed category, and are kept going mostly by enthusiasts. The numbers in these breeds are in the hundreds compared to the many millions of cross-bred pigs which are slaughtered each year. Hardiness, vigour and good mothering, combined with superior quality meat, make them popular for small-scale, free-range farms. Easy to recognise are the Gloucester Old Spots, decorative hardy pigs famed for their ability to fatten on windfall apples, and the Tamworths, an ancient breed with a coarse sandy-red coat. Tamworths have a well-deserved reputation for making the tastiest pork.

THE FUTURE

In the late 1980s it became more common to see pigs out in the fields. As farmers look for ways to increase productivity and cut costs, commercial breeders are pushing their specially bred free-range pigs hard, often as a profitable break crop to benefit arable land. But this does not necessarily mean a return to more natural methods. Huge sums of money are invested in commercial pig farming, and sophisticated new ways of increasing productivity are constantly being developed. Scientists are turning out a steady stream of products to be injected, fed or implanted in animals to stimulate fertility and growth. These are a less obvious but more insidious threat to the quality of the meat, and possibly to the health of the animal and those who eat it, than the mechanical constraints of factory farming.

HANGING

Pork has a high proportion of unsaturated fat which goes rancid quickly, and it is therefore not usually hung for very long, if at all.

WHAT TO LOOK FOR IN GENERAL

The lean should be pink, firm and close grained – the deepness of the pink will depend on the breed of pig, the feeding and whether it has lived outside. Free-range pork shows perhaps the most marked difference of any meat when compared with the intensively farmed equivalent. Don't be put off by the fact that it in no way resembles the stuff on supermarket shelves – some of the most delicious pork we have tasted has been quite dark coloured.

People worry about the safety of eating pork, as it taints more rapidly than any other meat, but so long as it smells fresh, looks moist without being wet or sticky, and the fat is firm, then it is fine. Cook it as soon after purchase as you can, but in your haste to get it into the oven make sure that you allow enough time to thaw the meat thoroughly if it has been frozen. Organic pigs will not have been heavily medicated against parasites, so as human beings and pigs do share the trichina worm it would be as well to observe the golden rule always to cook pork and pork products to at least medium done, and never to eat them rare.

FAT

In a pig the fat tends to be deposited in layers around the muscles rather than marbled through the meat, but

this differs from breed to breed. Free-range pork sometimes has more fat than intensively-reared pork, but it is
usually tastier, firmer and more palatable, and can be
put to good use by the cook.

Pork fat is fine-textured and can be used to make lard.
As it doesn't have a strong flavour it is also valuable for
larding any sort of lean meat for roasting, and for enriching stews and casseroles lacking in fat or containing
starchy ingredients like beans. Cut it away from the
meat, then mince or cut it up very finely so that it disin-
tegrates almost completely in the cooking. Raised pie,
pâté and terrine recipes often call for minced or finely
chopped pork fat, which keeps the game, poultry or
tender cuts of lean meat in these dishes well-basted,
preventing them from becoming dry and tough.

Pork fat will keep for a week to ten days in a cool, dry,
dark place, either buried in or thickly coated with a
mixture of flour and pepper. Rinse before use.

CUTS OF PORK AND HOW TO COOK THEM

Hindquarters

The hind leg, cut off at the pelvic girdle, is not usually
available whole unless from a very small animal. It
usually makes two prime roasting joints, the lower part
called the leg or knuckle end, and the more tender
upper part, the fillet. The leg is sometimes boned and
rolled, and is often butchered to make several leg joints.
The very bottom part is known as the knuckle or shank
and is tougher and more fatty, suitable for slower cooking methods. Try boiling it (skim thoroughly) to make it
tender, after which it can be roasted or grilled to crisp
the fat, or used for enriching bean stews or soup. The
fillet is sometimes cut into steaks for grilling or frying.

The tenderloin is the same cut as the fillet of beef and
is taken from under the loin. It is very lean and, as the
name suggests, very tender. It can be roasted as it is or

Cuts of pork

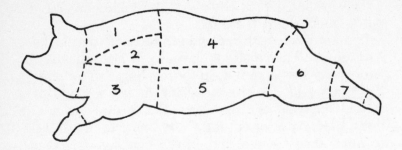

1. spare rib
2. blade bone
3. hand and spring
4. loin
5. belly
6. leg
7. hock

in a pastry crust, or cut into little steaks which are grilled or fried; it is often served with a creamy sauce.

Back

The whole of the back is called the loin. It can be jointed in sections, either bone in, boned and rolled for roasting, or cut into chops. The chump chops are the ones towards the rear and may have a piece of kidney attached. Then come the loin chops and the middle chops which have more fat between the lean. The shorter ribs of the loin can be bought in 'sheets' – they don't have much meat attached but are delicious marinaded and barbecued or baked in a piquant sauce. The Barnsley chop is one chop from each side of the backbone, unseparated.

Belly pork is cut away from the ribs. It is very fat and needs to be slow roasted, either on a rack to allow the

Knuckle end

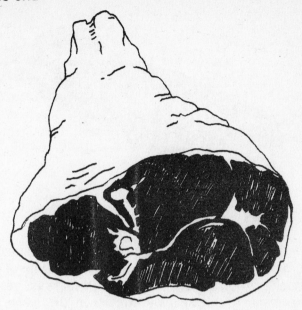

Fillet end

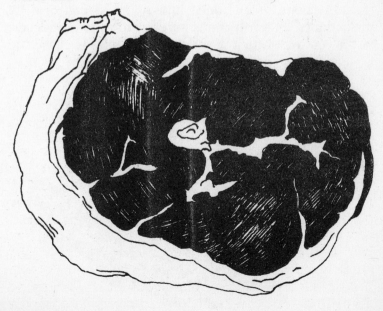

Tenderloin

fat to run away or stuffed with something starchy like rice or breadcrumbs which will soak up some of the fat. A small portion of stuffed belly pork makes a very satis- fying meal. It can also be braised in the same way as breast of lamb, boned, and then grilled or roasted in a hot oven. The neck, known as the spare rib, is good for roasting, bone in or boned and rolled. It can also be divided into spare rib chops for casseroles or barbecues, but if you are cutting it yourself be careful because the bone splinters easily.

Chump chop

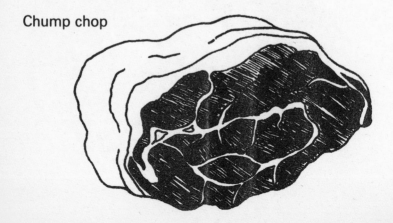

Loin chop

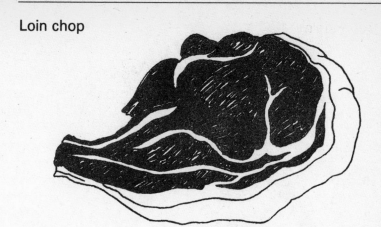

Middle chop

Belly pork

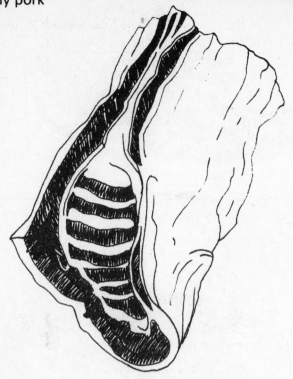

Spare rib

Forequarter

Blade bone is the shoulder blade joint, which is usually boned and rolled. It can be roasted, braised, or diced for casseroles. The lower shoulder and foreleg is known as the hand and spring and is cooked in the same way.

Blade bone (shoulder blade joint)

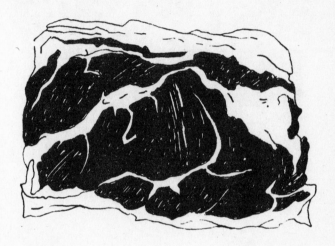

ROAST PORK

To roast a piece of lean pork first score the skin, push in cloves of garlic and herbs, rub with salt and pepper, brush lightly with melted dripping or oil, and cook in a moderate oven. (For times see Roasting pp. 69–76).

Lean pork is very close-textured, and as it has to be thoroughly cooked, larger joints can tend to be rather dry if care is not taken when roasting or grilling. Roasting with the bone in or with a stuffing to soak up the pan juices helps, as does basting with fat. You can cover the meat for a while during long roasting to keep some moisture in, but not for long or it will taste steamy and the crackling will be less likely to crackle. You can marinade the meat first if you want to.

Hand and spring

The fatty cuts make superb roasts if cooked carefully. Don't feel that the fat must be cooked and then left on the side of the plates and wasted. It is much better to trim some away and keep it for other dishes, or to slow roast the meat and render out the dripping. If there is a lot of fat on the outside of the joint, simply remove the skin and trim most of the fat away, leaving at least ½ inch. This exposed fat will then need protection from burning, so either replace the skin or cover the meat with a layer of breadcrumbs and parsley one hour before the end of cooking for a large joint (and for less time for it will absorb some fat and form a crispy coating which will help keep the meat succulent, just as the skin would have done. Alternatively you can cover the meat with greaseproof paper and tuck the skin underneath the meat, or save the skin to enrich other dishes such as cassoulet or beef casserole.

If the fat is in layers through the meat you can trim it out with a sharp knife and either fill the cavities with stuffing or tie or skewer the joint to hold it in shape. The stuffing will help to absorb the fat and make it more palatable.

Crackling

To make the crackling crackle the oven should not be too hot to begin with, in order to give the fat time to begin to melt before the skin hardens. The meat should not be basted with liquid.

Stuffings

For the base of the stuffing use breadcrumbs (particularly rye), cooked rice, flaked grains, etc., and to give flavour you can add most herbs (especially sage), most spices (especially nutmeg), onions and tart fruits such as apples, crab apples, gooseberries, quinces, plums, prunes, oranges and apricots.

Boiled pork

If you want to follow an old recipe for boiled fresh pork then you must use meat from a young pig, although boiled salt or pickled pork can be from an older animal.

Casseroling pork

The leaner cuts such as leg or spare ribs make good casseroles and stews, but the cheaper, fattier cuts are not suitable for these methods unless they are cooked with starchy ingredients such as the beans in a cassoulet, which will absorb the fat.

PORK CHOPS OR BELLY PORK SLICES WITH APPLES AND CIDER

This quick and easy recipe comes from Cotswold Stile in Gloucestershire. Made with belly pork slices it is very economical as well.

Place the chops or slices in a large casserole. Slice two medium onions and fry in a little oil, and while they're cooking, peel, core and chop some cooking apples (about half per person). Place the apples and onions on top of the meat and season with celery salt and black pepper. Add one pint of cider or dry white wine, cover and cook in a medium oven for about one hour, stirring occasionally. Serve with jacket potatoes and green beans.

CASSOULET

Cassoulet is a good way to use left-over meat, especially roasts, scraps of bacon, pork rind, the odd chicken leg or piece of tasty sausage. Fatty cuts of meat make the dish rich and satisfying, and the beans absorb the fat.

Soak some white beans (haricots are traditional but you could use soya or flageolet beans) and parboil them for thirty minutes uncovered in lots of water, leaving them to stand with the lid off. This will remove a lot of the flatulent properties! Fry some onions and garlic and add to the casserole with the drained beans, layering or mixing in pieces of cooked or uncooked meat and adding chopped tomatoes if you like. Add stock or water to cover the meat and season. Cover with a tight-fitting lid and cook very gently in the oven until most of the liquid has disappeared, adding more if necessary to prevent it becoming too dry. A nice variation is to uncover thirty minutes before serving, sprinkle with breadcrumbs and parsley, and brown. The finished product should be moist and succulent, but with not too much gravy. Serve with dry cider or any sort of dry wine or beer, and crusty bread and green salad.

TERRINE

Pork is a good basic ingredient for terrines and pâtés, because the fat content prevents other leaner ingredients drying out and allows their flavours to dominate. You can marinade the meat first if you wish, in which case strain the marinade and use it for cooking the meat in the terrine.

Choose a handsome and attractive oven-proof dish and line it with rashers of bacon. Coarsely mince or sliver the meat – use about a quarter fairly fatty pork to other meat such as game, poultry or beef (a small amount of minced or chopped liver is good). Layer the meat in the terrine with salt and pepper, ground spices, herbs, whole mushrooms, cranberries, blackcurrants, chopped apples, or nothing extra, whatever is appropriate to the meat you are using. Add a small amount of stock, marinade, wine or spirits – about half a wine glass to a pound of meat – to moisten it. Cover with grease-proof paper and foil, sealed quite tightly, or use a tight fitting lid. Put in a *bain marie* or roasting pan with water coming halfway up the sides of the terrine. Cook in a slow oven 150–170°C, 300–325°F, gas mark 2–3, making sure that the water doesn't dry up, until the juices run clear when a skewer is inserted – about one hour to a pound of meat.

Cool slightly and weight just a little until completely cold. If there is very little jelly round the terrine, add some jellied stock. It is better left for a couple of days in a cold place or fridge to let the tastes merge. Cover with melted fat if you want to keep it for more than a week. To turn it out, immerse the container in boiling water first. Carve and serve in slices.

This is a good dish to make well in advance as a centre piece for a buffet or party table.

PORK TENDERLOIN IN A CRUST

This is a good way of making an expensive piece of meat go further. It can be done with any lean, tender piece of meat, like fillet of lamb or beef or boned chicken breast.

Slit a piece of pork tenderloin along its length, open it out and beat it with a rolling pin to even out the thickness (putting the meat between two sheets of grease-proof limits the mess). Spread with chicken liver pâté and a layer of sliced tart apple, apricots or prunes. Fix the meat together again with wooden cocktail sticks or skewers. Fry the joint gently on all sides until golden brown and remove to a plate. Sauté a quarter of sliced mushroms in the pan juices and remove. Add a splash of sherry or something similar, and bubble it away until the juices are syrupy. When all is cold, roll out about one pound of shortcrust, puff or hot water crust pastry into a rectangle big enough to wrap the meat. Unskewer the meat and lay it in the middle of the pastry. Put the pan juices and the mushrooms on top. Fold the pastry round the meat, seal with cold water and decorate with pastry shapes. Bake at gas mark 6-7, 400–425°F, 200–210°C for fifteen minutes and then lower the gas to 4-5, 350–375°F, 180–190°C and cook for approximately thirty minutes per pound. Halfway through the cooking time paint the top of the pastry parcel with egg and water. Allow to cool for fifteen minutes before serving.

BACON AND HAM

Salting is one of the oldest methods of preserving foods. On small medieval farms only a limited number of breeding stock could be kept through the winter, so animals were killed in the autumn and the meat preserved to be eked out over the coldest months. This system lasted until comparatively modern times. Pork, mutton and beef were all commonly preserved or cured in this way, although nowadays what we know as bacon and ham is always made from pork. Ham is the hind leg which is cut off and cured separately; gammon is the hind leg which has been cured on the side and is milder than ham.

Traditional salting methods involve either rubbing dry salt into the meat or soaking it in brine. Other ingredients are often included, such as saltpetre (sodium nitrate), herbs and spices and some form of sugar, anything from white through all grades of refinement to molasses or honey. The purpose of the sugar is to tenderise the meat which is made tough by the salt, but it may also sweeten the flavour.

TRADITIONAL CURES

For traditional curing methods plenty of time is as necessary as plenty of salt. The salt has to be allowed to permeate the meat for days or weeks – the larger the piece the longer this process takes. In both methods the salt gradually draws the liquid from the meat and soaks in to replace it. The meat is then hung to dry to allow the salt to go right through the meat and mature the flavour. The finished product is dryer than fresh meat, and keeps well – a large ham with a strong cure will keep up to a year at room temperature. As part of the drying process the ham may be smoked over smouldering sawdust (usually oak in Britain), which improves the keeping qualities and gives a characteristic smoky flavour.

The curing of pork for bacon and ham was always an idiosyncratic process, and there were hundreds of different family and regional recipes, often kept a closely guarded secret. Many of them have died out, but famous name hams such as York or Wiltshire are still prepared by these traditional methods, as is most continental bacon and ham. You will find that producers are very enthusiastic in extolling the virtues of their own particular cure.

MODERN BACON

Many people bemoan the fact that bacon has changed more than any other meat product in recent years, and there are several reasons for this. Firstly we no longer need the salt to preserve the meat since we have refrigeration, so modern bacon is far less salty than it once was. Also factory cured bacon is not matured – the curing solution is injected into the meat with fine needles, and the bacon is then tumbled in a solution of polyphosphates – chemicals which make the cells of the meat swell up and absorb extra liquid. If the meat is going to end up as cooked ham, it is then steam cooked which retains the maximum amount of fluid. The whole process takes less than a day. Then there is the vexed question of fat: concern about animal fats has led us to favour less fatty bacon, as with every other meat, but with a corresponding loss of flavour.

The end result is the wet flabby products we have become used to – bacon which spits and dribbles in the frying pan and ham which slithers out of the packet onto the plate. The consumer has little or no choice, and bacon and ham manufacturers are merely required to state the water content and the method of manufacture on the pack in the small print.

HEALTH RISK?

Bacon and ham contain a lot of salt, nitrates and nitrites and, if smoked, tar deposits, all of which may be bad for us. In these days of high blood pressure and cancer scares, and now that we no longer have to preserve meat in this way, one may well wonder why on earth we eat salted, smoked meat at all. The answer is – for the taste. Bacon remains a very popular food, often the meat missed most by the reluctant vegetarian!

Because the flavour is strong, a little goes a long way. Cured meats can be used to their best advantage as a 'seasoning' rather than a main ingredient, and in amounts that will surely do no harm. If you search out 'real' ham and bacon, at least you will know that they only contain the traditional additives, and no added water, polyphosphates and so on.

If you are still worried about these ingredients there are ways of reducing them, although you might lose some flavour. A lot of salt can be soaked out of meat before cooking, as long as you remember to change the water frequently so that the salt does not have the opportunity to soak back into the meat. It is also possible to buy bacon prepared without nitrates, although it may be grey or brown instead of pink. Alternatively ascorbic acid may be used to help the rosy colour and the keeping properties. Some producers maintain that a very little saltpetre near the bone is a good safety measure against botulism and other forms of spoilage, and others maintain that it is an indispensable ingredient without which the meat becomes tasteless. Smoked bacon and ham can be avoided altogether – just buy green bacon.

CUTS OF BACON

Collar Rashers.

End of collar Small joint to boil.

Cuts of bacon

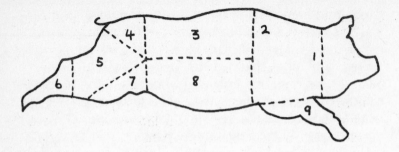

1. collar
2. shoulder
3. back
4. ham corner
5. gammon
6. and 9. hock
7. slipper
8. streaky

Shoulder and middle   Rashers and larger pieces to boil, roast and braise, sometimes separated into back and streaky for rashers.

Ribs   Bought in a sheet, good for soups, with pulses, or soaked and then marinaded and baked.

CUTS OF HAM AND GAMMON

Corner or slipper   Small joints for roasting.

Leg   Slices for grilling and frying, joints for boiling and roasting or braising.

Hock   Fatty joint used for soups and stews, but can be boiled and finished in the oven.

WHAT TO LOOK FOR IN GENERAL

Bacon should have a smooth thin rind, and the lean should be firm and finely grained. The colour will depend on the breed and feed of the animal and on the curing process used. Smoked bacon will be darker and drier. The fat should be even-textured, firm and overall white, but may have a pinkish tinge. It should not have a slimy feel and it should smell pleasant. Yellow streaks mean the bacon is 'rusty', and has reacted with air.

Ham should be firm and thin-skinned, dry with no oozing patches, and a pleasant, slighty salty aroma. As long as the ham is like this a little bloom or mould is usual and even desirable; it is harmless but should be scrubbed off with a stiff brush before cooking. The colour will so much depend on the cure that it is impossible to generalise.

SOAKING

Traditionally cured hams may be extremely salty for modern tastes. If you try to cook a large piece using a modern recipe, it will only be fit for putting on icy paths in winter. If you are adding the meat to other dishes you can use much less, but if you are cooking it in one piece soak it overnight or longer in several changes of water, and boil it first before roasting to get rid of some of the salt. If you are going to fry or grill a slice of salty bacon you can soak it for a while first, but not too long or you will lose the flavour. Dry it well before cooking. Always ask the producer or shopkeeper for their instructions, as they are the best judge of how much soaking the ham needs. An experiment gone wrong can be very expensive.

USING BACON FOR COOKING

Because bacon is so tasty there are many different ways to use it as a 'seasoning'. Add a small amount when casseroling or roasting poultry, game and beef and when making vegetable and bean casseroles and soups. It is also good for adding to pâtés and terrines, pies, pasties, stuffings and sauces.

161

A very small amount will add something special to cold dishes and mixed salads. Snip rashers into small pieces and grill or fry, or use left-over roast and boiled ham.

BARBECUE BACON OR PORK RIBS

There is not much meat on ribs but they are cheap and can be made very tasty and satisfying for a barbecue or buffet, served hot or cold. Boil the ribs for a few minutes and discard the water to remove the salt (not necessary for pork). For the marinade for two sheets of ribs, mix together three-quarters of a pint medium sweet sherry, 3tbsp of sugar, 3tbsp Worcestershire sauce, 1 heaped tbsp tomato purée, juice of one orange, 1tbsp hot pepper sauce (optional), 1 heaped tsp mustard powder and 2tbsp oil. Marinade for at least two hours and then roast or barbecue, basting frequently – this marinade is also good for chicken.

TRADITIONAL RECIPE FOR ROAST HAM

Soak the ham overnight in cold water. Drain, cover with fresh cold water and bring to the boil. Drain again, recover with cold water, bring to the boil again and skim off the scum which rises to the surface. This process takes out the extra salt. Remember to ask your supplier just how much of this process their particular ham needs.

Add the stock vegetables – celery, carrots, green/red

pepper, onions, etc. – and ½tsp peppercorns and fresh herbs. You can also add any spices you fancy, but they must be whole and not ground. Simmer for twenty-five to thirty minutes per pound for a joint under 4lb, twenty to twenty-five minutes per pound for a joint over 4lb.

When the ham is just cooked, pour off and save the cooking liquor for soup and discard the vegetables. Cut off the rind, and some of the fat as well if you want to. With a sharp knife cut a criss-cross pattern into the remaining fat and stud it with cloves. Paint the fat with apple juice, honey or brown sugar. Bake in a hot oven, gas mark 6, 400°F, 200°C for 20–30 minutes until the glaze is crisp.

FRUIT AND NUT VARIATION

This variation is for a 5½lb ham. Simmer with lovage, parsley, marjoram, carrots, spring onions, green pepper, mustard seeds and black peppercorns for one and a half hours. Cut off the rind and rub in a mixture of 1 rounded dsp mustard powder, 2tbsp nut oil, juice of two oranges, half a pint apple juice. Rub into the fat and bake and baste for one hour.

PEA AND HAM SOUP

A thick, delicious and economical soup which makes a winter meal in itself. Use bacon ribs or a hock. If the meat has a rind soak it first, bring to the boil in cold water, drain and rinse. Cover with fresh water, bring to the boil, skim thoroughly. Add pot herbs, peppercorns, etc., and simmer until the meat is cooked. Remove the bacon from the pan and cut the meat from the bone, strain the stock, add soaked pulses and the bacon meat, and simmer until the pulses disintegrate. Extra vegetables can be added if you want them. If the soup is very salty add plenty of potatoes.

BOILED HAM

Soak overnight in cold water, drain, cover with fresh cold water and bring to the boil. Drain and recover with cold water, bring to boiling point and simmer for about twenty minutes to the pound. When cooked, allow the ham to cool in the stock. When cold remove the meat, saving the stock for soup, and peel off the skin. You can serve it as it is, carved thinly, or press toasted breadcrumbs all over the fat in the traditional way. Or try the Real Meat Company's special glaze for a 2½–3lb joint; mix 4tbsp fine shred marmalade, 5tbsp clear honey and four to five drops tabasco together. Brush over the meat, put in a hot oven for ten minutes, and then repeat the process.

OFFCUTS

It used to be common practice when an animal was killed on its home farm for every part of the beast to be used. The larger joints and tongues were salted, pickled or smoked to keep them through the winter, and less meaty cuts were made into huge pies and sausages which would also keep. The offal and blood was used straight away for a host of ingenious dishes like black puddings, often taking a lot of time and effort to render them palatable.

It is not economic even nowadays for producers to throw away what amounts to a great deal of edible meat. Our tender sensibilities often baulk at the prospect of buying these offcuts, so they are sold to the meat processing industry where they undergo cosmetic treatment to give them 'eye appeal'. They are coloured, ground up, reconstituted in sausages, pies and so on, and given names which will not offend. This often leads us to accuse the industry of dishonesty, but while these accusations may have some truth in them, perhaps we could regain more control over what we eat if we accepted the poorer cuts and bought and cooked them in an appropriate way. To justify the eating of meat we are surely under an obligation to use every part of the animal that we can, and not allow any needless waste. This means using what we have called the offcuts – the offal, the fat and the skin and bones for making stock.

The offal is all edible parts other than the main carcass; some types of offal are familiar, others less so. Offal is extremely nutritious, especially the vital organs of the animal, because much of the nutrients from the animal's food are collected there. However, unpleasant residues are also concentrated in the offal, so special care should be taken to buy organic where possible. The same applies to the fat, which we tend to reject anyway these days, but it can be used as a healthy homemade alternative to factory produced lard. Home-made stock beats a stock cube any day, and can make the world of difference to many dishes.

It's important to remember when buying and cooking offal that it should be used as soon as possible, and always washed well.

BRAINS AND HEADS

Butcher, butcher, give us a sheep's head.
We can't afford to buy best meat;
But butcher, butcher don't take its eyes out
It has to see us right through the week.

This verse of a Northern folk song, although humourous, has a ring of truth, as these were the only parts which poorer families could afford. Unfortunately most people no longer have the option of using the brains and heads of cattle and sheep because of the possible risk of contracting bovine spongiform encephalopathy (BSE), the brain disease which has infected these species. If you can get meat from an enclosed herd or flock, however, and you want to try using these parts, then they can be used to make delicious meals.

Soak brains and remove the arteries and membranes, then simmer for about thirty minutes in clean stock or water. Slice and serve with a tasty sauce, or chop with breadcrumbs and seasonings and make into cakes to be fried. Heads minus the brains and tongue are first soaked in acidulated water, scraped of blood, then baked or boiled. Pig's head can be pickled after soaking, and the cheeks make particularly good small joints, called Bath chaps. The tongue is usually cooked separately.

BRAWN

Pickle one pig's head (split) overnight in brine, drain, wash and clean. Place the head in a saucepan with 1½–

2lb shin or brisket of beef, one large onion, a bouquet garni and some peppercorns, cover with water and bring to the boil. Simmer until the meat will easily come away from the bone. Remove the head and the beef, strain the stock and return to the heat to simmer. Using two forks, shred the meat into small pieces, pack into a brawn mould, adding plenty of pepper or ground mace, and just cover with stock. Allow to cool, then weight lightly. Leave for at least twelve hours before cutting, and serve sliced with a Cumberland or similar sweet-sour sauce.

OXTAIL

Oxtail contains the spinal column of the beast and may not be safe to use because of BSE. If you do have a safe supply it makes a delicious soup or casserole, and should be cooked until the meat falls off the bone. It can be very fatty, so thorough skimming may be necessary.

Bone marrow used to be a great delicacy, but again should be considered suspect because of BSE. The large bones were cooked whole for about three hours and served with a special long handled spoon to scoop the marrow out with, or the bones were cracked open and the marrow removed and braised.

HEARTS

Soak hearts in two changes of water with a little vinegar added, and scrape off the blood. Trim off the fat, valves and any other hard parts. To stuff and roast a heart you need carefully to make the two compartments into one, fill the cavity with breadcrumb stuffing, tie it together and cover it with fat bacon. Roast the heart, basting well, in a moderate oven until tender – about two hours for an ox heart, less for smaller ones. Serve with fruit sauce or jelly. Stuffed or unstuffed heart can also be braised with vegetables and stock with added piquant ingredients such as Worcestershire sauce. An ox heart will feed three or four people. Hearts of younger animals can be sliced after soaking and fried.

STOMACHS

Tripe is part of the ruminant stomach of cattle. Tripe stalls still exist on many markets in the north of England; the tripe that they sell is part cooked and probably bleached. Abattoirs do not usually have the facilities for processing it, so it is unlikely that you will be able to get tripe from an organic producer. If you do get it untreated it is very unpleasant to deal with, as it needs to be soaked and scrubbed repeatedly until the smell disappears, then cooked for hours to make it tender. It can then be eaten cold, sprinkled with vinegar, braised in milk and onions, or cut up and fried in batter or crumbs.

Haggis is made with a sheep's stomach (the 'pluck') turned inside out and scalded, scraped and soaked. It is then stuffed with a mixture of partly cooked shredded sheep's heart, lights and liver, shredded suet, toasted pinhead oatmeal, onions and seasoning. The stomach bag is then stitched up and boiled or steamed for several hours. Organic haggis is now available from several Scottish producers.

BLOOD

Fresh blood added to gravy helps to thicken it and gives flavour – the rich sauce of a jugged hare is made with the blood. Pig's blood is the main ingredient of black puddings; the blood is mixed with seasonings and sometimes with chopped fat, and then boiled in skins.

LIVER AND KIDNEYS

Liver and kidneys are often the only form of offal available, and they are familiar to most people. They are rich

168

in vitamins and minerals, especially those from plants which the animal has eaten. Both liver and kidneys can be grilled, fried or casseroled, and livers are also used for pâtés and terrines. Ox and pig's liver and kidneys are more strongly flavoured than those of lamb or poultry.

Wash and dry these organs before cooking them. You may like to soak kidneys for a while in acidulated water to remove the slight ammonia taste they sometimes have. To remove the core from a kidney, lay it on a board and cut it in half horizontally. The white part is the core and it has fine tubes running from it into the meat. Slide a sharp knife under each one and trim it out, and when you have freed all the tubes trim out the core.

LIVER AND BACON CASSEROLE

Sauté a chopped onion in a little fat and add 4oz of chopped bacon to it. Cook a little longer while you slice 12oz of liver. Coat the liver in 1 heaped tbsp of seasoned flour, brown on both sides and transfer to a casserole. Add the rest of the flour to the pan, stir and fry and amalgamate all the fat into it. Add stock or water, bubble and scrape up the pan deposits, adding them to the casserole with extra liquid to cover, together with chopped root vegetables if you wish. Add a bay leaf and some seasoning and cook gently in a slow oven for about one and a half hours. Serve with plenty of potatoes.

SWEETBREADS

These are the pancreas and thymus glands of the animal, usually only from lamb and young cattle. They are delicately flavoured, especially the pancreas, and easily digested, and used to be considered ideal food for invalids.

Wash sweetbreads thoroughly, simmer in acidulated water for about fifteen minutes, then plunge into cold water – this will firm and whiten them. Remove any membrane and tubes, then weight the sweetbreads down until cold and firm. They can then be sliced and crumbed for frying and grilling or braised or chopped into a creamy or piquant sauce.

TONGUE

Tongues of the larger animals, usually ox or pig, are more commonly eaten than those of the smaller animals and birds, which are more gristly. Tongue can be used fresh, pickled, or dry salted.

Wash and scrub well, and soak pickled or salted tongue in fresh water, fresh tongue in salt water for an hour. The tongue can then be cooked in stock or water with pot herbs, spice berries, herbs, etc., or just a little lemon juice or vinegar for thirty minutes to the pound, plus thirty minutes. Allow to cool completely in the liquid, then skin and take off the roots. Carve the cold tongue thinly across the grain and serve with a tasty sauce such as tartare or Cumberland sauce, or a salad containing fruit.

Tongue may also be served hot, but the skinning process is easier when it is cold. You can three-quarters cook it, skin and trim, then braise it whole on a bed of vegetables with a little stock, or slice it thickly and fry it gently with mushrooms and onions. Serve with a fruit or tomato sauce, or gravy and tasty vegetables such as spinach or spring cabbage. Palates (if you can get them) are cooked initially the same way, then skinned and fried or grilled. Elder is cow's udder, and is simmered as above and then usually skinned, sliced and served cold – only to those with an acquired taste for it!

TROTTERS

You can use both pig's and sheep's trotters. Those from the forelegs are said to be more tender than the hind. Soak trotters in a strong salt solution overnight, then wash and scrape off any hair or wool and simmer with pot herbs until the bones will pull easily out of the flesh. Allow to cool, then either egg and crumb the meat and grill or bake it, or stuff the bone cavity and bake the whole thing. A tasty sauce is needed with this dish. Cowheel is cooked in the same way.

BONES

Both raw and cooked bones are invaluable for making a tasty stock. When all the meat has been carved from the carcass of a bird or joint, simmer it in water for an hour. All the little pieces of meat will fall off and will make the basis of a tasty soup or stew.

Raw bones can either be made into white or brown stock. For white stock the bones are simmered with pot herbs, and for brown the bones are baked in the oven until browned, then simmered with pot herbs. Stock can be kept in the fridge for some time, especially if it doesn't contain any vegetable ingredients. It can also be frozen, but it will take up less space in the freezer if it is reduced by boiling first.

Bones from a younger animal make a stock with more body, which becomes jelly-like when cold. Sheep and pig's trotters and calves' feet also make jelly, and they are an essential ingredient of brawn beef or pork.

FAT

Caul fat

The caul is fat from around the internal organs, held together by lacy connective tissue. It is useful for laying over lean meat for roasting and is also sometimes used to wrap smaller pieces such as faggots, which are a mixture of minced offal and cereal or breadcrumbs, onion and seasoning, formed into balls and baked.

Suet

Suet is hard fat from the body cavity of cattle, and it melts at a higher temperature than other fats. This makes it useful for stuffings when the meat is lean, since it melts slowly and bastes the meat rather than running out as softer fats do. Suet makes very good and tasty pastry both for baking and steaming, different from conventional pastry in that it is very open textured. It is usually bought ready grated and mixed with a little flour to keep the bits separate, but you can buy suet and grate it yourself.

Dripping

Dripping is a delicacy which has disappeared from our kitchens, and is likely never to return. The generous amounts which kept our grandparents' families warm came from meat which was much fattier than we would find acceptable today. When cold, dripping separates into the meat juices and the fat; try saving what you do get and spread a little of each layer on bread or toast sprinkled with a little salt, or use it for frying other meats, roasting potatoes or Yorkshire pudding.

To clarify dripping
Dripping will keep for quite a long time if it is clarified, because it is the deposits which go off quickly. You can collect fat from the top of soups, stews and stocks as

well as from roasts. Scrape as much of the deposits from the fat as possible and put the fat into a saucepan with water to just cover. Boil without a lid for twenty minutes then strain into a bowl, and the deposits will be left in the water. When you use the clarified fat for frying, heat it steadily as it will contain water which may cause the fat to spit.

Clarified dripping used to be the favourite fat for frying chips. If you are shocked at the prospect of the saturated fat content, bear in mind that even unsaturated oils become more saturated when reheated, so the pan of oil used for frying time and time again is not a healthy alternative.

To render down fat
Collect the trimmings from fatty meat, removing any skin and gristle. Put the fat into a baking tin in a very slow oven, or in a heavy saucepan over a very low heat. When all the fat has rendered out you will have a clear liquid with tiny scraps of solid. Strain through a fine sieve or muslin. Lard is rendered-down pig fat: being so fine, it is perfect for pastry and deep frying. The fat from the belly is finer than that from the back. Render it down as described above and clarify it as described below.

To clarify fat
Put the rendered fat into a heavy saucepan with water to cover, bring to the boil and boil steadily until all the water has evaporated and the liquid fat is completely still. Let it cool a little then strain through muslin. When cold and set, any deposits on the underside of the fat must be completely scraped off. A little bicarbonate of soda can be added to the pan to make the cleaning process more efficient.

SAUSAGES

The sausages you buy from home producers will in no

way resemble the pale soft variety commonly available. They are usually made with coarsely minced meat with a proportion of fat to keep them juicy, sometimes cereal, and a variety of herb or spice seasonings. They will not shrink to half their original size when cooked and will taste of meat. One producer told us that you can make gravy from the drippings from her sausages.

You can make sausages at home yourself quite easily if you are prepared to invest in a mincer with a sausage filling nozzle and some real skins made from the intestines. All you need is a basic recipe and you can then create a thousand variations with different spices, herbs and other ingredients.

MINCED MEAT

Minced meat is very useful since it cooks quickly, a little will go a long way when cooked with other ingredients, and it is very versatile. It is usually made from less lean and tougher cuts of beef such as flank or neck. Pork or lamb mince is usually from the shoulder cuts. If you buy minced steak it should be just that and will be more expensive. Extra lean mince may appeal to those who want to reduce their fat intake, but will not make the kind of rich dish often associated with mince such as Bolognese sauce. Since minced meat does not keep well it is a good idea for extra freshness to make your own, which is easy to do with a hand mincer.

MINCED MEAT SAUCE

This is the basic method for making the ubiquitous Mediterranean dishes like spaghetti bolognese, moussaka, and so on.

Gently fry 1lb of minced lamb or beef (you can substitute up to 4oz of the meat with chopped chicken livers or chopped unsmoked bacon) until good and brown, either in a dry pan if very fatty or in some olive oil. Add finely chopped onions and garlic, and as variations to make the meat go further some finely chopped mushrooms, grated or chopped carrots, or chopped peppers. Sauté everything together and add chopped ripe fresh or tinned tomatoes, tomato paste and herbs and seasonings. Bring to the boil and simmer very gently until the fat rises to the surface.

A spoonful of this thick, rich sauce on pasta is enough. There are a lot of variations for main meals, and the sauce will also make a good topping for jacket potatoes, a filling for pancakes and pitta bread and, with the addition of some padding like breadcrumbs or flaked grains, a stuffing for vegetables like marrow, green peppers and aubergines.

MEAT LOAF

This forgotten favourite is versatile, foolproof and tasty, and is open to many variations. Mix together 1¼lb minced meat, all one kind or a mixture (but there must be some lean and some fat), 4oz breadcrumbs or flaked grains, plenty of fresh or dried herbs, one finely chopped onion, and optional seasonings such as crushed garlic, tomato purée, Worcestershire sauce, salt and pepper. Beat one egg and combine it well with the other ingredients. Pack the mixture into a greased loaf tin, cover, and cook in a *bain marie* or roasting tin with hot water for one and a half hours. Allow to settle for five to ten minutes, then loosen and turn out. Serve hot with a piquant sauce or cold with salad and bread.

BURGERS

This mixture is also open to many different flavourings and seasonings, and most cuisines have several. Always use good quality meat, minced and then pounded, or pulverised in a food processor. Add finely chopped onions, spices, herbs and seasonings of your choice, and if you want to pad out the meat add some breadcrumbs, flaked grains or gram flour and beaten egg to bind. Form into the desired burger or rissole shape, and allow to rest before frying, grilling or barbecuing.

CHICKEN

'Man works extremely hard for the chicken. The chicken works very little for man.'

Bill Mollison
The Parable of the Chicken

All modern chickens are believed to be descended from the Asiatic jungle fowl, and their habits still very much reflect their origins. Chickens like to scratch for their food in loose litter or on short vegetation, eating a wide range of insects, worms, seeds and young shoots of plants. They prefer a dry environment, needing some shelter from the rain as their feathers are not as well-oiled as those of ducks. They are otherwise extremely hardy, and if used to being outside will naturally be well-feathered. They like taking dust baths to help keep themselves clean and free from parasites, and on hot days can be seen stretched out motionless, soaking up the sun. At night time they become dopey and easy to catch, which makes them especially vulnerable. Consequently they have a strong instinct to roost as high up as they can get, which in the wild protects them from predators.

Chickens have been domesticated, especially in the East, since prehistoric times, but were probably introduced to these islands by the Romans. As they were easy to keep, most farms had them as a sideline to provide eggs and the occasional meal. They were allowed to wander freely, occasionally fed scraps from the kitchen but otherwise left to scavenge for their food. They cleared crop residues from arable fields, improving pasture by aerating the grass with their scratching and fertilising it with their droppings. They also dispersed the manure of grazing animals and ate their parasites. The chicken was thus a useful bird, even though the eating of chicken was a rare treat.

This is not the case today, however. Chicken has become the cheapest and most popular meat available. It easily beats pork and bacon to the title of 'most industrialised farm crop' – the vast majority of Britain's annual production of 600 million chickens is reared on just over a thousand farms. Recently, however, the true price of our favourite meal has begun to emerge – outbreaks of food poisoning have highlighted the inadequacies of the battery and broiler systems and reinforced public dissatisfaction with an inferior product. Hopefully this crisis will have prepared consumers to pay higher prices for good free-range chickens.

THE BROILER SYSTEM

Commercial production of chickens is controlled by multinational companies who supply stock and feed on a contract basis to farmers. After hatching, the chickens are kept in broiler houses containing from 5,000 to 100,000 birds. These are large, windowless, dimly lit sheds, which a passer-by may justifiably assume to be the scene of some industrial activity. As chicks they enjoy some space and their new litter is clean and fresh, but by the end of their brief seven-week lives they have grown so rapidly that they are crushed together almost into a solid mass. At this stage the smell and the noise is likely to be overwhelming.

This is mass production with no pretence at individual attention. Approximately one in sixteen birds fall ill and die before slaughter. 'Husbandry' consists entirely of administering feedstuffs laced with routine medications to keep down disease levels and growth promoters to get the birds to the right weight as soon as possible. It is quite common to have one worker in charge of hundreds of thousands of birds. Dead, wounded or diseased birds are not guaranteed to be noticed or dealt with until the shed is cleared out ready for the next batch. At the packing station the birds are slaughtered and plucked by machine, packed and usually frozen. Unfit carcasses or pieces of carcasses are discarded at this stage. Although the farmer will be penalised if the number of unfit birds is too high, a certain percentage of wastage is allowed for in the costings.

This system is clearly inhumane, and its product unhealthy and unpalatable. What's more it is not cheap. It uses a great deal of 'hidden' resources in the form of energy to control the chickens' environment, and vast amounts of water and intensively grown cereal feed to convert them to food for us. It causes massive pollution, both directly with 2.5 million tonnes of effluent and corresponding quantities of processing waste to be disposed of each year, and indirectly because of pesticide use on the cereal growing land. It also completely wastes the beneficial side effects which could and should help to justify the keeping of poultry.

BREEDS

Traditionally some breeds were more suited either to egg laying or meat production, but most were general purpose. All the pure breeds are now the province of the enthusiast, having been overtaken by the commercial hybrids and first crosses, which have become popular with smallholders as well as poultry farmers.

Commercial breeding is so far advanced that it has probably already reached its ultimate point. The national flock is now firmly comprised of two separate parts – the egg-laying hens and the table-meat chickens – each so well suited to its purpose that they are useless for any other. The meat hybrids of today weigh twice as much at the same age as the equivalent bird of twenty-five years ago. They are usually white birds with a characteristic deep body. In the broiler unit this extra large body causes problems with weak, easily injured legs and feet, and the problems can persist even on free range.

FREE RANGE

In response to the distaste felt by many about the intensive poultry business, most supermarkets have started to sell some 'free-range' chickens. It is felt that the consumer will want these birds to be as tender as their familiar intensive cousins, and not too much more expensive, so they need to grow as fast to reach the required weight before they become tough. They are usually kept in sheds for their first four weeks and then turned out to range – as many to the acre as the land can bear – for the next four weeks before being slaughtered. They are fed a similar diet to the broiler house birds.

Although an improvement on the excesses of the completely intensive system, supermarket free range is often a compromise. If chickens were hatched and reared by their mother on true free range, in the story book way, they would be a very pricey meal, only available in the warmer months of the year. However there are acceptable compromises which allow the birds a greater freedom, a better diet, and sometimes a quick and humane death on the farm, without the necessity for a stressful journey to the slaughterhouse. Birds from these systems will still be more expensive than their mass-produced counterparts.

Deep litter/free range

Once out of the warmth of the brooder, young birds are kept in a shed on a deep layer of straw or wood shavings which absorbs their droppings. The chickens will turn the litter with their scratchings and it should, if well maintained, decompose gradually without odour. Although they may have some access to the outdoors for exercise and fresh air, they will not gain much food from their environment and will need either home grown or bought-in feed. They will be slaughtered at a few weeks older than broiler house chickens.

For a more flavoursome but possibly tougher meat, birds can be kept longer on the same system or allowed more free range, perhaps alongside other stock or in an orchard or in woodland. Culled laying hens also make delicious stews and casseroles. They were once commonly available as boiling fowls, but the sorry discarded birds of the present battery systems are only considered suitable for the processors. Older hens from well-run free-range egg laying units could become the source of a plentiful supply of good meat.

COOKING CHICKENS

Young birds weighing 2–4lbs are suitable for roasting, frying, grilling and barbecuing. Older birds weighing from 4–6lbs may be better braised or casseroled, or made into pies and other made-up dishes. If you want to roast an older bird try boiling it first to tenderise it, and then finish it in the oven to brown it. A 4lb roast chicken will easily feed six people.

How to make sixteen servings from one large chicken

The usual way of getting the most out of a chicken is to roast it and then use the left-overs for pies, casseroles, soups and so on. This method can work, but only if the diners have more than average self-discipline. Our families and friends tend to eat most of it in one go, leaving a rather mean-looking carcass which is just asking to be picked at by the washers-up! If you do succeed, by the second or third chicken dinner in a row, you're thinking of going vegetarian.

Our method does involve a freezer, but even if you haven't got one you probably know someone who has who could find space for a few extra little bags. Most freezers are half-empty anyway. The trick is to buy a *fresh* free-range bird, joint it, wrap each piece separately and freeze them. Out of sight, out of mind. If you're very virtuous and organised you will then have enough once-a-week meat meals for about a month; for the rest of us, about a fortnight.

CHICKEN SALAD

Put one leg, or for preference one breast, in a small pot or heavy saucepan with white wine, orange juice, a few thin slices of orange peel, fresh herbs and salt and pepper. The liquid should be about one inch deep. Poach gently until cooked. Allow the meat to go completely cold in the stock. Scrape off the fat and the jellied stock and put to one side. Cut up the meat into bite-size portions. Toss the meat, some nuts, pieces of orange and the juice, and fresh herbs in nut oil. This can stand for up to one hour to absorb the flavours. Just before serving add salad greens, such as crisp lettuce, chicory or watercress and toss. Serve at room temperature with other mixed salads and fresh bread.

CHICKEN BUNDLE

This is a sort of mini-roast with lots of flavour, good with rice or new potatoes and steamed vegetables, or the usual roast dinner accompaniments. One breast, even though it looks small, will serve four people.

Slit the breast open and put in a stuffing – cheese, garlic or herb butter (with or without breadcrumbs), ham, bacon and chopped onion – it must be fatty and have a strong flavour. Wrap rashers of fat bacon round the parcel to hold it together, tuck slivers of garlic under the bacon, and roast in a medium to slow oven for thirty to forty-five minutes or until it is done and the bacon is starting to go crisp.

CHICKEN CASSEROLE

Brown the joint gently all over in a little oil and remove. Sauté whole shallots and carrot chunks. Pour off excess fat, add chopped tomatoes, garlic, red wine or stock, or cider and apple chunks, and herbs, salt and pepper. Return the chicken joint to the casserole and simmer gently, or bake in the oven until tender. Skim if necessary and thicken with *beurre manié* if liked.

CHICKEN PIE

Either poach the chicken as for the salad recipe, dice and add to sauce when it is ready, or cut up a joint and sauté it in butter for three to five minutes. Remove and add chopped vegetables such as leeks, carrots, mushrooms, and sauté until beginning to soften. Sprinkle in flour and cook, adding stock, water or milk to make a thick sauce. Add the chicken, turn into a pie dish, top with pastry and bake until the pastry is cooked.

STOCK

Use the remainder of the carcass to make stock – either simmer slowly with or without stock herbs for several hours or cook in a pressure cooker for half-an-hour. Strain and leave liquid to cool. Carefully pick the meat from the bones, and make a hearty stewy soup with lentils, vegetables and bacon. Or you can use the meat for a salad, pie or sandwiches, and the stock for a non-chicken soup.

CHICKEN LIVER PÂTÉ

You can use turkey or goose for this recipe if you wish. If you are using a food processor, you will need at least 8oz of livers, because a small amount tends to get lost amongst the blades. Livers freeze well, so you can save them up from several free-range birds to make this dish.

Clean and trim the livers of connective tissue and cut into slivers. Melt 2oz of butter in a frying pan and soften one small finely chopped onion, and one clove of crushed garlic. Add the livers and stir and fry gently until just cooked and they are no longer pink inside. You can add a splash of wine or brandy at this stage and bubble it away. Remove from the heat, add some chopped fresh or dried herbs, such as thyme, marjoram or oregano and season. Allow to cool for five minutes, then add another 2oz of butter cut up into pieces. While the liver is still warm, whizz in a food processor for a smooth pâté, adding 1tbsp of cream if desired, or for a coarse pâté bash with a rolling pin. If you have enough, I find that for an interesting combination of coarse and smooth the best texture is achieved by whizzing half and bashing half. Turn into a serving pot, and allow to go cold and set before using. Covering the top with melted butter will help it to keep longer.

Chicken liver pâté will make a concentrated basis for a main meal if served with crusty bread or crackers and plenty of salad. It also makes a good stuffing for lean, tender pieces of meat such as boned chicken breast or pork tenderloin, and can be used as the bottom layer of a savoury pie.

TURKEYS

The turkey is a native of North America, 'discovered' by the settlers of the New World who nearly hunted them to extinction as they were an easy source of food. Fortunately they had the foresight to start farming them at the same time, and they were taken back to Europe as a domesticated bird. Until fairly recently turkey was a Christmas treat, and many farms fattened just enough to meet local demand as a seasonal sideline. As the birds were only present on the farm for less than six months of the year, problems of disease associated with over-stocking were kept to a minimum. Modern intensive techniques have enabled specialist turkey farmers to keep them in large numbers all the year round, so that they have become a much more common meal.

INTENSIVE SYSTEM

Commercially raised turkeys are reared in broiler houses under much the same regime as chickens. As with chickens, all commercial turkeys are hybrids, usually white, and come in three sizes – 'maxi', 'midi' or 'mini', weighing from 14kg to 4kg. They have almost completely overtaken the traditional breeds such as the Bronze, the Blue, and the Norfolk Black, which are now almost museum pieces even though they have more flavour. Selective breeding has emphasised the heavy breasts and short legs of the turkey, so that natural mating is impossible and the hens have to be artificially inseminated.

Even though turkey is comparatively cheap, the shopper looking for a convenient meal for a small family will baulk at the size of a turkey. Big commercial producers have overcome this marketing problem by processing the meat into small 'roasts' and ready-prepared dishes. This increases profits by giving the producer the opportunity to reconstitute the meat with fats, water and additives to bulk it up, putting turkey high on the list of 'adulterated' meats.

BETTER SYSTEMS

Turkeys tend to be a specialist livestock line – they are not easy birds to rear, being unwieldy and rather nervous, and not totally adapted to our climate. But they do have a certain charm, their soothing musical warblings belying their strange appearance. Because of their susceptibility to disease they are best not kept near any other poultry. It is standard practice for all turkeys to be given preventative medication against blackhead, a disease to which they are particularly prone.

The young chicks, or poults, need to get off to a well-protected start under carefully controlled conditions, so most are reared by specialists. The more fresh air they get as they grow larger the better. They can be kept on free-range, sometimes even given the opportunity to roost in trees or on top of buildings out of harm's way. The more usual method is to keep them in pole barns or open sided sheds, on deep litter, so that they will fatten quicker in the more confined conditions, but are still well ventilated. They can be fed similar rations to chickens, and will find plenty of green food if they can graze on good land.

The method of slaughter is dislocation of the neck, and they are usually bled immediately so as to give a whiter meat. Traditionally they were hung for about seven days to develop the flavour but, predictably, commercially-produced turkeys are moved into the freezer after slaughter without further ado.

COOKING TURKEY

Young birds can be roasted, fried or grilled, and bigger birds roasted or boiled. The meat of the hen is more delicate than that of the cock, which can grow as big as 30lb. At that weight it would need very careful cooking! A 10lb roast turkey will make a good meal for a large party of ten people.

TURKEY AND HAM PIE

This is a basic raised pie recipe and the filling can also be made with a mixture of game, poultry or other meats, as long as there is some fat and some lean. Vary the flavourings to suit the ingredients, and make the stock with the offcuts. To make a large pie to feed between sixteen and twenty people you will need 3–4lb of mixed ham and turkey meat. Trim the fat off the ham and cut it into very thin slivers, and cut the lean ham and the turkey meat into bigger ones. Mix it all together with 6oz cranberries (optional), two teaspoons ground nutmeg, black pepper and some chopped fresh marjoram or other herbs.

Mix 2lb hot water pastry and use it as hot as your hands can bear, so that the pastry doesn't crack. Working quickly, cut off a piece for the lid, and put the rest into a loose bottomed ring mould lined with greaseproof paper. Push the pastry into the mould and up the sides, allowing some overlap at the top. Pack the meat mixture into the pie, piling it up slightly in the centre to make a gentle domed shape. Moisten the edge of the pastry, roll out the pastry lid and put it on, tucking it into the sides. Trim off the excess and crimp or flute round the edge, making sure it is well sealed. Make a 1cm hole in the centre of the pie (this is to pour the stock into when the pie is cooked, and will also help to stop the juices bubbling through the joints). Decorate, and bake in a moderate oven for three to four hours. If necessary, cover it with greaseproof paper before it has finished cooking to prevent it over-browning. About one hour before the end of cooking remove the mould and the paper and paint the surface with beaten egg and water to give it a good shine. After fifteen minutes when the pie comes out of the oven, carefully pour a good jelly stock, just warm, through the hole in the lid, using a funnel if you have one.

Serve warm or cold with cranberry and orange sauce for a special occasion. The flavour will improve if left uncut, wrapped in greaseproof paper, and stored in the fridge for up to ten days.

GUINEA FOWL, DUCKS AND GEESE

GUINEA FOWL

Guinea fowl are members of the pheasant family, originally from Africa. They are pretty birds with speckled white and grey feathers. They have always been prized for their delicate gamey flavour and the firm texture of their white flesh, and there is still a good demand for them at the luxury end of the market. Consequently they are kept intensively in broiler houses and fed similar rations to chickens, although they cannot tolerate some of the routine medications which are added to chicken feed. In these conditions they can be fattened to killing weight in nine or ten weeks.

Although they have been domesticated for a long time, when guinea fowl are kept on free range they hang on to their wild habits, preferring to roost in trees and nest in the hedge rather than in a shed. They are difficult to catch and tend to be nervous, making a lot of noise at any disturbance. Despite these drawbacks for the farmers, once past the brooder stage they are hardy, and very good at grazing and getting much of their food from insects and plants. This is said to make the flavour of a free-range guinea fowl far superior to that of an intensively kept one.

As with other poultry the commercial hybrid 'rules the roost'. On free range the hybrid will fatten in sixteen weeks, compared to an older ornamental breed which may take up to six months. The three most common varieties are the Pearl, the White and the Lavender, which are similar in appearance, and hybrids will most likely come from these stocks.

Cooking guinea fowl

Guinea fowl is rather like pheasant, but with a whiter meat which can be rather dry. Guinea chicks up to 2lb can be fried or grilled, and larger birds up to 3lb are suitable for roasting, well basted, or pot roasting. A 3lb roast guinea fowl will feed four people.

DUCKS

All domesticated ducks, except for the Muscovy, are descended from the wild mallard. They used to be kept for their eggs, their meat and their feathers, and were a familiar sight on many farms, scavenging for food in the fields and around the farm yard and taking full advantage of the farm pond. Nowadays, like most other livestock, they have disappeared indoors.

Modern commercially-produced ducks are not kept on the same scale as chickens and turkeys, but like them they live all their lives in sheds, either on wood shaving litter or on wire mesh flooring. They fatten quickly to a slaughter weight of around 3kg in six to seven weeks. It is uneconomic for the farmer to keep them any longer, as they naturally moult when they reach this weight and suffer a check in growth. Growth promoters are not used as much for ducks as they are for chickens as they pass through their digestive systems too quickly to have any effect.

Many of the good points of the duck are wasted indoors. If a farm has suitable ponds, streams and grasslands, where their mess won't create a problem, they can get a lot of their own food to satisfy their hungry appetites. They will also help clear slugs from arable and horticultural crops, without doing as much damage as chickens. They do not need elaborate shelter, and are more hardy and resistant to disease than chickens.

Breeds

Commercial hybrids are usually white. They have been developed mostly from the Pekin breed, but the Aylesbury, the famous traditional meat breed, is still sometimes used. Some other breeds of duck also make good table birds – the Welsh Harlequin, the Rouen and the Buff Orpington, and one or two of the ornamental breeds have a good gamey flavour. The Muscovy duck, a large, ugly, black and white bird with a red skinned head and a vile temper also makes good eating.

Cooking farmed ducks

The flesh of prime duck should be fine and pink and the livers pale. Ducklings from six to twelve weeks old are suitable for roasting, grilling and barbecueing, if basted. Very young ducklings will be juicier if stuffed. Ducks up to one year old are suitable for roasting, grilling, etc., and ducks over one year are best casseroled or made into pâté, terrines and other made-up dishes. They can also be braised or steamed and then roasted. A 4lb roast duck will feed six people.

GEESE

Geese have been domesticated since ancient times, and were kept by the Egyptians, Greeks, Romans and Chinese. In traditional British farming they were a valuable bird, providing rich meat for festive occasions as well as eggs, feathers and quills. They also supplied large quantities of much prized soft fat known as goose grease, which had a hundred and one uses in the household. Being aggressive and noisy they also made good 'watchdogs'. They were often fattened on the stubble after harvest, sometimes having been raised on grassland farms and on common grazing land, then driven on foot to the arable areas.

Geese could be said to be the poultry equivalent of

sheep – both are good grazers and unsuitable for intensive rearing. Grass is their main foodstuff, and if it is good quality and they have enough of it they need little supplementary feed. By tradition their production is usually linked to the growth of the grass, so that some were slaughtered as 'green' geese at Michaelmas, which falls at the end of September. Those left were fattened with a cereal supplement to be killed and eaten at Christmas time.

Geese are very long lived birds and can go on laying eggs for up to twenty years. They are extremely hardy and like living outside, often ignoring any housing provided for them, although this does make them vulnerable to foxes. They have always been kept in orchards to help keep the grass down and eat up the windfalls during the autumn and winter. Now that young trees are often protected with guards they could usefully perform a similar function as weed controllers in new plantations, reducing the need for chemical weedkillers. They also fit in well with larger livestock, as they prefer a closely cropped sward.

Slaughtering is preferably a two-handed job as they are such large powerful birds. The bird may be stunned and then have its throat cut, or the neck may be dislocated. Traditionally geese were hung for about two weeks, but nowadays commercially produced geese are likely to be frozen straight after plucking.

Breeds

Domesticated geese are probably all descended from the wild Greylag goose. The Embden, which is white, and the Toulouse, which is grey with a dewlap under its throat, are the most important pure breeds today. In France the Toulouse has to suffer the unfortunate custom of force feeding, so that *pâté de foie gras* can be made from its unnaturally large liver. In Britain it is often crossed with the Embden, and sometimes with other mixed strains of common farmyard geese, to make a heavy table bird.

The delicate looking Chinese goose has dark flesh and is less fatty than other geese, which makes it a good table bird.

Cooking geese

Goose flesh is pink and the fat yellow. Young geese have yellow feet and bills which gradually get more orangey as they get older. As 'green' geese up to three months old they are suitable for roasting and quick cooking methods. Geese up to one year old are suitable for roasting. A 10lb roast goose will feed ten people. Older geese can be very tough. Boiling or casseroling will make them tender but the stock or sauce will have to be well skimmed of fat.

PREPARING AND COOKING POULTRY

Poultry includes all the domestic fowl which are suitable for eating. Although they all have their distinctive characteristics – in general chickens and turkeys have lighter meat and less fat than ducks and geese – the methods of preparation are similar. The following instructions apply specifically to chickens, but can be adapted for all other birds.

CHOOSING POULTRY

In general the skin should look fresh, not discoloured or shrunken. There should be no green or blue tinge or unpleasant smell. Young birds for roasting should be plump and the skin smooth and moist, not wet or sticky. Young birds will have smooth legs with barely formed scales, and a pliable breast bone. If you buy the bird unplucked, look for small combs if they have them, soft feathers with down under the wings, and long wing feathers which pull out easily.

Older birds, which can be tastier but will need slower cooking, are usually heavier. They will not necessarily yield more lean meat because the bones will be bigger and they may have more fat. The skin will be coarser, the necks and legs longer, the legs more scaly, and their combs and spurs larger. The breast bone will be fully formed, more prominent and rigid than that of a younger bird.

HANGING

Birds can be plucked, drawn and cooked on the same day as they are killed if this is done before they are cold, but older birds especially do benefit from hanging to mature the flavour and increase tenderness. They can be hung plucked or unplucked, although the feathers come out more easily immediately after killing. Hang them in a cool, dry, well-ventilated place, protected from flies in summer. The length of time will depend on the age of the bird and the temperature – if the bird is young or the weather is hot or damp the flesh will deteriorate more quickly.

Duck and geese can be hung for one to fourteen days, turkeys and chickens up to one week, longer in winter. Opinions vary as to whether hanging should be head or feet downwards. If a blue or green tinge appears where the innards are resting against the carcass then the bird has hung too long. If only slightly discoloured, dress the bird immediately, cut the discoloured parts off and discard them, wash the bird thoroughly in vinegar and water, and cook straight away until well done. If in doubt throw it away.

DRESSING

Plucking

To make plucking easier you can dip the bird in very hot water, but this may 'cook' the skin and could be dangerous if the bird is to be hung in warm weather. Do the job outside for preference, in a sheltered place, over a bin or dustbin liner to catch the feathers as they fall. Place the bird on a board or hold it with its feet towards you, and begin plucking the wings, pulling the feathers in the opposite direction to which they lie and working back towards the body. If the wing tips are difficult to pluck try scalding them. When both wings are plucked start the body from the base of the neck, again pulling the feathers against their growth. The downy feathers which are difficult to pluck can be singed off over a gas jet or a little methylated spirit set alight in a shallow plate. If any broken quills remain in the skin pull them out with tweezers. Bend the wings back and tuck them behind the body.

Drawing

The ideal place to do this is on the draining board. You need a very sharp knife, newspaper to wrap the intestines in, and a clean cloth, both to help you get a grip on your slippery opponent and for wiping everything down.

To remove the feet make an incision in the skin right round the leg just below the drumstick joint, taking care not to cut through the tendons. Put each leg in turn over the edge of the table and bend the joint back on itself to break it. Now grip the foot, using a cloth to prevent slipping, twist it and pull. This should pull out the tendons from the leg, but if it doesn't work try wrapping the tendons around a fork or skewer to get more leverage. With a big old bird it may degenerate into a wrestling match and the tendons may break inside, but it is worth trying to remove them as the leg will be more tender when it is cooked.

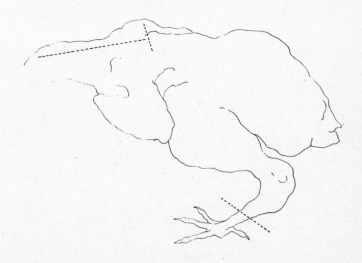

Drawing poultry/game birds

Drawing poultry/game birds

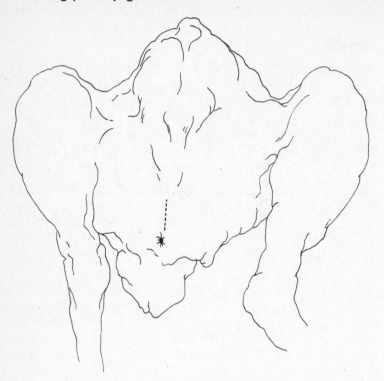

Cut off the head, and with the back uppermost make an incision in the skin from the base of the neck to the top. Fold back the skin and cut the neck off at the top of the spine, leaving the flap of skin intact. Pull out the windpipe and feel under the skin for the crop, which is a membraneous sack attached to the skin near the breast. This is the bird's first stomach. If may contain food if the bird was not starved before slaughter, in which case it will be quite big, hard and lumpy.

Turn the bird over onto its back. Make an incision below the breastbone down towards the vent, just large enough to get several fingers into, being careful only to cut through the skin and the underlying fat (see above). If you go deeper you will cut through the intestines which will make a horrible mess (if it does happen wash the bird thoroughly under cold running water). Drawing the skin tight with the other hand makes cutting easier. Insert two or three fingers into the gap and close your eyes! This will help you to feel your way up under the breastbone and loosen the innards all round by breaking through the thin membranes which hold them to the carcass. You may also insert your fingers through the neck cavity to loosen from that end as well. When you get to the top you will come across a firm lump which is the gizzard. Get your fingers round it and pull it gently and all the intestines should come out. Take the sharp knife and cut them away carefully from the rectum so that they come away completely.

Find the liver amongst what has come out and carefully cut away the small dark green gland attached to it. This is the gallbladder and it must not be punctured because the contents will give a bitter taste to anything they touch. If it does break, discard the liver immediately and wash the bird with lots of cold water. Put your hand back inside the bird and scoop out the lungs which are bright pinky-red and spongy and attached to the backbone. The kidneys are attached to the back lower down the body cavity.

You can keep the liver, kidneys, heart and the outer skin of the gizzard for stock. The gizzard is the second stomach which has a muscular outer layer and an inner sack which holds the digesting food. Slit through the outer layer and peel it off the inner layer, wash it and discard the inner layer. Wipe the whole bird inside and outside with a clean cloth rung out in cold water. Bend the legs close up to the body. The bird is now ready for trussing and cooking, or for freezing.

Trussing

The object of trussing the bird is to keep the wings and the legs close to the bird during cooking. There are many complicated ways of trussing requiring specialist equipment, but if you bear in mind why you are doing it, a simple figure of eight (with the crossover on the back of the bird rather than the breast) with strong thread or fine string will do the job. Be sure not to truss too tightly as this will prevent the bird cooking evenly. The flap of skin which covered the neck should be folded over and held in place underneath the wings.

Jointing

Poultry shears are ideal but sturdy kitchen scissors or a sharp heavy kitchen knife will do. Jointing is a good idea if you are going to freeze a large bird and want to decide later what to do with it – if you freeze it whole it will have to be cooked all at once when it has been defrosted.

Pull the leg away from the body, breaking the joint closest to the body by bending it back on itself, and cut through the skin and the flesh. The leg can be divided into the drumstick and thigh joints by feeling for the centre joint, cutting the flesh around it, and breaking it gently.

Cut off the wing tip and pull the wing away from the breast, break the joint and carefully cut round it without tearing the breast meat. Alternatively you can leave the wings on.

If the bird is young you can cut down the centre of the breast bone, cutting through the wishbone or trimming it out, and opening the chicken up completely. An older bird is more difficult because the bone is harder. Cut as best you can to one side of the central ridge of the bone.

Trim the ribs away from the underside of the breast meat, leaving the ribs and back.

If you remove the skin from the back of the bird you will find two tender lumps of flesh in cavities either side of the backbone. These are the 'oysters' which can be cut out with a sharp knife – succulent tiny additions to a stir fry.

You then have two legs, two breasts, two wings, two

oysters (optional) and the back and ribs which can be used for a stock or stew.

Boning poultry

Boning the bird and then stuffing and rolling or reshaping it makes for easier carving, and is also good for serving a cold roast at a party. It also makes the meat go further because you can fill it with plenty of stuffing. If the whole bird is boned the leg and wing meat is tucked inside, but you may leave the legs and wings unboned and just remove the central bones of the bird, reshaping it with the legs and wings outside.

To bone a whole bird, with the back uppermost cut through the skin and flesh down the full length of the backbone. With short clean cuts start to work the meat away from the ribs, using your other hand to pull it away as you go. Keep the blade of the knife against the bone all the time. Work your way down over the rib cage and make a long cut down the inside of the wing and the leg and then work round the bones to get them out. Go right round to the breast bone but stop short of the ridge, and then do the other side, stopping at the same point on the other side of the ridge. If you want to keep the skin intact, on a young bird you can cut away a little of the gristly breast bone with the meat. Otherwise the skin may tear. On an older bird the skin may tear away from the breast bone here but it can be sewn back together.

ROASTING POULTRY

Lean poultry, particularly young chicken and turkey, will need some added fat, at least to begin the roasting before its own fat starts to .melt. You can do this by covering the breast with fat bacon, smearing or brushing it with fat, or inserting solid fat such as butter or dripping (perhaps flavoured with herbs) between the skin and the breast meat. As the fat drips out start to baste the bird with it. You can also cook the bird breast side down for part of the time, especially as it is the breast meat which is most likely to dry out. If you don't want to add fat, cover with greaseproof paper and foil, removing it a little while before the end of cooking to brown, or cook in a chicken brick or self-basting roasting pan.

Fattier birds can be cooked on a rack to let the fat drain away, but you still need to baste the breast or protect it from drying out in some way.

To make an older bird suitable for roasting, put a few scraps of bacon rind or fat in the bottom of a flameproof casserole dish and put on a low heat until the fat starts to run. Add some diced pot vegetables – carrots, celery, leeks, etc. – to make a layer which covers the bottom of the pan. Put the bird upside down on top of the vegetables, fit the lid tightly, and either put in a low oven for half an hour or leave on a low heat. At the end of this time roast in the normal way and use the contents of the pan for stock or gravy. This steaming process helps to tenderise the meat.

Frothing

For a crisp brown finish to the roast, baste the bird and then sprinkle it with flour about fifteen to twenty minutes before the end of cooking. Then return it to the oven.

Gravy

Prime birds will give the richest drippings for making gravy. Skim off most of the fat, add a rounded dessertspoon of flour for each pint of gravy to the drippings, cook and stir for about a minute. Whisk in hot stock or wine and simmer until the flour is cooked.

Poultry lends itself to serving with fancy sauces. For a light sauce it is usually better to use a white stock made with bones and vegetables, reduced and mixed with egg yolks, cream or whatever. For a fruity dark sauce use the well-skimmed drippings from the pan.

Stuffings

There are many ways of using stuffing. You can stuff the body cavity or the neck cavity, or put an onion, fresh herbs or pieces of lemon inside the bird and cook the stuffing separately. Stuffed birds take longer to cook and the timing is more difficult, so with larger birds such as turkeys it is a good idea to stuff just the neck cavity, or cook the stuffing separately. Add fat to stuffings for lean birds and for stuffings cooked separately.

For a basic stuffing for chicken mix 8oz breadcrumbs, 3–4tbsp finely chopped fresh herbs (or a smaller amount of dried herbs), one small finely minced onion (can be browned or parboiled first), 2oz suet or melted butter (optional) and a little liquid such as milk to moisten if necessary. To this you can also add grated lemon or orange rind, chopped mushrooms, grated or chopped dried or fresh fruit, olives, capers, spices, chestnut purée, celery, watercress, nuts and oatmeal or cooked rice in place of breadcrumbs. You can also stuff birds with forcemeat made with minced meats such as pork, ham, liver or sausage meat.

Accompaniments

For chicken, turkey and guinea fowl the traditional type of accompaniments are brown or cream gravy and bread sauce, small sausages and bacon rolls. For a change try grated celeriac in a *rémoulade* sauce, apple sauce, or egg and lemon sauce. For duck and goose, fruit sauces or jellies are good, particularly orange, and grilled pineapple or apple slices. Try stewed red cabbage and crisp croutons.

GAME

PIE IN THE SKY

In the past wild meat or game was an important source of food for everyone. Country people have always supplemented their diet with a rich variety of game, both legal and illegal, and even comparatively recently professional hunters, called market gunners, supplied the industrial areas with large quantities of wild birds. Even small song birds and finches were netted and eaten, and in mining areas sparrow pie was a popular stand-by for hard times. For many years game has been disappearing from the shops and markets, so that now most people never cook it and only rarely eat it when dining out in a restaurant. To many a town dweller even the once ubiquitous wild rabbit is as unfamiliar as wild elephant.

Many social, political, economic and environmental factors have contributed to the present low profile of game. One main reason is that the supply has simply fallen away. Intensive chemical farming has crushed wildlife, and the post-war years saw a violent and careless acceleration of this process. Cooking and eating habits have also changed; the traditional has largely given way to the exotic, and we have become a nation of supermarket shoppers, unwilling and perhaps unable to tackle anything that isn't marketed and pre-packaged.

The city dweller often has a prejudice against shooting and its proponents, and an understandable mistrust of guns. But modern game shooting is no longer, if it ever was, 'the murderous habit of crusty colonels'. Today it is a sport open to anyone who cares to take the trouble to seek it out. With tight controls it is not a threat to wildlife, but has become an influential driving force behind the maintenance and restoration of some of the most beautiful areas of a crowded island.

A NATURAL HARVEST

Game shooting is thriving as a sport, with some twelve million pheasants alone shot each year in Britain. Lack of interest in the end product, however, means that most of it is exported to the Continent, where it is in great demand. This is a pity because, generally speaking, game is a cheap and healthy natural food. Although some commercial shooting is almost like farming and shares the same excesses, the ancient lore of hunting remains strong among enthusiasts. At its core is an almost lyrical respect for the environment, the careful management of wildlife to produce and maintain a harvestable natural surplus, and the ultimate aim of providing something for the pot. It's up to born-again carnivores to search out game and take advantage of it!

THE JIGSAW OF THE COUNTRYSIDE

In densely populated countries such as Britain, every natural and artificial feature of the landscape, pond, hedgerow, wood or mountainside has long been used and changed by the owners or occupiers. Our need to use the land has never diminished, but increases all the time as the population grows. All wildlife is affected by that use, and complicated food chains connect the whole system in a delicate ecological balance. Our abuse of natural resources has upset that balance, and we have a responsibility to make good the damage. But with many millions of people to be accommodated, our efforts must be active rather than passive. If we want to eat fresh, wholesome food and not be dependent on food processed from increasingly dubious raw materials, we cannot afford to allow land to become derelict or pass out of food production for ever.

The game that we eat today fits into the jigsaw of a healthy countryside in several ways, and the traditional sport of country shooting gives a reason for the conservation of habitats which may otherwise be destroyed. The lowland game birds prefer to live in our traditional much-loved landscape – the varied crops, hedgerows, and woodlands of mixed farming, with minimal or no use of pesticides. They don't compete with any farming activities, and they can be a useful interim crop during the establishment of new broad-leaved woodlands, which are desperately needed everywhere and for which grants are now available. Already many arable farmers who would never consider going organic have nevertheless recognised the benefits of 'conservation headlands'. These are the outer edges of the fields, always difficult to cultivate and relatively unproductive, which are left unsprayed by pesticides to provide cover and food for young game birds and a host of insects, butterflies and plants.

The birds and deer of the highlands can provide a useful harvest from land which can only support a few sheep, and would probably otherwise be covered with a monocrop of conifers. Then there are the water birds whose wetland habitat would be threatened with draining for cultivation. Other sorts of game – hares and rabbits, pigeons and sometimes deer – do sometimes compete with crops and damage land. The shooter, or hunter as they are known in North America, as well as providing a source of food, can perform a useful service to the farmer by controlling their numbers. It is much safer and more 'organic' than the alternative method of pest control, which is poisoning. This simply adds to the burden of pollution, kills other wildlife and wastes the meat.

HOW GAME IS SHOT

Everyone who shoots needs a suitable gun (usually a shotgun), a gun licence, permission to shoot from the landowner, and possibly a game licence. Previous target practice is essential, and so is some basic knowledge and advice. This has traditionally come from family and friends, but as shooting becomes more popular it is inevitably becoming more organised. Not every beginner will be able or willing to learn on a commercial shoot where everything is laid on. Joining a club or organisation which gives education and advice to the novice (and to the old hands) is the best way of learning about country shooting.

There are three main types of shooting; rough shooting, driven shooting and wildfowling.

Rough shooting

Rough shooting is the most basic informal form of hunting with a gun; it is where most people start and many stay. There is no organisation; the responsibility is upon the individual to learn the skills of shooting, to ask permission, and get to know the particular piece of land and its wildlife. Rough shooters usually hunt alone or in pairs with a dog, 'walking-up' the game in front of them as they move across the land or hunt hedgerows, woods and cover. All legal game may be taken, and many rabbits and pigeons are shot this way. Rough shooting works best when done on a small scale, where everyone concerned knows one another and knows the habitat in intimate detail. Over-shooting is avoided and the landowner, who is often a farmer, gets the benefit of pest control and a maintained balance of wildlife.

Although the shooting itself is not formally organised there may well be some land management by the landowner or the hunters. Sheep may be fenced away from woodland, trees and shrubs planted for cover, and small strips of special crops planted for foodstuff and cover for the game birds. This has obvious beneficial side effects for the environment.

Driven shooting

The leap from rough shooting to organised or driven shooting is a big one. Much bigger 'bags' are taken, although it's not just a question of scale. A driven shoot is organised by the landowner or a syndicate which rents or owns the shooting rights. Gamekeepers are employed to manage the land, look after the birds and rear new stock. On the day of the shoot teams of unarmed beaters drive the game towards the guns, usually about eight, who are told where to stand and when to shoot. There may well be extra workers to load the guns and pick up the birds.

The driven shoot has always been a formal social event, and contines to be so even now that many are run commercially. As it can cost up to £17 to get each bird into the air, there may be strong financial pressures to over-stock and over-shoot, and to rear and release too intensively. These practices don't make for testing sport, and can create problems with disease and vermin. General improvement and care of the habitat, with a minimum of disturbance, is a much better long-term strategy, just as organic methods are better for the continued health of agricultural land.

Wildfowling

Some wildfowl are shot on walked-up and driven shoots, especially inland, but most shooting over coastal waters is controlled by wildfowling clubs, who lease the shooting rights to the foreshore from the Crown. These clubs often have waiting lists, and have strict training and probationary periods – wildfowlers must be particularly safety conscious and knowledgeable to avoid shooting the many protected species of water birds. Mostly the hunters go on foot, but sometimes they use a special punt which lies low in the water.

Wildfowling continues the traditions of the professional wildfowlers who used to shoot large numbers of birds to sell. It often takes place in the hardest conditions and demands a great deal of skill and perseverance.

THE BRITISH ASSOCIATION FOR SHOOTING AND CONSERVATION

The BASC is probably the most influential force in the shooting world. It was founded in 1908, and was known originally as the Wildfowlers' Association of Great Britain and Ireland. Its present membership of 100,000 is drawn from all sections of society and all sorts of shooting. The stated ideal of the BASC is 'that all who shoot conduct themselves according to the highest standards of safety, sportsmanship and courtesy, with full respect for their quarry and a practical interest in wildlife conservation and the well-being of the countryside'. The organisation encourages these high standards by promoting strict codes of practice for hunters, gamekeepers and managers, and by running a Proficiency Award Scheme.

Due to the increased illegal use of firearms, there have been calls for stricter controls on the ownership and use of guns, and a new Firearms Act is now being implemented. The BASC promotes very high standards of safety and security, and continues to emphasise the need for conservation, education and research. The address of the BASC headquarters is:

Marford Mill,
Rossett,
Wrexham,
Clwyd LL12 0HL.

THE GAME CONSERVANCY

The Game Conservancy Trust is a research organisation whose objective is to ensure the future of game in its natural habitat. They conduct research programmes on every aspect of game ecology, offering valuable scientific information to policy makers in agriculture, forestry and conservation. Their work has an important practical application through the advice and training in game management they give to those working in the field.

WHERE TO BUY GAME

If you live in the country you might be offered some game by a shooter looking for a good home for his or her bag. If you have to buy game (with the exception of rabbit), then it must be from someone with a game dealer's licence. Just because the local butcher's shop isn't permanently festooned with fur and feathers don't assume that it doesn't have a licence, although the words 'Licensed to deal in game' should be displayed somewhere. Customers might have to place a special order, especially for anything more unusual than pheasant. You may be able to persuade a butcher to get a licence if you can convince him that there is a demand.

Otherwise look in *Yellow Pages* under 'Game Dealers' for the nearest wholesale dealer, who will probably sell you some direct. Most big supermarket chains also sell a limited range of game, although it will probably be frozen and may have come from a farm rather than the wild.

Don't bother to go looking for game out of season. It is only legal to sell it, fresh or frozen, during the open season and for up to ten days after the season closes. All frozen game should have been killed in the same season, but it's possible that an unscrupulous dealer might buy up, kill and freeze spent pheasant hens from laying pens, offering them for sale after the start of the following open season.

POACHING

Game dealers'˙ licences and restrictions on sales are likely to remain on the statute books as a check on the sale of poached game. Unfortunately while legitimate shooting is becoming more common, so is its illegal counterpart, poaching. The excesses of bad hunters and poachers are anathaema to those who care about animals. This is why the responsible organisations need support in their efforts to educate newcomers and old hands alike.

HYGIENE

At present game is not subject to the same inspection regulations as farm meat, which is one reason for its relative cheapness. With the current debate about food hygiene it is possible that the situation may change at any time. A European Community Game Meat Directive has been drawn up (apparently in response to problems with farmed rabbit), which proposes that game be brought under the same regulations as meat. Although the suggestion that a vet be present at every shoot may be laughably unworkable, tighter regulations will inevitably mean big changes and more expensive meat.

If you go shooting yourself, or receive game straight from the shoot, you must be your own meat inspector. Be careful when gutting and skinning not to break the gallbladder or intestines; if you do, wash and dry the meat immediately and thoroughly. Inspect the internal organs, especially the liver, for signs of disease and parasites, and discard meat which is discoloured. If you are unsure get guidance if you can from an expert.

RESIDUES

It is difficult to say how much pesticide residue there is in game, but there will not be as much as in farmed animals. Artificially reared birds shot too early will have been given similar feeds to those given to poultry, perhaps with added medications. Truly wild birds are usually free from these residues, although they might eat chemically treated cereals on farm land. Grouse may be treated for parasitic infection with wormers, being caught and dosed at night, or given medicated grit to peck at.

GAME BIRDS

PHEASANT

Pheasants were probably introduced into this country as captive birds, raised for meat, but they have lived wild here for more than a thousand years. Their exotic plumage is a common sight in many parts of the country, but their favourite habitat is a mixture of open fields and woodland with good ground cover. They nest on the ground and at night go to roost, very noisily, in trees. During the day they like to spend most of their time on their feet, searching for a wide range of natural foods from insects and worms to fruits, seeds and leaves.

Like all game birds pheasants will run for cover and hide when threatened, only taking to the wing as a final resort. Ironically this is an inappropriate strategy for survival when the beaters come to flush them out. The birds rise vertically in a burst of energy and noise and then glide away looking for an early opportunity to come down again, making them an excellent target for guns.

Compared with many traditional game birds pheasants have adapted well to the unfriendly environment of modern agriculture. This, and the fact that they can be successfully reared artificially and released, has led to them becoming the main quarry for driven shoots. Despite the large numbers of reared birds, an estimated two-thirds of birds shot are bred in the wild.

Rear and release

Pheasants can be reared from a permanent breeding stock, or poults (baby birds) can be bought in from a game farm. The eggs are usually incubated and the poults kept in a brooder, as hen birds in captivity keep dirty nests and losses can be too high if they are left to hatch the poults themselves. They are fed proprietory pellets, similar to poultry feeds and with the same medications. At six to eight weeks the birds are ideally put in release pens with access to the wild, although they will return to the pen to be fed and to roost. Within four to six weeks they are effectively wild.

Unfortunately management on some driven shoots is more like a production line, with the birds released ready to be shot, almost too tame to bother to get into the air. This is not considered good sport at all and only serves to bring shooting into disrepute. It can hardly be claimed that the meat of such birds is wild or additive-free.

Poached pheasant

Strictly for its curiosity value, here is a tip from Dorothy Hartley's *Food in England* for getting a troublesome pheasant who is stealing your peas into the pot. Make a paper cone and smear the inside liberally with treacle or gum, and stick a few raisins in the bottom. Prop it up amongst the peas. When the bird sticks its head in to investigate, it won't be able to get the cone off, and will wander around, unable to see, waiting for you to come and dispatch it. Well, it's worth trying, especially as if you own your house you do have a right to take and kill by legal means any game which comes into your garden!

Preparation

The open season for pheasants is October 1st–February 1st. Pheasant is probably the commonest and most read-ily available of game birds, and can be bought frozen from many supermarkets and fresh from game dealers and butchers. Pheasant is always hung, from two or three days in warm humid weather to up to two weeks in the cold.

GREY PARTRIDGE

The grey partridge was the most important British lowland game bird until numbers fell dramatically after the Second World War. Heavy use of pesticides destroyed the insects which are food for the chicks, and the rooting out of copses and hedgerows radically altered the varied habitat which is necessary for the shy partridge to thrive. Some are now reared artificially and released, although this is not as successful a way of keeping up numbers as good land management. Fortunately the population is now growing again, but is still a fifth or sixth of what it once was.

The grey partridge is a small brown bird, notable for laying more eggs in one clutch than any other bird – in Britain it may be between fifteen and nineteen. Both parents conscientiously look after the nest and the chicks. They eat mainly plant food and some insects. When not breeding they feed and sleep together in large flocks called coveys.

RED-LEGGED OR FRENCH PARTRIDGE

This bird was introduced here in the late eighteenth century. It has grown in popularity as a quarry because it is easier to rear and release than the grey, and its flight habits are more suitable for driven shooting. It is similar in size to the grey partridge, but more strikingly marked with a black neck ring. As a parent it is not as enthusiastic, but will usually compensate by building two nests and laying eggs in each of them.

Preparation

For both sorts of partridge the methods of rearing and releasing and the circumstances of the shoot are similar to that of the pheasant, as is the hanging, plucking and preparation. The open season is September 1st until February 1st. Partridge are best eaten young. Older birds can be used for pies, casseroles, terrines and salmis.

RED GROUSE

The red grouse is a truly wild bird, as are its less common grouse cousins, the black grouse (called black-cock in old recipe books), capercaillie and ptarmigan. The grouse is a creature of the moorland, and is only found in the lonely open spaces and high hills of the north and west of the country.

A medium-sized brown bird with a comb, the red grouse is recognisable by the whirring of its wings as it flies fast and low over the moor. It cannot be artificially reared because the heather which shelters it constitutes the main part of its diet, therefore good management of the moors is the only way that landowners have of ensuring the continued existence of grouse as a shooting quarry. The heather must be burned in patches to ensure a plentiful supply of young shoots, and legally controllable predators must be kept down, as being ground nesting birds, the eggs and the young are particularly vulnerable.

Since grouse are considered to be the best of sporting quarry their habitat has been maintained, even in the face of increased competition from deer and sheep. The latter were described to us by a shooting man as 'woolly maggots' – they also like the heather and over-grazing can disturb the delicate ecological balance of the grouse's habitat. Moorland conservation has had fortunate consequences for many rare species of plants, birds and insects, but not for some protected birds of prey; some gamekeepers have been guilty of killing them, as well as the legitimate quarry of foxes and crows, but these attitudes are now changing slowly.

The open season for grouse, as most people know, starts amid a lot of bally-hoo on August 12th and goes on until December 10th. Grouse are sometimes 'walked-up' by rough shooters, but are usually shot on organised shoots. The beaters drive the birds towards the butts, permanent or semi-permanent walls of stone or wood usually half sunk into the ground, behind which the guns are concealed.

Preparation

Grouse have dark meat and a stronger flavour than other game birds. A grouse should be hung for about a week. The young birds can be roasted or cut in half and grilled, while the older birds make good casseroles and pâtés.

The black grouse, the capercaillie and the ptarmigan are less common quarry, and shot only in small numbers on specialised shoots. They vary a lot in size – the capercaillie can reach the size of a turkey, but the ptarmigan is smaller than the red grouse. The capercaillie feeds naturally on pine needles and the meat tastes of resin, rather like the Greek wine retsina. It is said that burying the bird, or soaking it in milk and then vinegar, will remove the flavour, but others say it is best buried and forgotten!

PIGEONS

Pigeons used to be kept in this country for meat, and still are in many parts of the world. Old manor houses sometimes still have dovecotes with a myriad of holes high up near the roof, or on a tower or gable end, for the birds to fly in and out. Nowadays pigeons are usually kept for racing and pigeon fanciers would probably be affronted at the mention of eating their birds. Since there are large flocks of wild pigeons plaguing crops all over the country and no close season, there are plentiful supplies available for the cook.

The wood pigeon probably mates for life, and lays two or three clutches of eggs each year. There are an estimated three to five million breeding pairs in Britain. They have very elastic crops and can eat their own body weight of food every four days; in six days they can eat enough wheat to make a large loaf of bread, and in one day enough barley to make a pint of beer. Modern monoculture creates a concentrated food source which just asks to be ravaged and pigeons take full advantage of it, just as other pests do. As well as cereals they also relish arable weeds, so possibly to an organic farmer they may be less of a nuisance.

The pigeon shooter may attract them down into an open field with decoys and shoot them from a hide, or take to the edges of woods and shoot them when they come to roost, to digest their food or to sleep.

Although small, pigeons make good eating. Most of the meat is concentrated in their plump breasts, and you can make them go further by cooking them with other meats. They are at their best in the spring and summer when their food is full of protein. Young birds, which are known as squabs, are good for roasting or grilling, and don't need much cooking. Older birds are best casseroled or made into an old favourite – pigeon pie. Pigeons are not usually hung.

WADERS

There are three species of waders which can be shot in Britain – the golden plover, the snipe and the woodcock. Until the beginning of the century they were a common food and were shot by professional market gunners. Nowadays they are not so easily obtainable, but they are held to be among the best of game birds to eat. The golden plover are usually shot by wildfowlers, and the woodcock as a 'side-product' of a pheasant shoot. The open season is roughly September to the end of January.

All three are ground nesting birds, favouring open spaces, heaths, bogs and wetlands, although the woodcock, as its name suggests, prefers the shelter of trees for breeding and resting. Insects form the main part of their diet, with worms being a favourite. The snipe and the woodcock are both brown birds with long beaks, ideally suited for rooting out their food. The golden plover is easily recognised by its eyecatching gold and black mottled plumage.

These birds are traditionally eaten barded with fat

bacon and roasted whole, and served with the innards in, known as the 'trail', spread on toast. The long beaks were left on and used as a skewer to truss the bird. They may also be grilled whole or split, and again they should be barded or basted. They are usually hung for a very short time, especially if they are to be left undrawn before cooking – this is a matter of personal preference, but they can be drawn. The crop and gizzard should *always* be removed through the neck opening, and they should be thoroughly cooked. If they have been drawn, keep them succulent by filling them with a fat-enriched stuffing.

WILD DUCKS

The open season for wild ducks is September through to February. Nowadays they are mostly shot by wildfowlers, although in the past large numbers were shot or netted by professionals. There are three species of quarry diving ducks, the pochard, the goldeneye and the tufted duck, but their meat is not as good as that of the dabblers – the mallard, teal, widgeon, gadwall, pintail and shoveler. The divers swim down for their food to the muddy depths. The dabbling ducks eat mostly vegetation, with some insects and small water life taken near the surface in shallow waters, or on shore. There are also four species of wild geese on the quarry list, but it is illegal to sell them.

Mallard

The familiar wild mallard is happy to live near any sort of water, even in urban areas. They usually mate for life and nest some way away from the water. The duck can hatch two broods of ducklings a year, not many of whom will survive – perhaps only two from a brood of ten. Because of their adaptable nature mallard are easy to rear artificially, but this has led in some cases to large numbers of virtually tame ducks being released as easy targets for commercial shoots.

Teal

The teal is also a common duck, with the winter population boosted by many immigrants. It is smaller than the mallard but similar in looks, except that the drake has a brown and green head. It favours small patches of water and bogs and is always wild.

The other dabbling ducks frequent the marshes and wetlands of coastal areas, often in huge flocks. Numbers of resident birds are very few, but there are many winter visitors.

Preparation

The most common wild duck is the mallard, and it makes excellent eating. One bird will usually feed two people. The meat is very lean and can be dry, so it should be cooked carefully with added fat in the form of stuffing or barding. The gadwall and the pintail are also good, but the widgeon and the shoveler can be more difficult to cook, with a flavour which varies according to the nature of their diet. If you suspect a fishy flavour poach the bird for about twenty minutes in salted water to take away taint, then cook, reducing the recipe time accordingly. Hang wild duck for about two days.

CHOOSING GAME BIRDS

One way in which wild meat differs from farmed meat is that the age and condition of the animal or bird is unknown. If you have a little basic knowledge you are better placed to make a judgement about the age and to choose the right cooking method. Young birds are suitable for roasting – they will have a pliable breast bone, beak and feet and soft smooth feathers. Older birds are better pot roasted, casseroled or used for pâtés and terrines. Their breast bones will be harder and their legs and feathers will be coarser. In some species the cock will have spurs. Hen birds are smaller and usually more tender than cock birds, but cocks have a more pronounced flavour. When you buy a brace of birds it will usually be a cock and hen.

HANGING

Game birds are always hung to bring out the flavour and increase the tenderness, but now that we are more squeamish about our food, and perhaps better informed, it's no longer common to hang them until they are so rotten that the maggots drop out. Hang the bird feet down in a cool place for two days to two weeks, according to the weather and the age of the bird, older birds needing longer. The Continental way is to hang the bird head down so that the guts fall into the body cavity and increase the flavour.

It's a good idea to pluck the bird before you hang it. The flesh will not tear so easily, it helps to keep the body well ventilated, and enables you to see what condition the bird is in. If the bird has been wounded, for instance, or if the legs are wobbly and obviously broken, don't hang it for too long. The same applies if there is a lot of shot in it, although if you are unlucky enough to swallow any it will go straight through you! If it is really badly damaged, cut off the good bits, cook them as chicken (unhung) and discard the rest. Watch out for flies, especially in early autumn – it is a good idea to enclose the bird in a muslin bag which will help to protect it.

PLUCKING

Plucking is the same as for poultry but more care is needed, especially if the bird has hung for a long time. Small birds can be wet plucked by dipping the bird in hot water and pulling off the feathers carefully into the sink, but as wet plucking will make the bird go off quicker, it is better not to wet pluck before hanging.

DRAWING A SMALL BIRD

Cut off the head and feet, slide the skin down the neck and cut the neck off close to the body. Work the crop loose and remove. Pull up the pointed end of the breast bone with your left thumb, making the skin tight above the vent. Make a horizontal slit with a sharp knife. Put two fingers inside the hole, loosen the entrails and shake them out. Keep the liver, heart and gizzard for stock. Fold the wings under the body, tie the legs down as you would a chicken, and truss or skewer the bird together.

SKINNING

It is easier to skin pigeons and other small birds rather than pluck them, unless you particularly want to roast them with the skin on. Ideally you will need a very sharp large-bladed knife, and a filleting or thin-bladed knife. Place the bird on its back. Cut off the wings before the first joint and cut off the legs above the shank. Pinch up the loose skin and feathers on the breastbone and nick it with a sharp knife, then it's a simple matter to work your fingers in under the skin and pull it back over the breast. If you only want the breast meat, cut it carefully away from the breast bone and ribs with the thin pointed knife.

If you want to skin the whole bird, continue pulling the skin off, easing it over the wing joints and up to the neck. Cut the head off and pull out the wind pipe. Then pull the skin down over the legs to the vent and cut off the parson's nose (where the tail feathers were attached) which will free the skin from the carcass.

ROASTING

Game birds have very little fat, and although this is a health advantage for the eater it can make the flesh dry and tough unless additional fat is used in cooking.

221

Young birds for roasting and grilling should be barded (wrapped over the breast) with fat bacon rashers, basted with dripping or butter, or finished with a rich sauce made with fresh or soured cream. These are all ways of making the rich, rather dry meat more succulent. When roasting game birds you don't usually get much juice in the pan after cooking, so you will need a good stock made from the giblets if you want to serve gravy.

Stuffings and accompaniments

Fruit of almost any kind is a good accompaniment to game dishes, whether in stuffings, sauces, jellies and relishes, or side salads. Chestnuts and buttered vegetable purées are also good. Traditionally small game birds are served on a piece of bread fried in the drippings, which aren't enough to make gravy but are necessary to help digest the meat. Alternatively, because the meat is quite dry, a plain roast can be served with creamy dressings and sauces. Depending on the gaminess of the bird, use herbs with a strong or delicate flavour.

ROAST AND STUFFED PIGEONS

This recipe can also be used for other small birds. For four birds mix together four good handfuls of tasty breadcrumbs (ryebread is good), half a small finely chopped onion, 3oz of melted butter, seasonings and fresh chopped herbs. Stuff the cavities. If the birds have been plucked and still have the skin on, baste with butter and roast. Wrap skinned birds in rashers of fat bacon. Roast until tender in a medium oven for about twenty minutes. Young birds can be successfully barbecued using this recipe.

COOKING OLDER BIRDS

Older birds, which may be tough but will be full of flavour, are best used for casseroles, pies, soups or salmis. Watch out for small bones.

CASSEROLING GAME BIRDS

Brown the birds gently and remove. Brown some bacon and root vegetables. Turn everything into a casserole, cover with stock or water and simmer very gently. Add new potatoes, barley or pasta if liked. Serve from the dish.

SALMIS

This is a game stew where the meat is first roasted, then finished in a thickened sauce with vegetables. Lightly roast a bird. Make a slightly thickened stock by sautéing vegetables in fat and sprinkling with flour, adding stock and cooking until the vegetables are tender, then straining and sieving them. Carve the meat from the bird and keep warm. Chop up the carcass and put it into the thickened stock, then cook for about thirty minutes. Strain the stock over the carved meat, add sautéed mushrooms, peppers, etc. Cook very gently in a moderate oven for twenty minutes. Serve with croutons, fried bread, watercress and orange salad.

COLIN BLANCHARD'S PIGEON BREASTS WITH MUSTARD SAUCE

Small birds have very little meat other than on their breasts. Cut off the breasts and cook them in this way, and use the rest of the bird for a stew or stock. Allow two to four breasts per person, depending on the size of the bird and the appetite of the diner.

Top each breast with butter and black pepper and grill them under a medium heat until just pink inside, basting with the butter while they cook. Remove and keep warm. For half a pint of mustard sauce take 2tbsp of the cooking butter into a saucepan, add 1oz wholemeal flour, stir and cook gently for a minute. Stir in 1tsp mustard powder, remove from the heat, and gradually mix in a half pint of liquid. This can be stock, water, white wine, cider, milk, or a combination. Mix thoroughly to avoid lumps, bring to the boil and cook for five minutes. Adjust the seasoning and pour the sauce over the pigeon breasts. Serve with plain bread and a green vegetable.

RABBIT AND HARE

RABBIT

Rabbits have always been hunted for food, and are good consumers of waste, just like pigs and poultry, so they have long been kept on small farms and in gardens. Until the nineteenth century they were also kept by large landowners in extensive warrens, surrounded by wooden fences and banks. The meat was a valuable source of income to the estate.

As agriculture developed and became increasingly intensive, rabbits became more and more of a pest to the farmer. It is believed that the disease myxomatosis was deliberately introduced into Britain in the early 1950s in order to control the rabbit population. It did this most effectively, wiping out an estimated sixty million rabbits within the first year. It has taken about thirty years for the disease to run its course, and there are now only small localised outbreaks. Perhaps because of the shortage of wild rabbits and revulsion at the disease, rabbit meat lost its appeal, but rabbit farming and the importation of frozen rabbit from China has kept the trade going, and we can expect to see further expansion in the future.

In their natural state rabbits are grazing animals which like a mild climate and light soil, with plenty of cover provided by hedges, walls and woodland. They live in large colonies with a strict social order, each colony being dominated by a queen doe and the most powerful buck. The rabbit's reputation for prolific breeding is well deserved – each year a doe can produce an average of twenty kittens, in up to six litters.

Rabbits can severely damage arable and horticultural crops and pasture, and have a particular fondness for young saplings. This is why they can be hunted all the year round, although some hunters will not take them during the main breeding season so as to sustain a surplus for the future.

WILD RABBITS

Wild rabbits may be shot with a gun on a rough shoot, or sometimes during a driven shoot of game birds. Ferrets are also used to flush them out of their burrows into nets – this method makes better meat as there is no wounding or gun shot. Once trapped in the net the hunter will either break the animal's neck or kill it with a sharp blow. The hunter will then empty the bladder to avoid tainting the meat, and, especially if the weather is warm, 'paunch' or gut it on the spot. If it ends up at the game dealers or butchers they will complete the job by skinning and possibly jointing the meat.

FARMED RABBITS

Keeping rabbits in cages or hutches is nothing new – modern rabbit farms are simply bigger and more intensive. The rabbit has perhaps the biggest potential output of any farm animal, and is now being exploited to the full. According to the British Commercial Rabbit Association a commercial doe can produce between forty and sixty meat rabbits per year, up to twenty times her own weight. The industry produces a yearly total of over a million meat animals.

Adult rabbits will fight if confined together, so they are inevitably kept indoors in cages, sometimes in two or three tiers. Sometimes young rabbits being fattened are kept together in larger pens with a wire mesh floor. The cages, usually six square feet, are made from steel mesh for ease of cleaning, and will hold about eight fatteners, a doe with a litter, or an adult buck.

To keep the does breeding all year round they must have seventeen hours of light, so artificial lighting is necessary. The doe gives birth in a nest box and feeds her own young. She will be mated again ten to fourteen days after giving birth, and the current litter weaned just before she is due to give birth again. The young rabbits are fattened to a minimum weight of 5½lbs, which takes about eight to ten weeks, and are then sold, either to a commercial packer/processor or at the farm gate or market.

All rabbits are fed proprietory pellets, but some farmers will provide hay and straw for the animals to pull through the holes in the cage to give them something to do. Although some medication is used in the feeds and antibiotics given for infection such as mastitis, rabbits are not likely to be given medication on the same scale as larger intensively reared animals, as their value does not justify the expense. Seriously diseased animals are automatically culled.

PREPARATION

If you live in the country you may be given, or be able to buy, rabbits with the skin on. The rabbit should always have been gutted in the field. It is not usually recommended to hang rabbit, so the task has to be done soon after death. *In extremis* the rabbit can be frozen with the skin on (in fact it will be easier to skin when defrosted), but do make sure that it is completely sealed in a thick plastic bag before going into the freezer.

SKINNING

It is not difficult to skin a rabbit but, as with most practical tasks, the best way to learn is to watch someone else doing it first. You must have a very sharp knife – one with a long blade makes the job even easier.

Cut all the legs off just above the joint nearest the body. Turn the rabbit on its side, and start to part the skin from the flesh where the guts have been taken out of the rabbit's belly. Loosen all the skin round the body from both sides of the cut, so that the middle of the body is free. Grasp the skin and pull it over and off the back legs, cutting off the tail at the vent. Do the same at the front end up to the top of the neck and cut the head off. Pull out the wind pipe.

JOINTING

Lay the rabbit on its back, cut through the body just above the hips, then cut through lengthways to separate the legs. Cut the central body section through twice to make three joints. Cut the shoulders lengthways to give two joints.

GUTTING

If you keep rabbits for meat yourself you will need to know how to kill and gut them. If you want to break the rabbit's neck, which is a swift, clean method, get an expert to demonstrate it to you. Otherwise consult the forthcoming book on humane killing available from the Humane Slaughter Association.

To gut a rabbit, make a cut up the centre of the abdomen with a very sharp knife, taking care not to cut in too deeply and puncture the innards. Pull out all the organs, and keep the liver, kidneys and heart as they make good stock. Details of how to remove the skin in one usable piece will be found in any specialist book.

COOKING RABBIT

The meat of wild rabbits will vary a lot according to the age and condition of the animal. Obviously the size of the rabbit will be a good indication. The ears of a young rabbit will tear easily, there will be plenty of white fat around the kidneys, and the bones will be pliable. You can roast a fairly young rabbit in quite a hot oven for about an hour, or for about one-and-a-half hours in a moderate oven. If in doubt as to the age of a wild beast, use for casseroles and pies. Farmed rabbit is liable to be more tender than wild, but all rabbit meat is lean and therefore may dry out if not cooked carefully.

HEATHER'S RABBIT PIE

This is a rich and warming pie which does just as well for a dinner party as a family meal.

Stew or pressure cook a jointed rabbit with a chopped onion, celery stick, carrot and a bay leaf. When it is cool enough to handle drain off the stock and set to one side. Pick the meat off the rabbit carcass and place it in a deep pie dish. Chop one leek finely and fry it in 1oz of butter until soft. Add a chopped green pepper and 4oz of chopped mushrooms, cook for a few more minutes and then add 1oz of flour and enough stock to make a fairly thick sauce. Add ¼–½ tsp of chilli powder and 2oz of grated mature cheddar cheese. Pour the sauce over the meat and top the pie with wholemeal pastry. Bake at gas mark 6, 400°F, 200°C, for approximately twenty minutes.

RABBIT WITH MUSTARD SAUCE

Fry rabbit joints or diced pieces and chopped shallots or onion gently in butter until lightly browned. Sprinkle in 1 level tbsp flour mixed with a heaped tsp dry mustard powder per pint, stir and add white wine or stock to cover. Season with salt and pepper, parsley or tarragon, and simmer gently for one hour. Sauté a few mushrooms lightly in butter, add to the casserole and simmer for fifteen more minutes. Reduce the sauce if necessary. Serve with creamed potatoes.

HARE

There are two species of hare in Britain, the brown hare of the lowlands and the smaller mountain or blue hare. Despite the Bible admonition that hares are unclean meat, both species have always been a valuable food for large country families. There is no close season for hares, but they cannot be sold from the beginning of March until the end of July.

Hares are more solitary than rabbits, and not such prolific breeders. The doe can raise from six to twelve young in a year. Her nest is a shallow scrape in the ground called a form, and when the young hares or leverets are born they already have their fur.

The brown hare is a good sized animal, weighing up to eight pounds. It looks like a large rabbit, with longer ears and legs, and a fast and energetic sprint. Its favourite habitat is old-style arable farmland, with cereals and plentiful vegetation for food, and hedgerows, woodland and long grass for cover. The widespread use of chemicals, the huge prairies of modern farming and increasing numbers of foxes have all contributed to a decline in numbers since the 1960s, and in many areas of the country the brown hare is no longer hunted. Since it is regarded as an agricultural pest where the population is higher, there are still some driven hare shoots which take place after the end of the game-shooting season. It is also a target for rough shooters.

The mountain hare is smaller, and in very high areas it may shed its brown summer coat in the autumn and grow white fur for camouflage in the snow. It likes the same habitat as the grouse, and shares its taste for heather.

PREPARATION

Hang the hare whole by the back legs, head down, for up to a week. The older the animal the longer it needs to be hung. Gut and skin like a rabbit before cooking. The meat of a young leveret is very different from that of an older hare, which has a more gamey flavour. The fur of a young hare will be soft, with pliable ears and sharp white teeth. With age the teeth become irregular and yellowish, the coat starts to turn grey, and the cleft in the lip becomes bigger. Game or lamb recipes can be adapted for cooking hare.

JUGGED HARE

When the hare is hung the blood which collects under a piece of membrane in the ribs should be saved for the gravy. Marinade the hare in red wine and spices first if you prefer. Brown the pieces in bacon or pork fat, add diced fat bacon (optional), and remove to a casserole. Add vegetables, whole spice berries or a bouquet garni, salt and pepper, and the juice and rind of a lemon (optional). Just cover with stock and cook very slowly for two to three hours. Strain off the stock from the vegetables and meat. Thicken the gravy slightly with *beurre manié* and cook the flour out. In the meantime add a few spoonfuls at a time of the hot stock to the blood to bring it up to the temperature of the casserole before adding it to the dish. Add some fruit jelly as well if you have some. Put back the pieces of meat and heat through without boiling. Add port. Serve with creamy mashed potatoes, boiled parsnips and dark green cabbage.

VENISON

Since prehistoric times the deer has been valued for its meat, its skin and its horns. It has always been hunted, but the mediaeval aristocracy maintained large areas of forests in which they kept herds of deer for sport and as a source of food. Ordinary people only ever tasted it at clandestine meals – Shakespeare was a deer poacher in his spare time!

Gradually, as agriculture grew in importance, venison was overtaken in popularity by beef and mutton. Cattle and sheep could be overwintered, and provided more fat and other useful by-products. Now the tables have turned, and deer are being farmed themselves. Deer farming is growing rapidly, and such is the demand for wild breeding hinds that they currently command a higher price alive than as venison.

WILD DEER

There are six species of wild deer in these islands. Venison is technically the meat of the red deer, but the meat of the fallow, roe and Sika deer is also commonly known as venison. They are found in most parts of rural Britain, and can make use of the most inhospitable terrain where even mountain sheep and cattle cannot survive. They are alert to danger, quick and strong, and will travel long distances to take shelter. In times of shortage their lack of fat is a serious disadvantage, as they have fewer reserves of energy to fall back on. It is normal for deer to become emaciated in the winter, but because the population expands rapidly in good years, when conditions change they can suffer from mass starvation and become serious pests to trees and crops. This is the main reason that culling is necessary for the maintenance of a healthy deer population.

There are a few packs of hounds in the south of England who still hunt deer, but the vast majority are shot for sport or as part of a cull. By law the authorised stalker may only use an appropriate high velocity rifle and ammunition, in order to maximise the chances of a clean kill. All deer are protected by a close season, but unfortunately the increased demand for venison has led to more poaching. Poachers often use crossbows, traps and dogs as well as guns, and their methods can cause much suffering.

Since deer are heavy animals and most are shot in remote places, for convenience most stalkers 'gralloch' (gut) the carcass on the spot. The butchering of venison involves as much skill as the butchering of cattle, sheep and pigs, and is usually done professionally. It is likely that it will soon come under some of the same regulations as farm meats.

Advocates of wild venison praise it for having more flavour, and for being truly additive-free, free-range meat which doesn't waste precious resources of food and land. Sales of wild venison still exceed those of farmed venison, and much of it goes for export to Germany and other European countries.

PARKLAND DEER

In lowland areas, herds of deer have traditionally been kept by landowners as ornamental features in large enclosed parklands. Nowadays these herds are likely to be managed in order to help pay their way. Conditions will fall somewhere in a broad spectrum between the wild and the farm, but good husbandry is needed in order to minimise stress for a virtually wild animal when it is caught and handled.

FARMED DEER

On a farm, deer are kept in a similar manner to beef and

sheep – out to grass in the spring and summer, and housed in the winter and fed hay, silage and concentrates. They grow extremely fast, and research has shown that even without any special breeding the calves can grow as quickly as fat lambs.

Predictably, as with every other branch of farming, there are moves afoot to control fertility and step up production. Deer naturally give birth in June, but some farmers would prefer it to be earlier in the year so as to gain the maximum benefit from a longer growing season. Ovulation can be artificially induced with hormones, but it remains to be seen whether this type of management will backfire and damage the 'healthy' image of venison.

Deer, being outsiders in agricultural terms, are still allowed to be shot in the field, although a few abattoirs do exist where the deer get preferential treatment over other farm animals. If and when the regulations are changed and slaughtering can take place in abattoirs on a commercial scale, the big farming interests are likely to get involved. Farmed venison is young, tender and succulent, and with its low fat advantages has great potential for the mass market. The British Deer Farmers Association issues a British Prime Venison mark, for venison complying to their standards.

PREPARATION

Hanging is similar to beef, anything from ten days to three weeks depending on age and condition. Butchering is more like that for lamb and goat, although the meat is usually cooked like beef. Red deer have the strongest flavour and roe deer the most delicate. As venison is very low in fat, about 5 per cent, it may be necessary to lard roasting joints with fat or cover with fatty bacon to prevent the meat drying out.

AVAILABILITY

Wild venison is protected by a close season in the spring and summer. Farmed venison is available all the year round, although in the summer it may only be available frozen.

CUTS OF VENISON AND HOW TO COOK THEM

Prime roasting cuts Haunch and saddle, and shoulder of farmed venison.

Pot roasting Flank and shoulder.

Casserole Shin, neck and flank.
Wild venison may be of doubtful age and condition, and demands the traditional methods of cooking – marinades and slow cooking – to counteract any toughness. Old recipes for cooking venison are always for the wild meat and must be adapted for cooking farm venison, which takes less time to cook and is not so strongly flavoured. Deer farmers are always keen to point out that their product is guaranteed young and tender.

ROAST VENISON

Marinade first if you wish – the traditional flavourings are juniper berries, ginger, nutmeg and cloves. Lard the meat with fat or cover with fat bacon, or plan to baste frequently with dripping throughout cooking. Farmed venison is best cooked rare to medium by a fast method, as for beef. For older meat and for shoulder, or if you prefer the meat well done, cook by a slower method as for beef. Take care not to let the meat dry out. The British Deer Farmers' Association recommend cooking vegetables such as onion, carrots, celery, tomato, courgette, etc., until soft, then puréeing them and adding them to the pan juices to make the gravy.

ACCOMPANIMENTS

The traditional accompaniments are rowan and redcurrant jelly and Cumberland sauce, but other fruit sauces are worth trying.

MANOR FARM VENISON CASSEROLE

Brown two medium onions and one clove of garlic in some oil. Add 1lb sliced carrots and three rashers of streaky bacon cut in strips and brown them. Coat 1lb diced casserole venison or shin in seasoned flour, and brown as well. Turn into a casserole, add ½lb quartered mushrooms, enough stock, wine, cider or beer to cover, and a bay leaf, parsley and seasoning. Cover tightly and cook in a moderate oven for two to three hours. For delicious extra flavour add about 2tbsp bitter marmalade about half an hour before the end of cooking, or 1tbsp dry vermouth and 3fl oz cream just before serving.

Part 4
DIRECTORY

USING THE DIRECTORY

Unfortunately, good quality meat cannot be found in every high street butchers and supermarket. But with a little searching you should be able to find good meat wherever you live, and for once those in the remote countryside won't be at a disadvantage. We have compiled this directory to help you in your search, and also to give farmers an opportunity to air their views.

Many sorts of producers and retailers are included, small and not so small, ranging from simply additive-free to Soil Association Symbol organic, so that you can see what is available. You may care less about home-grown organic feedstuff than you do about animals being able to range freely; or you may suffer from allergies and want meat which is as residue-free as possible; or simply want meat that tastes like it used to. When you come to buy you will have to decide what your own criteria are.

In the course of compiling the directory some fears were expressed by our correspondents that false claims are sometimes made, both knowingly and unknowingly. We couldn't make personal checks on every entry, so we thought the fairest thing to do was to let each farmer put their own case in more or less their own words, and leave it to you, the consumer, to make your own decisions. The comments are theirs, not ours. Buyer beware!

What has been said in the rest of the book – and asking the right questions – should help you decide for yourself whether what you are buying is what it is claimed to be. When buying direct from a farm remember that you are visiting the farmer's place of work. If you don't take up too much of their time we're confident that, like us, you will meet some charming people who will probably be pleased to explain their enterprise to a sympathetic listener. By the nature of their work many farmers are cut off from the community and they feel unjustly attacked by the rest of us, so you have an ideal opportunity to bridge the communications gap.

Once you have found a delicious product from a producer that you can trust, making the effort to buy regularly should become a habit. The power of the consumer should never be underestimated. Campaigning organisations have fought doggedly for years for better food produced in better conditions; legislation has been passed, although sometimes ignored, to improve animal welfare; but nothing has such impact on producers and retailers as a fall in demand. Factory-farmed meat could disappear if people stopped buying it.

By buying good humanely produced meat from small producers you are helping to keep them going, and encouraging them and others to produce more. We feel that it's a positive way for the individual to support causes such as the welfare of animals and the protection of the environment.

Prices are mid-1989 and have been included as a guide only. The reader will notice that they vary in a predictable way – by and large the bigger the range and more organised the supply, the higher the price. By comparison, some smallholders are charging what seem like almost giveaway prices, but it would be unfair to expect a regular supply from these sources. As with all fresh produce, there are seasonal variations in price and availability. Other details may also have changed, and some people may have gone out of business, so we suggest that you always phone or write first.

Directory entries are organised alphabetically by county and then town. The map opposite will help you to find your nearest supplier. The numbers on the map refer to entries in the Directory. If you wish to buy organic meat produced in Eire, please contact the Irish Organic Farmers' and Growers' Association for an up-to-date list of suppliers (see page 333 for the address).

ORGANIC SYMBOLS AND STANDARDS

When you buy meat which is claimed to be organic, the chances are that it will have at least one symbol which certifies it as such. There are several different sets of standards, although they are all quite similar in essence. Full details can be obtained from the organisations involved. The Government's own organic certification scheme – UKROFS – is also expected to get off the ground in 1990.

Organic standards are ideals, as well as practical rules, and will never be compromised by those who cherish them. But farmers who for legitimate reasons can't, or don't want to, apply for a symbol might still be producing excellent food, and their produce should be considered on its own merits.

OTHER SOURCES OF SUPPLY

The National Federation of City Farms encourages all its members to use organic methods, and city farms often have small amounts of meat for sale to visitors. In country towns, Women's Institute market stalls sometimes have free-range poultry. There are also moves afoot to bring organic meat into some of the major supermarket chains. There are many problems to overcome whenever retailing giants get supplies from small producers. The supermarkets need a uniform product, packaging and regular supplies. Small producers need to be well organised to meet their demands and keep their independence. But this is an opportunity for good meat to become available to more people, and it would remove the problems of marketing that many farmers don't have the resources to tackle.

Groups such as Compassion in World Farming and the RSPCA are also pressurising supermarkets to label meat clearly, so that consumers know how it has been produced and slaughtered. Shoppers should watch out for interesting labels, and keep asking for the sort of products that they want to buy.

DIRECTORY

1.

Radford Mill Farm
Timsbury
Bath
Avon
BA3 1QF
tel: 0761 72549

2.

Radford Mill Farm Shop
Picton Street
Montpelier
Bristol
Avon
tel: 0272 245360

<u>Opening times</u>   Direct sales from farm to order, half pigs and lambs, beef as required. Frozen meat always available from the shop, 9a.m.–7p.m. Mon–Sat, 10a.m.–1p.m. Sun.

<u>Products</u>   Organic beef, all cuts and 100 per cent meat beefburgers. Organic lamb, half lamb ready butchered (average weight 20lb). Additive-free pork, half pig ready butchered (average weight 40lb). Fresh and frozen.

<u>Price guide</u>   Beef from £1.40/lb for cheap mince to £5.50/lb for fillet steak. Half beasts – pork 75p/lb (including head), lamb approx. £1.40/lb.

Radford Mill Farm pigs are fed on vegetable waste, whey from a local sheep and goat milking enterprise, and feedstuffs mixed to their own specifications at the local mill – no additives or meat and bone offal. The sows are on

243

free range and weaners are fattened inside on straw with natural lighting and ventilation. Lambs are kept to Soil Association standards, fed home-grown grass, hay, silage and cereals, and are always outside in natural conditions. Beef calves are raised on milk powder (without antibiotics), organic cereals and some proprietary rearing feedstuffs for the first six months, then grass, hay and silage. They are reared in peer groups and not individually penned.

All animals are taken to a local abattoir first thing in the morning, so that they are not waiting too long in the lairage.

Soil Association Symbol for sheep only (not for beef because calves have been bought at markets in the past).

3.

Manor Farm Deer
The Manor Farm
Brockley
Backwell
Bristol
Avon
BS19 3AQ
tel: 027 583 2313

J. and E. Ridge

Opening times   Farm shop open 2p.m.–7p.m. Mon–Fri, 10a.m.–7p.m. Sat, 10a.m.–2p.m. Sun. Or by prior arrangement.

Products   Prime British venison, normally sold fully butchered and frozen but fresh to order. Packaged in individual and family sized packs, bulk and catering discounts available. Cookery information is given in the shop. Primitive lamb seasonally available.

Price guide   Venison from £2.20/lb pot roast–£4.90/lb sirloin steaks. Lamb prices available on application.

No artificial growth promoters are used and all feedstuffs are based on natural ingredients. Venison is from grass fed animals no more than three years old and of a consistently high quality, guaranteed free from disease. Venison stags are shot and butchered on the farm, the meat is inspected by the Local Authority Meat Inspector and then hung for ten days. Manor Farm venison complies with British Prime Venison requirements. Lamb is naturally reared and grass fed, killed at local family-run abattoir and butchered as for venison.

4.

Windmill Hill City Farm
38A Doveton Street
Bedminster
Bristol
Avon
BS3 4DU
tel: 0272 633252

Opening times   10a.m.–4p.m. Tues–Sun.

Products   Additive free beef, pork, lamb and kid, fresh and frozen. Half carcasses or butchers' cuts.

Price guide   Beef mince £1.30/lb–sirloin steak £3.60/lb. Lamb's liver 80p/lb–leg fillet £2.50/lb. Belly pork 75p/lb–leg fillet £2/lb. All meat sausages with real skins £2/lb.

All animals are reared in stress-free conditions, and the farm intends to go organic in the near future. Poultry is free-range, pigs are loose-housed and free-range, cattle and sheep loose-housed in winter and grazed in summer, and goats are grazed untethered. Feedstuffs are proprietary mixes, some organic, brewers' grains and vegetable and green waste. Animals are slaughtered at a small abattoir just outside the city and collected the next day, except for beef which is hung for two weeks. The meat has flavour and is lean.

5.

Real Food Supplies
36c and 38 Gloucester Road
Bishopston
Bristol
Avon
BS7 8AR
tel: 0272 243474/232015

Phil Haughton

<u>Products</u> Full range of fresh and frozen meats and meat products to Soil Association standards, and additive free meat if organic is not available. Also organic wholefoods, fruit and vegetables and dairy products.

<u>Price guide</u> Beef brisket £1.70/lb–fillet steak £5.40/lb. Belly pork 75p/lb–leg of pork £2.60/lb. Rib and breast of lamb 75p/lb–leg of lamb £2.65/lb. Chickens £1.45–£1.75/lb, ducks £1.94/lb, geese £2.39/lb and turkey £2.15/lb to order for Christmas.

Animals are fed on home-grown and bought-in feedstuffs from registered organic feed merchants, and kept to Soil Association standards of husbandry. Many of the shop's suppliers use the normal slaughter facilities, others arrange to have their stock put through the abattoir immediately after arrival to limit the stress.

Phil Haughton says that Real Food Supplies meat is tender and well-textured, and very few people who try it want other meat again. He is committed to the Soil Association Symbol, which represents the only sustainable agriculture, and feels that any less stringent codes of practice will open the door for a general lowering of standards, so that 'before we know it there won't be much difference between "real" meat and other meat'. He is hoping to develop a retailers' scheme with the Soil Association.

6.

Clutton Hill Farm Shop
Clutton Hill Farm
Clutton
Bristol
Avon
tel: 0761 52458

Mr Appleyard

Opening times 8a.m.–1p.m. Mon, 8a.m.–5p.m. Tues, 8a.m.–3.30p.m. Sat.

Products Beef, pork, lamb and chickens frozen and fresh, additive free turkeys.

Price guide Chicken livers 75p/lb–large cockerels £1.04/lb. Beef from £1.35/lb mince–£3.95/lb sirloin steak. Pork from 74p/lb for belly pork. Cooked ham £2.40/lb, smoked bacon £1.98/lb. Leg of lamb £1.65/lb, lamb chops £2.20/lb.

Loose housed pigs kept on straw and slatted floors. Grass and silage fed cattle, sheep and lambs. Home-grown and home-mixed feedstuffs are used as well as proprietary mixes, with no use of imported substitutes or waste products. Medication is only used in case of sick animals. Animals are transported by the farm to a local abattoir for immediate slaughter with a minimum of stress.

Clutton Farm believes that the main requirements for good, tender, tasty meat are the right breed of animal with good quality foodstuff and comfortable, stress-free conditions at all stages, correct chilling of the meat and, in the case of beef, correct hanging time.

7.

St Werburghs' City Farm
Watercress Road
St Werburghs
Bristol
Avon
BS2 9YJ
tel: 0272 428241

<u>Opening times</u> 8a.m.–6p.m. summer, 8a.m.–5p.m. winter, seven days a week. There is nearly always frozen meat available, but the farm prefers to take orders in advance, particularly for fresh meat and freezer orders.

<u>Products</u> Additive free pork, pork sausages, lamb and goat meat, all frozen, occasionally fresh. Christmas poultry should be available as from 1989.

<u>Price guide</u> Half lamb freezer pack at £1/lb. Quarter pig freezer pack at 75p/lb. Individual cuts; breast of lamb 75p/lb–£1.60/lb for best cuts. Belly pork 75p/lb–£1.25/lb for best cuts. Sausages 100 per cent meat £2/lb.

Pigs are kept in deep litter and yards, poultry are free-range and in straw yards. Animals are fed on proprietary mixes without additives or growth promoters, but the farm hopes to mix their own feeds in the future. Animals are taken to a small slaughterhouse about ten minutes away, where the slaughter is carried out quickly and quietly.

St Werburghs' animals are not just kept for meat, but play an invaluable part in the educational role of a city farm, giving city dwellers a first-hand experience of farm animals.

8.

Garland's Organic Farm Shop
Gardener's Lane
Upper Basildon
Berkshire
RG8 8NP
tel: 0491 671556

9.

Springhill Organic Farm Shop
Cuddington Road
Cuddington
Aylesbury
Buckinghamshire
tel: 0296 747334

Elizabeth Trethewey

<u>Opening times</u>   Retail shop 9a.m.–4p.m. Mon–Sat, no need to phone in advance. A delivery service is available for orders over £10.

<u>Products</u>   Organic beef from the farm, also lamb, pork, chickens, sausages, bacon, etc., from other producers, all Soil Association Symbol holders. Garland's also sells a wide range of other organic produce – fruit and vegetables, dried goods, cheese and wine.

<u>Price guide</u>   Sirloin steak £3.05/lb–mince £2.20/lb. Chickens £1.89/lb. Lamb shoulder £1.60/lb.

The animals are fed on home-grown and other feedstuffs to Soil Association Symbol requirements, giving an excellent flavour and quality. Elizabeth Trethewey feels that at present slaughterhouses deal inadequately with organic meat.

Soil Association Symbol.

10.

Woodlands Farm
The Vale
Chesham
Buckinghamshire
HP5 3NS
tel: 0494 783737

M.D. How and Son

<u>Opening times</u>   Farm shop open 9a.m.–12.30p.m. and 2p.m.–5p.m. Mon–Fri. 9a.m.–12.30p.m. Sat.

<u>Products</u>   Oven ready turkeys, turkey portions, mince, sausages, liver, etc., all frozen.

<u>Price guide</u>   From £1.20/lb–£3.05/lb.

Young birds are kept in an enclosed building for the first six weeks, then moved to outside open-air barns (although protected from wind, etc.). The farm also grows wheat, barley and oats which provide the basic ingredients for the various food rations mixed on the farm for the turkeys, and straw for bedding. No growth promoting additives are used, and no preservatives or colours in sausages, jumbo burgers, meat loaves or plain stir-fry. The birds are killed on the farm, plucked and then hung before gutting and preparation, unlike most commercially produced turkeys. The hanging gives a superior flavour, tenderness and appearance. Turkey is economical and tasty, and low in fat and cholesterol.

11.

Naturally Yours
The Horse and Gate
Witcham Toll
Ely
Cambridgeshire

CB6 2AB
tel: 0353 778723

Roland Finn

<u>Opening times</u> Customers may call any day of the week from 8.30a.m. onwards, but please phone first. Monthly delivery service to London and East Anglia. Nationwide deliveries by overnight carrier.

<u>Products</u> Additive-free beef, lamb, pork, traditional and nitrate-free bacon, kid, game, chicken, duck and turkey, fresh and frozen.

<u>Price guide</u> Beef mince £1.94/lb–fillet steak £7.40/lb. Breast lamb £1.25/lb–leg £2.52/lb. Belly pork £1.15/lb–chump chops £1.74/lb. Chicken from £1.45/lb. Bacon from £2.05/lb. Casserole kid £1.25/lb.

Naturally Yours is a group of small farmers co-ordinated by one of their members. They have a detailed Code of Practice for their producers which, among other things, puts restrictions on the distances which animals are allowed to be moved. All animals are reared as naturally as possible and allowed to grow at their own rate in a stress-free environment. Some of the suppliers have the Soil Association Symbol; the Finns are working along similar lines, but have no supply of organic grain. Feed is home mixed from straight grains, with no growth promoters or routine antibiotics. They also use potatoes and green vegetables in feed mixes. Bacon is made both with a traditional cure and without nitrates for allergy sufferers.

Animals are slaughtered at a small local abattoir which is run by 'a kindly old man who talks to the animals instead of hitting them'. The Finns are concerned about the demise of small abattoirs in favour of large 'factory' type places. The meat is then hung for the proper period of time, and butchered to customers' requirements by a master butcher.

12.

Manor Farm
Glatton
Huntingdon
Cambridgeshire
PE17 5RR
tel: 0487 830247 and 0733 242525

Mr J. Williams and Mrs S. Robinson

<u>Opening times</u>   Direct from the farm or Huntingdon market, Wednesday and Saturday, and St Ives market on Friday.

<u>Products</u>   Pork and pork products, i.e. fresh pork, sausages (with or without additives), pork pies, haslet, faggot, bacon, ham, etc. Everything sold is produced on the farm, including home-cured bacon and gammon.

<u>Price guide</u>   Prices kept at about average shop level.

Mr Williams has been a pig farmer all his life, as was his father before him. He has strong views against modern production methods, and keeps his pigs in the old fashioned way, housed in kennel-type sties with open yards. He takes the pigs to a small local slaughterhouse, with which he is satisfied. No artificial growth promoters or routine antibiotics are used. The feedstuff is mixed on the farm from straight ingredients, and only top quality white fish meal is used, to avoid a fishy taint. Pigs are always fed 'wet', producing a better quality of meat than dry fed animals.

Mr Williams is finding a growing market for 'good, old fashioned meat from well-housed, well-fed animals', and is striving to produce a top quality product. He is suspicious about the organic issue, which he believes is 'likely to become one of the biggest "con tricks" of our time'. Organics 'is good in theory, but not in practice, because of human nature.... How could I, as a farmer, produce organic grain at perhaps a ton or so an acre, and feed it to pigs? Who would pay a big enough premium for the pork?'

13.

Karma Farm
8 Fen Bank
Isleham
Cambridgeshire
CB7 5SL
tel: 0638 721112/780701

Will and Sheila Taylor

<u>Opening times</u> Please telephone to order. The Taylors prefer customers to collect their meat but they will send orders on an overnight carrier at cost price, which is usually around £10.

<u>Products</u> Beef and lamb, fresh, ready to cook or freeze. Beef is sold as an eighth of a beast, and comes in labelled freezer bags of an equal selection of all parts – 2–3lb joints, steaks, mince, etc. Total weight 50–70lb. Lamb is sold as half a beast in labelled bags, approx. 2lb, of joints and chops. Total weight 20–25lb.

<u>Price guide</u> Beef £2.30–£2.80/lb (boned out). Lamb £1.50–£2/lb, depending on season.

All the stock at Karma Farm live outside in family groups, mostly on organic grass and clover leys or water meadows. They are also fed home-grown hay, straw and locally-grown untreated potatoes. During the lambing season the sheep are also given the local mill's own sheep nuts without additives. The Taylors catch the animals and load and deliver them to the slaughterhouse themselves to minimise stress. They feel that the quality and flavour of their meat, especially the two-year-old grass-fed beef, means that it only needs simply cooking and no special recipes or fancy sauces. Visitors to the farm are welcome.

14.

Philip Warren and Son
1 Westgate Street
Launceston
Cornwall
tel: 0566 2089

Philip Warren

<u>Products</u> Traditionally reared and fed steer/heifer beef, mostly South Devon breed and other native breeds, including English Shorthorn. Also pork, lamb and chicken bought privately from local farms, so that the quality can be verified.

<u>Price guide</u> Chuck mince £1.40/lb–fillet steak £5.70/lb. Farm chicken 88p/lb. Pork joints £1.20–£1.46/lb.

All supplying farmers use the old-fashioned methods traditional in the area, and there is no bull beef or boar pork. Animals are fed mostly on home-grown cereals, hay and dry silage, and pigs on skimmed milk from a cheese factory.

Mr Warren chooses eighteen- to thirty-month old bullocks with a soft muscle texture and a good cover of fat – this means the native breeds such as South Devon, Devon, Angus, Galloway, Shorthorn and the pure-bred Charolais (which he says only produces tough and tasteless meat when crossed with a Friesian). Everything is fasted for sixteen hours before slaughter in 'a very quiet, old-fashioned, *clean* abattoir'. He feels that the modern system is 'all about killing vast numbers, which is too stressful for the animal and causes toughness in the muscles'. Beef is hung without being chilled for four days, then quartered and hung for a further eight or more days under refrigeration. The fat is then trimmed off so that the customer can have the lean meat they want but with traditional flavour and tenderness. The meat is jointed and trimmed as freshly as possible, and still looks red and fresh after a fortnight of proper care. Mr Warren aims to produce meat which is 'a joy to eat, not a chore to eat'. He has perhaps one complaint a month, usually from the same people!

Mr Warren rejects the modern trend towards the more economic production of lean bull beef, preferring the quality of meat from the castrated animal. He says '... down in our little corner we have kept to our past and not let profit be our main motive ... pride in our product and pride in our name is more important. Luckily the majority of my farmers feel the same as me ... and are sticking to the way their forefathers did it, for it was they who knew the way to produce the flavoursome product we strive for.'

15.

Trenerth Organic Foods
Hewas Field Farm
Trenerth Bridge
Leedstown
Cornwall
TR27 5ER
tel: 0736 850637

Squadron Leader T.W. Jones (Proprietor)

<u>Opening times</u> Customers can call at any reasonable time at the smallholding, but better to phone in advance, especially for larger orders.

<u>Products</u> Beef, lamb, pork, ham and bacon, other pork products, chicken, duck, geese/turkeys for Christmas. Poultry is oven-ready, fresh or frozen. Normally meat is sold frozen, but can be bought fresh within two days of butchering. Beef has the Soil Association Symbol, and the rest is in conversion from additive-

free to organic, and will be organic by July 1989. Trenerth Organic Foods' main enterprise is the production of escargot, and they also sell organic vegetables and herbs.

<u>Price guide</u>   Beef mince £1.40/lb–fillet steak £4.90/lb. Belly pork 98p/lb–pork tenderloin £3.30/lb. Bacon £1.50–£2.10/lb. Chicken £1.10/lb, duck £1.20/lb, goose £2/lb. Please phone for availability and price of lamb.

All animals are kept on free-range, with access to shelter. Pigs kept through the winter are housed in sties. Animals live in family groups to reduce stress in the meat and the parent stock. Feed is home grown, changing to home grown supplemented with bought-in Soil Association standard feed, but free-range stock find their own minerals and trace elements from the soil, and herbs for effective self-medication.

Poultry is slaughtered on the farm, and other animals slaughtered by a private butcher with no other animals present, eliminating stress which might adversely affect the taste of the meat.

Trenerth organic meat is lean, and is killed younger than conventional meat to reduce the gristle and fat content. Consequently the carcasses are just over half the conventional weight at slaughter. Unfortunately Squadron Leader Jones finds that he is unable to charge even a 10–20 per cent premium to compensate for this as customers are unwilling to pay more for the extra quality. He also feels that organic standards should be rigorously enforced, and breaches in standards disciplined in order to stop the sale of non-organic produce under an organic label when the supply does not meet the increase in demand.

Soil Association Symbol.

16.

The Priory
Woodeaves
Fenny Bentley
Ashbourne
Derbyshire
DE6 1LF
tel: 033 529 238

Angela Hughes

Opening times   Prefer customers to phone and order in advance.

Products   Frozen beef quarters, whole lambs, pork sides, all butchered to customers' own requirements. At present Mrs Hughes is only producing sufficient for present customers but she could expand. She is investigating the possibilities of making sausages.

Price guide   Prices vary (July 1989 £1.15/lb for lamb and pork).

Pigs are yarded but will eventually be free range. Cattle are outside for most of the year until January or February, and then out again from May. Animals are fed on home-mixed feedstuffs, so that the ingredients can be monitored. The farm makes more than enough organic hay, but has difficulty in finding organic barley to buy in. Animals are taken to a nearby slaughterhouse by a local driver, and the carcasses are collected by the butcher.

The meat is much appreciated by long-standing customers, many of whom suffer from allergies, and they often travel miles to collect it.

17.

Tordean Farm
Dean Prior
Buckfastleigh
Devon
TQ11 0LY
tel: 0364 43305

Adrian and Sue Dawe

<u>Opening times</u> Direct sales to the public, 7a.m.–5p.m. Mon–Fri, late opening 6.30p.m. Fri by appointment. Closed for lunch 1p.m.–2p.m. The Dawes also run Murray Meats, supplying vacuum-packed meat by mail order. Locally they prefer customers to phone their order through first, especially larger orders. They also supply six local shops.

<u>Products</u> Natural meats, beef, pork, lamb, kid goat, veal and venison, duck and chicken. All the meat is free of hormones, implants and antibiotics in feed-stuffs, and there is no intensive indoor feeding. The livestock is from Tordean farm and other selected farms within a fifteen-mile radius. Organic meat is available at 20 per cent premium.

<u>Price guide</u> Mostly minimum packs of 5lb. Beef mince from 69p/lb–fillet steak £6.99/lb. Pork spare ribs from 49p/lb–pork steaks £1.38/lb. Breast of lamb 28p/lb–leg of lamb £1.89/lb. Half or whole carcass veal £1.25/lb–escallopes £2.25/lb. Additive-free chickens (oven ready) 92p/lb. Offal from 38p/lb ox liver.

Cattle and sheep are fed on brewers' grains, sugar beet nuts and hay in winter and on solely organic land grass in the summer. Half the farm is now organic, and although they do not yet have an organic symbol, they find the Soil Association useful when selecting livestock suppliers. Pork is drawn from one good source on a standing order basis. Poultry is from one farm, where they grind their own feed, and the birds run and feed in large outdoor runs.

The Dawes have a long-standing arrangement at a local abattoir, using their own carefully controlled transport. They prefer the old method of wiping down the carcass, rather than the present wet hosing, which diminishes keeping quality. Tordean Farm meat has a good reputation for the way it is packaged and presented, which has been developed and perfected over twenty years. Great importance is attached to hanging times – beef is hung at least ten to fourteen days before boning, and because of this and because of thoughtful and humane treatment of the livestock before, in transit to, and at the abattoir, the meat is more tender as a result.

18.

Blackdown Farm
Loddiswell
Kingsbridge
Devon
TQ7 4EA
tel: 054 882 387

<u>Opening times</u> The farm shop is due to open June 1989. At the moment please order in advance, and collect.

<u>Products</u> Organically* produced, additive-free goat and kid meat, sold fresh, whole or half, jointed if required.

<u>Price guide</u> £1.50–£2/lb.

Goats are organically fed and allowed to range on grass, kids are milk fed with organic concentrates. Food is home-mixed to keep control of protein sources. Animals are slaughtered locally.

Blackdown Farm milk-fed kid meat is tender and

roasts well. They recommend a marinade to improve the flavour.

*Blackdown Farm has not applied for a symbol as they feel that the cost of inspection is too high for small producers.

19.

The Pure Meat Company Ltd
Moretonhampstead
Near Newton Abbot
Devon
tel: 0647 40321

<u>Opening times</u> Two retail butcher's shops: 1 The Square, Moretonhampstead, and 8 Bath Place, Taunton. Nationwide delivery service of fresh vacuum-packed meat, despatched Tuesdays, Wednesdays and Thursdays for delivery next day, suitable for freezing on arrival. Presently negotiating to sell the meat pre-packaged into supermarkets.

<u>Products</u> Full range of additive-free meat and poultry, turkeys and geese at Christmas, game in season. Many specialist cuts and prepared roasts. Traditional Wiltshire cure bacon and ham. Several different sausages, will make to customer's own recipe if desired. All the meat is fresh and produced under the guidelines of the Guild of Conservation Food Producers.

<u>Price guide</u> Mail order prices, including delivery, minimum 25lb (deduct 40–50p/lb for shop prices). Beef mince £2.50/lb–fillet steak £8.80/lb. Veal mince £3.20/lb–escalopes £7.50/lb. Leg of pork (on bone) £2.65/lb–pork cutlets £3.75/lb. Shoulder of lamb £1.80/lb–cutlets £5.50/lb. Sausages from £1.85/lb. Roasting chicken £1.85/lb. Wiltshire cure bacon from £1.95/lb and ham from £2.25/lb.

Poultry is free range, and cattle, pigs and sheep are kept outdoors in fields. Pigs farrow outdoors, weather permitting. Only natural fertilisers are used on the land. No chemically treated mixes, routine antibiotics, artificial hormones or other growth promoters are allowed, but dipping for fly strike and scab and worming are permitted if necessary for the welfare of the animal.

The Pure Meat Company uses a unique, truly additive-free feed, which is supplied to all their producers. It is made by an associated company – Multigerm – and has as its basis sprouted grains held in suspension with lactic bacteria. The grain used is grown to Conservation Grade and Organic standards. The animals are killed at a small family-run slaughterhouse which is within easy reach of all their present producers. They are particularly concerned that animals going to slaughter should not have too long a journey.

Traditional native breeds are favoured for all the livestock, for size and quality as well as taste. The smaller breeds of sheep, such as the Welsh Mountain, produce a family sized leg joint which does not need to be halved, thus detracting from the quality. All the beef is well hung.

Members of the Guild of Conservation Food Producers.

20.

Sydenham Estate Ltd
Sydenham Farm
Lewdown
Near Okehampton
Devon
tel: 082 286 410/242

<u>Opening times</u> Direct sales to the public, and mail order. Orders must be placed in advance by phone, giving as much notice as possible.

<u>Products</u> Organic, additive-free beef and lamb, finished to order.

<u>Price guide</u>   Supermarket prices, plus 10–20 per cent.

The Sydenham Estate uses hardy and thrifty traditional native breeds noted for their meat – Longhorns, South Devons, Aberdeen Angus, Ryland and Soay. All stock are kept unhoused and on pasture, and fed only home-grown feedstuffs, to ensure the quality of the ingredients. Currently they are arranging for new slaughtering facilities, as most of the existing facilities are considered injurious to the quality of the meat. Stress and incorrect and insufficient hanging will lead to poor meat.

Soil Association Symbol.

21.

Lipton Farm
East Allington
Near Totnes
Devon
TQ9 7RN
tel: 054 852 252

Mr and Mrs Jones

<u>Opening times</u>   Direct sales from the farm. Please phone at any time to make an appointment.

<u>Products</u>   Organic beef and lamb. Quarter or one-sixth beasts, butchered, labelled and frozen – approximately 112lb. Maximum wait for beef is no more than three and a half weeks, but lamb is only available March–September.

The Jones have an organic dairy herd which supplies milk to Unigate. The beef animals, mainly Angus and Murray Grey cross, are born and reared from the herd. The calves are suckled three or four to a foster mother for about twelve weeks, then gradually weaned onto a diet of grass (with some home-mixed organic cereal concentrates for six months only). Free grazing of the organic herbal leys produces a lean meat with a superb flavour when they mature at about two years of age. Sheep graze with the cattle and receive no concentrates, wormers or vaccines.

The animals are very humanely slaughtered at Miller Down abattoir, Newton Abbot. They are hung for two weeks and then 'beautifully butchered' by Mr Dawe of Tordean Farm.

Soil Association Symbol for beef, lamb and dairy herd.

22.

Heal Farm Meats
Heal Farm
Kingsnympton
Umberleigh
Devon
EX37 9TB
tel: 07695 2077
fax no: 07695 2839

Anne Petch

Opening times 9a.m.–5p.m. Mon–Fri, 10a.m.–4p.m. Sat. Phone orders in advance of a visit to the farm would be helpful. Speedy and efficient telephone mail order service by overnight delivery. Visa and Access are accepted.

Products Pork, beef, lamb, venison and wild boar in season. Oak-smoked or plain hams, cooked and uncooked, and bacon, eleven varieties of sausages, pâté, hogs pudding, salami, smoked fresh pork tenderloin, salt beef. All naturally reared from old-fashioned rare breeds without the use of any antibiotics or growth promoters.

Price guide Prices vary according to quantity ordered, carriage, etc. A full price list is available on application. Lean beef mince £2.50/lb–fillet steak £9.85/lb. Belly pork £1.78/lb–tenderloin £4.55/lb. Neck of lamb £2.18/lb–leg of lamb (off bone) £5.88/lb. Bacon from £2.34/lb. Ham from £3.68/lb. Comprehensive recipe leaflets with orders.

Only farmyard manure is used, and all feedstuffs are mixed to the farm's own specification without antibiotics, growth promoters, blood and bone meal or other animal derivatives.

The pigs – Gloucester Old Spots, Tamworths, Berkshires, Large Blacks, Middle Whites, British Lops and Saddlebacks – are reared without the routine use of antibiotics or growth hormones on specially produced foods. Breeding stock and litters are outside in grass paddocks in the summer where they can be viewed by visitors, and inside in large pens with plenty of straw in the winter. The pedigree North Devon cattle are single suckled, and in winter fed on hay and silage only. Cattle are grown on slowly to twenty-six months of age before slaughter, carcasses are hung for three weeks. Ten rare breeds of lamb, both primitive and conventional, are born and reared on grass with no artificial fertiliser, and their carcasses are hung for two weeks. Deer are kept by the same system as the lambs. All the stock is reared and handled with care and consideration, and dispatched with the minimum of stress at a small local abattoir.

Anne Petch believes there is much confusion between the different symbols and standards and she prefers to set her own, based on humane farming principles and common sense, with emphasis on value for money, honesty and integrity. The stock is slow to mature, thus producing meat which is infinitely superior in quality, texture and flavour. As the meat is well hung the cheaper cuts of meat are very tender and represent good value for money. 'The methods of meat production are as old-fashioned as the livestock and you can taste the virtues of both.'

Rare Breeds Survival Trust Approved Centre.

23.

Higher Birch
Bere Alston
Yelverton
Devon
PL20 7BY
tel: 0822 840257

N. and M. Willcocks

Opening times   Direct sales to the public. It's essential to phone and order in advance. Availability is seasonal – usually beef around November and lamb in June/ July.

Products   Organic beef and lamb. Beef – minimum quarter beast (100–150lb). Lamb – minimum whole carcass (40–55lb). Mutton available by arrangement. All sold fresh for the freezer.

Price guide   Commercial wholesale rate plus 5–10 per cent.

All animals live out all year, and are fed on home-grown feedstuffs generally plus small amounts of sugar beet in winter. Animals are slaughtered locally, as well as can be expected, but as the output is small there is no other option.

The Willcocks' meat held the Soil Association Symbol from 1982–88, but the bureaucracy and cost, being out of all proportion to the scale of their activities, have persuaded them not to reapply. They continue to keep to the standards however. Customers are queueing up to buy the meat and are well satisfied, often saying that they have not tasted this sort of meat since before the war. Contrary to some claims they find that the Channel Island breeds, crossed with Limousin or South Devon, have provided them with some of their best beef.

24.

Manor Farm Organic Produce
Manor Farm
Godmanstone
Dorchester
Dorset
DT2 7AH
tel: 03003 415

W. and P. Best

<u>Opening times</u> Please phone to order or make enquiries, and call to collect.

<u>Products</u> Organic pork and lamb. Quarter pig and half lamb, approx 20–25lb, jointed ready for freezer. Sausages made from organic pork, rusk, salt, herbs and spices. Any quantity, fresh or loose-frozen.

<u>Price guide</u> 1988/89 season: lamb £1.20/lb, pork 90p/lb, sausages £1.50/lb.

The pigs and sheep are part of a balanced farming system on 250 acres, which also includes cereals and dairy cattle. They are fed on home-grown products, but on occasions bought-in feed may comprise up to 20 per cent of the ration. If illness occurs then homeopathic medicine is used. Antibiotics may be used to save life but no animal so treated is sold as organic. Animals are delivered in small batches at pre-arranged times for slaughter at a small local abattoir.

The Bests feel that it is most important that the whole farm is run to Soil Association standards, which guarantee ecologically sound farming and humane living conditions, and prohibit artificial chemicals. They find that although their customers initially want their meat because it is organic, they always come back for more because the taste is excellent.

Soil Association Symbol.

25.

Ryewater Farm
Holnest
Sherborne
Dorset
DT9 5PL
tel: 096 321 248

Mr and Mrs I.W.T. Loftus

<u>Opening times</u> Direct sales to the public, please phone to order in advance.

<u>Products</u> Organic lamb sold fresh, whole and half lambs and cuts to order. Additive-free beef sold fresh in quarters, cuts to order.

<u>Price guide</u> Lamb 20 per cent above price of non-organic meat, beef 5 per cent above price of non-additive free meat.

Both sheep and cattle live outside on Soil Association Symbol grass all year round. In a very hard winter they are fed a supplement of home-grown hay. Animals are slaughtered and butchered by a local butcher, producing top quality meat free from all growth promoters and chemicals.

Soil Association Symbol for lamb.

26.

Cross Hands Distribution
Caeau Newydd Farm
Milo
Llandybie
Ammanford
Dyfed
SA18 3LZ
tel: 0269 842698

Peter and Jemima Mitchell

<u>Opening times</u> No direct sales to the public, but supply meat in cuts or carcass form by refrigerated vehicle to shops in the south of England, including Brewers Basics, Leominster; Only Natural, Malvern; Wye Organics, Stow on the Wold; Garlands Farm Shop, Upper Basildon; Carrot Connection, Woking; Wholefoods, London; Natural Foods, London: Cherry Tree Farm, Rickmansworth.

<u>Products</u>   All types of Soil Association Symbol meat.

<u>Price guide</u>   Prices are available on application.

Meat is usually collected 'on the hook' and has to go through the conventional slaughter and inspection process. The Mitchells feel that many abattoirs are humane and efficient, but are worried about the large organisations where responsible management does not always extend to the slaughterhouse floor.

Cross Hands Distribution only handles meat which is produced under the Soil Association Symbol scheme, humanely and free from chemical adulteration. It is reasonable to suppose, especially in pork and poultry, that these systems lead to better tasting meat. The Symbol is especially important in their business, because the chain between producer and consumer is such that the consumer cannot inspect the production personally.

27.

Glynhynod Organic Farmers
Glynhynod
Llandysul
Dyfed
SA44 5JY
tel: 023975 528

Opening times   Direct sales to the public, 9a.m.–
5p.m. Mon–Sat. Please phone first.

Products   Organic beef, lamb and pork.

Meat is organic and completely additive free. Animals
are free range and fed on home-grown and home-mixed
feedstuffs.

28.

Ty-Hen
Pedbryn Sarnau
Llandysul
Dyfed
SA44 6RD
tel: 0239 810347

P. Knifton and A. Degen

Opening times   Customers can buy meat from the
farm or from Mr Ted Harries, Butcher, Aberporth,
Cardigan, Dyfed.

Products   Organic beef and pork.

Deep-litter pigs fed on whey and home-grown barley.
Animals are slaughtered at Cardigan slaughterhouse.
The meat is organically produced and chemical free.

Ty-Hen have the Soil Association Symbol for their dairy
products and vegetables, but not for pigs and beef yet.

29.

Evan Owen Jones
Briwnant
Pumsaint
Llanwrda
Dyfed
SA19 8UT
tel: 055 85 410

Opening times Direct sales to the public, please phone in advance. Mail order, and wholesale to various shops and restaurants.

Products Organic beef, pork, lamb, mutton, chicken and turkey, all produced to Soil Association standards, freshly packed for freezing.

Price guide Subject to seasonal variations.

All animals are kept free range, fed mainly on home-grown feedstuffs, and are slaughtered at selected abattoirs. The meat produced is of a high quality, from properly finished animals which are reared in a stress-free environment. The meat is free of any residues and tastes as it should.

Soil Association Symbol.

30.

Newhouse Farm
Radwinter
Saffron Walden
Essex
CB10 2SP
tel: 079987 211

M.F. and D.G. Ridsdill Smith

Opening times Open at all reasonable times. Lamb available July–November, beef available December–April.

<u>Products</u>   Organic lamb and beef, jointed, packed and frozen.

<u>Price guide</u>   Whole or half lamb £1.50/lb. Mixed beef joints and stewing cuts £2.50/lb.

Sheep are grazed and lambs fattened on grass, cattle are housed in winter and fed on home-grown hay and cereals. All feedstuffs are home grown. Animals are taken direct to local slaughterhouse.

'The meat looks good, tastes good, and is good!'

Soil Association Symbol.

31.

Reediehill Deer Farm/Fletchers Fine Foods
Reediehill Farm
Auchtermuchty
Fife
KY14 7HS
tel: 0337 28369

John and Nichola Fletcher

<u>Opening times</u>   Farm shop open 9a.m.–5p.m. Mon–Fri, 10a.m.–6p.m. Sun, or at any time by arrangement. Also available by mail order from autumn 1989, and at The Scottish Deer Centre, By Cupar, Fife, KY15 4NQ, tel: 0337 81391.

<u>Products</u>   A wide range of naturally reared, additive-free frozen venison and venison products, including steaks, joints, stewing cuts, sausages, pâtés, haggis and 'Veniburgers'. Fresh vacuum-packed venison needs to be ordered.

<u>Price guide</u>   Mince £1.95/lb–fillet steak £7.20/lb, carriage extra.

Dr and Mrs Fletcher aim to produce meat with 'as little

outside input as possible while still remaining in business'. In winter young and adult females are kept in large open sheds to protect them from the weather, and in spring they are moved to grass paddocks which are fertilised with a small amount of artificial fertiliser, supplemented with dung. The exercise keeps the deer happy, and they can be seen playing on fine summer evenings. It also helps to stop any extra fat being laid down.

During their first winter the calves are fed a diet of home-grown silage, locally produced hay, potatoes and carrots, and a proprietary deer compound made from vegetable proteins and oils (not ground-up animals). They then graze summer grass and are fed hay or silage without concentrates until they are slaughtered at fifteen to twenty-seven months. This young age ensures a tender and succulent meat.

The deer are shot with a rifle in the field and dressed out, hung and butchered in the farm's own meat unit. The Fletchers feel that this is a stress-free system which produces better quality meat because the animal has produced no adrenalin prior to death. It also suits the small producer who may only want to kill six animals at a time. The meat is hung for two to three weeks in a chill room, giving a fine, highly distinctive flavour preferred by most people to that of game venison which is stronger. They can, however, produce the game flavour to order.

British Prime Venison quality standard mark.

32.

Organic Meat and Products Ltd
Endrigg
Jamesfield Farm
Newburgh
Fife
KY14 6EW
tel: 0738 85498 (24 hours)

Mr Ian Miller

<u>Opening times</u>   Deliveries of fresh, vacuum-packed meat within twenty-four hours anywhere on the mainland. Please phone to order.

<u>Products</u>   Prime Aberdeen Angus cross organic beef and organic Scottish lamb, wild venison, and additive-free pork and bacon.

<u>Price guide</u>   Beef mince £2.10/lb–fillet steak £7.50/lb. Boned and rolled shoulder of lamb £2.75/lb–double loin chops £3.45/lb. Venison sausages £1.20/lb–haunch £3.95/lb. Organic black pudding and haggis both £1.45/lb. £10 delivery charge, free on orders over £100.

No pesticides or chemical fertilisers are used in the soil and there are no hormones or antibiotics given to the livestock. Animals are out to graze and bedded on organic straw. Mr Miller went organic in the early 1980s when, despite producing record yields from conventional farming methods, he realised that he was not going to live up to the advice given him by his father when he took over the farm, to 'hand over his farm to the next generation more fertile than when he first received it'. He started with organic vegetables and cereals, but spent two years setting up the meat marketing company by searching out producers who were using natural methods who could easily convert to organic.

Member of Scottish Organic Farmers and Growers. Soil Association Symbol.

33.

Brentlands Cotswold Beef
Brentlands Farm
Brookthorpe
Gloucestershire
GL4 0UT
tel: 0452 813447

Mr and Mrs Warner

Opening times   Direct sales to the public; usually people telephone their orders or make an appointment to buy direct from the freezers. Also delivery fresh or frozen, by Datapost or overnight carrier, vacuum packed. Visitors welcome.

Products   Additive-free beef, fresh, frozen or vacuum packed. Beef mainly sold in three packs – Family (approx 50lb), Gourmet (approx 20lb) and Hotpot (25–30lb). Meat can be delivered fresh on the same day that the meat is packed.

Price guide   Family Pack £2.50/lb, Gourmet Pack £3.50/lb, Hotpot Pack £1.90/lb, Beefburger Pack £7.50.

Two-week-old top quality calves are bought from Gloucester market. The animals are kept on the farm until ready for slaughter at about eighteen months to two years old. In summer they are out to grass, and a large percentage of their winter feedstuff, including oats, barley and silage with no additives, is home grown. Only organic fertilisers are used and no artificial growth promoters or additional hormones are given. Animals are taken to a small slaughterhouse eight miles away and killed almost immediately. This produces top-quality well-hung beef from animals which are well fed and looked after compassionately.

34.

Cotswold Stile
The Old Bakehouse
17a Long Street
Wotton-under-Edge
Gloucestershire
GL12 7ES
tel: 0453 844994

Henrietta White

<u>Opening times</u> Please phone for order collection service.

<u>Products</u> Naturally reared beef, pork and lamb sold frozen, cut to customer's requirements and packed in strong clear polythene bags for ease of use from the freezer. Own range of sausages, burgers and prize-winning faggots. Bacon from Mr R. Keen of Sandridge Farm, Bromham.

<u>Price guide</u> Lean beef mince £1.39/lb–sirloin steak £5.49/lb. Belly pork 99p/lb–tenderloin of pork £3.39/lb. Bacon from £1.39/lb. Sausages from 98p/lb. Lamb is sold at market prices.

The meat is from various farms in the area, where the animals are able to free range in fields, although are often kept in large buildings in winter. They are kept in traditional, low density conditions, and fed home-grown and home-mixed feedstuffs, with occasional proprietary mixes which must be additive-free.

Cotswold Stile feel that strict organic conditions, although commendable, make the costs of production too high and therefore put the meat beyond the means of ordinary people. They believe that balanced traditional methods of natural rearing are more realistic.

35.

Cumber's Farm
Rogate
Petersfield
Hampshire
GU31 5DB
tel: 073080 840

Meriel Rogers and Guy Ballard

<u>Opening times</u>   July–January, Saturday morning and other times by arrangement, but please phone in advance. No mail order.

<u>Products</u>   Organic whole or half lambs, butchered, packed and frozen.

<u>Price guide</u>   £1.45–£1.50/lb.

A hundred and thirty sheep graze on grass/clover/herb leys throughout the year. Home-grown hay is fed in winter and some organic oats and a small percentage of bought-in feed prior to lambing. Ewes come into the barn for a few days for lambing. The grassland is rotated with the arable crops around the farm, and a clean grazing system is operated to avoid intestinal worms. The whole farm has the Soil Association Symbol.

The lambs are slaughtered, butchered and frozen in Newbury. The meat has a good flavour with just the right amount of fat and is very tender.

Soil Association Symbol.

36.

Larks Barrow Market Garden
Kingsclere Road
Whitchurch
Hampshire
RG28 7QB
tel: 0256 892933

<u>Opening times</u> Open all day, every day. Please phone first to check availability of meat.

<u>Products</u> Organic beef and additive-free pork sold in joints and packs from the freezer. Half pigs also available.

<u>Price guide</u> Beef mince £1.80/lb–fillet steak £5/lb. Pork heads/hocks 50p/lb–chops £1.60/lb. Half pig 85p/lb.

Beef is pasture reared on organic grass and hay. Piglets are born on open range, then weaned at eight weeks and reared in strawed pens. They are fed on a special proprietary mix without additives. A local wholesale butcher purchases the meat, or butchers it for return to Larks Barrow. The butcher organises the direct delivery of the animals to their slaughterers.

Customers comment on the good flavour of the meat, and Larks Barrow say 'the proof of the pudding is in the eating!' They would like to see more publicity on what the different standards mean, so that consumers know what they are getting.

Soil Association Symbol for beef and vegetables.

37.

Batchley
Grendon Bishop
Bromyard
Herefordshire
HR7 4TH
tel: 0885 483377

Mr and Mrs Wakefield-Jones

<u>Opening times</u> Direct sales to the public. Please phone first for details.

<u>Products</u> Organic beef, pork and lamb, frozen and sometimes fresh.

All the livestock is reared to Soil Association standards, and fed on home-grown and home-mixed feedstuffs. The animals are slaughtered at a local abattoir.

Soil Association Symbol.

38.

Green Acres
Dinmore
Hereford
Herefordshire
tel: 056 884 7045

David and Sheila Jenkins

<u>Opening times</u> Farm shop open 9a.m.–5.30p.m. If customers require large amounts of meat please phone first to order.

<u>Products</u> Beef and lamb from organically fed animals; also hormone and additive free. All meat is frozen except by prior arrangement.

<u>Price guide</u> Beef mince £1.60/lb–sirloin steak £5.50/lb. Shoulder of lamb £1.90/lb–leg of lamb £2.30/lb.

All stock is housed during the winter months, and fed on home-grown feedstuffs with a small amount of proprietary mix. They are then taken to a local trusted abattoir for slaughter. Customers say that the meat tastes as they remember it in their youth.

Soil Association Symbol.

39.

Brewers Basics
15A Broad Street
Leominster
Herefordshire
HR6 8BT
tel: 0568 2154

Linda and Ian Kaye

<u>Opening times</u>   Normal shop hours.

<u>Products</u>   Organic beef, lamb, pork and poultry, all joints, cuts and offal. Occasionally fresh but mostly frozen, vacuum packed when possible. Brewers Basics only like to sell Soil Association produce.

<u>Price guide</u>   Chicken £1.70/lb. Beef mince £2.20/lb– fillet steak £7.50/lb. Pork chops £2.45/lb. Lamb chops £2.25/lb–leg of lamb £2.50/lb.

Animals are kept on free range and fed on organic home-grown and home-mixed feedstuffs. Organic meat from free range animals has a different tissue structure, and the fat is less harmful, without stored toxic substances.

40.

Cherry Trees Farm
Olleberrie Lane
Belsize
Sarratt
Rickmansworth
Hertfordshire
WD3 4NU
tel: 09277 68289

Michael and Mary Bell

<u>Opening times</u> Direct sales to the public, 9a.m.–8p.m. Wed, 10a.m.–5.30p.m. Thurs, Fri, Sat. 2p.m.–6p.m. Sun. Please phone first to order large amounts.

<u>Products</u> Organic beef (Organic Farmers and Growers, Soil Association and Demeter standards). Organic Farmers and Growers standard pork and lamb. Oak smoked hams and bacon. A limited number of Soil Association standard chickens.

<u>Price guide</u>   Beef mince £2.90/lb–sirloin £7.00/lb.

Laying birds and fattening pigs are free range, all feeds are milled on the farm, and cereals are covered by a recognised organic symbol. The Bells are very unhappy with slaughterhouses – they consider the slaughtering of most animals to be disgusting, degrading and disrespectful. They feel that caring farmers should bring pressure to bear to create an independent organisation to govern the rearing, feeding and slaughtering of animals. They have experienced countless problems in reaching an organic standard they are happy with, and consider that organic meat production has a long way to go since all farmers 'use modern technology in one way or another, which condones maltreatment of animals'. Every year several thousand schoolchildren are shown round the farm and educated in humane farming methods.

Conservation Grade.

41.

Fordhall Organic Farming System
R.M. Cornmell (Butcher)
459 Halliwell Road
Bolton
Lancashire
BL1 8DE
tel: 0204 46844

Ray Cornmell and Arthur Hollins

<u>Opening times</u> Normal shop hours. Also delivery anywhere on mainland by carrier of fresh vacuum-packed meat. Customers can also phone Fordhall Farm for brochures, information and to order – 0630 83 255.

<u>Products</u> Organic beef, pork, lamb, veal, poultry, bacon, hams and oak smoked meats. All from Fordhall Farm, Market Drayton, Staffordshire.

Arthur Hollins is a pioneer organic farmer who, over a period of many years, has perfected his own system of permanent pasture, a blend of herbs, grasses and clovers which protects the micro-organisms in the soil, builds fertility, and produces healthy 'wild' meat. Both sheep and cattle are a mixture of breeds, for maximum health and virility. They live outside all year round, and are never fed any supplements, finding all they need from the carefully maintained pastures. The dairy breed cows are trained by Arthur Hollins to suckle two extra week-old calves in addition to their own. The breeding ewes are allowed to live out their entire lives on the farm. Sheep and cattle are kept to Soil Association standards.

Poultry and pigs are kept under the Fordhall organic system, bought in as day-old chicks and weaners, and not bred on the farm. They are rotated round the pasture, the pigs rooting up the soil which is then sown with a special mix for the poultry. They are both fed

281

home-grown organic and steam-cooked cereal, with some fish and soya meal, and chopped grass.

Arthur Hollins has teamed up with Ray Cornmell, a Bolton butcher who was looking for supplies of organic meat for customers with allergies. Mr Cornmell sells all Fordhall Farm meat, and also sends it by carrier around the country.

Soil Association Symbol for lamb and beef.

42.

Bank House Farm
Silverdale
Carnforth
Lancashire
LA5 0RE
tel: 0524 701 280

Richard and Rosemary Harward

<u>Opening times</u>   Please order in advance. Supplies are limited and very much seasonal. Occasionally available at Booth's supermarket. Visitors welcome on farm walk in August.

<u>Products</u>   Organic beef and lamb, fresh, whole or half. Additive-free pork, reared outdoors, whole or half. Boiling fowl, free range and additive free, fresh and frozen.

<u>Price guide</u>   Average local butchers' prices, plus approximately 10 per cent.

Twelve suckler cows and calves, and one hundred and twenty sheep and lambs are kept according to Soil Association standards, and fed mostly on home-grown fodder and small amounts of additive-free bought-in food. A few outdoor pigs and two hundred and seventy free-range hens are fed on additive-free bought-in food as well as grass. Particular attention is paid to the wellbeing of the animals, to make their environment as natural as possible within farming limits.

The Harwards voiced some dilemmas concerning slaughter. They prefer to take the animals to a small local slaughterhouse where the meat is hung properly, and butchered in the attached shop. Unfortunately it is too small to have a Ministry grader present, which means taking them to market first to obtain the subsidy, causing the animals greater stress. They also strongly object to their old ewes most likely ending up as *Halal* meat, and feel there is nothing they can do to ensure a more humane ending. If they don't send them to market, but direct to the slaughterhouse, they are dependent on what the slaughterhouse decides to pay, and are not guaranteed the market price.

Soil Association Symbol for beef and lamb.

43.

Middle Wood Trust
Roeburndale West
Lancaster
Lancashire
tel: 0468 21880

<u>Opening times</u> Direct sales to the public, please phone to order in advance. Also on sale occasionally at Booth's supermarket, Scotforth, Lancaster.

<u>Products</u> Organic whole or half lambs to Soil Association standards.

Animals are kept free range and fed on organic grass and hay, except for the six weeks prior to lambing when bought-in nuts are used. A local abattoir is used, but Middle Wood Trust would prefer to slaughter on the farm. Where possible homeopathic medicines are used which makes the meat extra safe for allergy sufferers. In September 1989 a new flock of South Country Cheviots was bought for the farm.

Soil Association Symbol.

44.

Chevelswarde Organic Growers
Chevel House
South Kilworth
Lutterworth
Leicestershire
LE17 6DX

Opening times Direct sales to public 8.30a.m.–
6.30p.m. Please phone first to order and for up-to-date
prices.

Products Additive-free pork, ready for freezer, cut to
order only.

Pigs are kept on a kennel-based straw system, which is
best for viability and health, fed special proprietary mix,
and slaughtered at a local abattoir.

45.

East Farm
Normanby By Stow
Gainsborough
Lincolnshire
DN21 5LQ
tel: 0427 788629

Dr T.D.and Mrs P.M. Organ

Opening times Orders must be placed in advance, so
new customers are asked for a deposit of £25 per
quarter beast.

Products Organic beef sold fresh, jointed, bagged
and labelled to the customer's requirements, in quarters only. Organic vegetables are also available.

Price guide Normal local prices, no organic premium
is charged. Forequarters 70p/lb, hindquarters £1.30/lb.
Liver and heart included at no extra cost, if asked for.

All the cattle sold for meat are born and bred on the farm, kept outside in summer and housed in winter. The calves are single suckled and stay on their mothers until the next calf is born. Polled cattle are used as often as possible to eliminate the stress caused by disbudding the calves.

The grassland has been farmed organically since 1976. Apart from the grass, the animals are fed on what are essentially waste products – steamed potato peel from chip factories, straw which would otherwise be burnt, and leafy waste from the vegetable enterprise. To improve rumen efficiency fish meal acceptable to the Soil Association is used, and mineral supplements to compensate for any deficiencies in the feed. There is never any need for antibiotics, and growth promoters would certainly not be used. A relatively safe anthelmintic is considered necessary for keeping the cows well wormed, and therefore producing plentiful milk for their calves.

The farm is gradually changing over to pedigree polled Welsh Blacks, which have been found to be most suitable for producing high-quality lean meat on this system. Animals have been slaughtered and butchered without problems for ten years at Hughes of Skellingthorpe, a small abattoir ten miles away, where they are individually handled with the minimum of stress.

The Organs feel that their system is philosophically sound. They used to hold the Soil Association Symbol for beef and vegetables, but they recently left the scheme. The fee represented a disproportionate part of their takings and they found that the symbol did not help them to sell their produce. Also regulations governing the amount of bought-in feed were tightened and anthelmintics and minerals are not allowed, which they feel is detrimental to the animals' health and fertility.

46.

F.A. and J. Jones and Son
Red House Farm
North Scarle
Lincoln
Lincolnshire
LN6 9HB
tel: 0522 77 224

Mrs Jones

<u>Opening times</u> Direct sales to the public. 9a.m.–
12.30p.m. and 1.30p.m.–5p.m Wed, Thurs, Sat. Late
closing 7p.m. Fri. (Closed for two-week holiday every
year.) Mrs Jones prefers orders one or two weeks in
advance, but customers are welcome to call in and
take 'pot luck'.

Local deep freeze orders are delivered monthly.
Nationwide mail order deliveries are despatched
Wednesday afternoons and delivered to customer's
door Thursday (usually mornings). Meat is packed with
polystyrene insulation.

<u>Products</u> Fresh or frozen additive-free beef, pork,
lamb, chicken, sausages, pork pies, potted beef, etc.
Meat is cut to customers' requirements, packed and
labelled if frozen. For the first time duck will be available, summer 1989, and will be continued if there is
enough interest.

<u>Price guide</u> Half pig 98p/lb. Pork chops (10lb or over)
£1.78/lb. Ox liver (10lb or over) 99p/lb–fillet steak
£5.49/lb. Half lamb £1.88/lb. Leg of lamb £3.28/lb.
Chicken (plucked weight) £1.63/lb.

Pigs and poultry are kept on straw litter with plenty of
fresh air and animals are never overcrowded. Cattle are
kept on grass except in very bad weather, when they are
housed in straw-littered yards. Sheep are kept on grass.
Animals are fed on feedstuffs especially mixed to the

farm's own specifications by a small miller, with no growth promoters or disease repressants.

Animals are personally delivered to a local abattoir at a time when it is known that the animals will be dealt with quickly to avoid stress. However, the family would like to see more careful handling of the animals before slaughter.

Mrs Jones has been farming since the 1950s, and gave up conventional practices when the shop was opened in 1974. For chicken especially she favours recipes from the 1950s, as modern books give times to suit supermarket chickens. 'Our meat is of extremely high quality, the animals being more mature than most butcher's animals, which gives more flavour to the meat. The beef and, when necessary, the lamb is properly hung, and this also enhances the flavour.'

47.

C. Lidgate (Butchers)
110 Holland Park Avenue
London
W11 4UA
tel: 071-727 8243

Mr David Lidgate

Opening times   Shop hours.

Products   A vast range of English, Continental and American cuts of fresh meat, cut to an extremely high specification and trim. Additive-free Scotch beef from the permanent pastures of the Aberdeen Angus country of the Grampian hills. Free-range pork from Piccards Farm, Guildford, fed on additive-free feed, containing no bone meal or animal offal. Free-range chickens from Gold Label products, Stafford, fed on a diet free of antibiotics and animal by-products. Grass-fed lamb from the West Country and Wales.

Mr David Lidgate personally selects the meat, and (except on occasions in winter) looks for animals fed on grass in the open air; non-intensive systems; a regular diet free of growth promoters, antibiotics and animal offal; and cereal-based feedstuffs, home-grown where possible. He feels that organic symbols are important, but are certainly not a guide to quality.

48.

Natural Foods Ltd
Unit 14
Hainault Road Industrial Estate
Hainault Road
London E11
tel: 081-539 1034
fax no: 081-539 9469

<u>Opening times</u> Delivery service in Greater London only. The phone is manned 8.30a.m.–7pm. Mon–Thurs, 8.30a.m.–5p.m. Fri. Answer machine outside those hours. Please note that Natural Foods is not a shop.

<u>Products</u> Organic beef, lamb and poultry, free-range poultry and pork, bacon, cooked meats, sausages, burgers. Frozen beef, lamb and chicken. Natural Foods use non-PVC clingfilm, and meat trays which are not manufactured using CFCs.

<u>Price guide</u> Fresh beef mince £2.35/lb–fillet steak £7.40/lb. Stewing lamb £1.80/lb–chump chops £3.85/lb. Spare rib pork chops £1.60/lb–pork steaks £2.10/lb. Chicken from £1.80/lb. Turkey from £1.55/lb.

All meat and poultry is from livestock that has been reared at its own pace, and in surroundings as near to natural as possible. Antibiotics, sex hormones and other artificial stimulants for growth have not been used. Natural Foods does not sell meat that has been reared in intensive factory-farmed conditions.

49.

Unique Butchers
217 Holloway Road
London
N7 8DL
tel: 071-609 7016

Miss D.L. McCrae

<u>Opening times</u>   Shop hours.

<u>Products</u> Organic lamb, pork, poultry, turkey. Naturally reared beef. Bacon 10 per cent salt. All fresh.

<u>Price guide</u> Beef mince £2.29/lb–steak £4.29/lb. Chickens £1.60/lb, turkeys £1.60/lb. Also sell free-range eggs.

Animals from Unique Butchers' suppliers are kept on free range, under humane conditions, and fed on organic grain. No hormones or antibiotics are used, and only homeopathic medicines. The result is tasty meat which doesn't need a lot of cooking. Miss McCrae, who recently took over the management of Unique Butchers, is a member of the Soil Association and only sells Soil Association meat.

50.

Wholefood Butchers
31 Paddington Street
London
W1M 4DR
tel: 071-486 1390

<u>Products</u>   Organic beef from Scotland, organic lamb from the West Country, and additive-free, free-range pork, chickens and turkeys. Game and wild rabbits in season. Bacon cured with no added chemicals. Sausages (no bread, rusk or additives) bound with

free-range egg. Wholefood Butchers buys whole animals and all products are sold fresh.

Price guide   Beef mince £1.98/lb to boned and rolled sirloin £5.90/lb. Lamb from £1.98/lb for shoulder. Pork spare rib £1.38/lb to bone leg £2.28/lb. Oven-ready chickens £1.86/lb, turkey £2.20/lb, ducks £2.20/lb. Offal from 98p/lb for pig's liver. Sausages from £1.68/lb.

Mary Langman, secretary of Wholefood Ltd, is a founder member of the Soil Association, and their standards are adhered to wherever possible. Poultry has been reared on free range in small groups, and fed a cereal-based diet which is supplemented by their foraging. Pigs are also kept in small numbers in purpose-built housing, bedded on straw with access to grazing. Beef and lamb are all Soil Association standard. All feedstuffs are completely free of additives, growth promoters, sex hormones and antibiotics, and pigs and poultry are fed organic grain where possible, and the next best when organic is not available. Animals are allowed to grow at their own natural slower rate, which gives a distinct and excellent flavour and tenderness. Animals are slaughtered humanely at nearby abattoirs, and the carcasses labelled with the name of the farmer and the farm.

51.

Greenway Organic Farms
Freepost
Edinburgh
Lothian
EH1 0AQ
tel: 031-557 8111

Stewart McKenna, Peter Harvey and Charlotte Mitchell

Opening times Delivery by overnight carrier of fresh chilled vacuum-packed meat to home and business addresses. Please phone to order.

Products Organic beef, lamb, venison, chicken. Seasonal availability in poultry and venison, and occasionally in lamb.

Price guide Beef mince £2.10/lb–fillet steak £7.50/lb. Boned and rolled shoulder of lamb £2.55/lb–double loin chops £2.70/lb. Haggis £1.90/lb. Delivery charge £6, free on orders from Scotland over £60, rest of UK over £100.

All the animals are kept to Soil Association standards, and some of the beef and lamb is also bio-dynamic. A humane and sensitive approach is applied to all aspects of animal husbandry. At least 90 per cent of foodstuff is organic, and is mostly home grown.

Venison is shot by the grower in the animal's natural environment. For all other meat Greenway use a fully qualified vet to supervise the slaughter and cutting of the beasts. They consider that well-run abattoirs are capable of clean, trauma-free slaughtering to a very high standard, and would consider it an insult to the organic farmers who supply them were they to 'mishandle and abuse their carefully (and often lovingly) produced livestock'. They disagree with some current slaughterhouse practices, such as goading and tenderising injections.

Greenway say that organic meat is not only safe to eat, it tastes better, as borne out by a recent tasting trial at the East of Scotland College of Agriculture. Slower roasting and pot roast stewing beef is 'mmmmmm!' Organic symbols are 'necessary as an absolute guarantee of source and purity ... additive free is almost meaningless or at best a slightly vain hope.'

Soil Association Symbol, and some Demeter Symbol beef and lamb.

52.

Tolly (Oxhey) Ltd
4 Main Avenue
Moor Park
Northwood
Middlesex
HA6 2HJ
tel: 09274 21665

Opening times   Shop hours.

Products   Additive-free beef, pork and spring lamb butchered fresh, individual cuts vacuum packed and frozen if necessary. Free-range chicken, whole and gutted or quartered as chicken portions. Bacon (tastes like it used to) rashered on the premises. From Gold Label Ltd, Staffordshire, and Dorset Farms, Beaminster, Dorset.

Price guide   Beef mince £1.80/lb–fillet steak £6.95/lb. Belly pork £1.25/lb–pork chops £1.85/lb. Stewing lamb £1.25/lb–chops £3.75/lb. Bacon £2.98/lb for throughcut. Whole chicken £1.28/lb, portions £1.80/lb.

Although Tolly's find that their additive-free meat is always good quality, they do not find it better than other meat and only offer it as an alternative for customers who want it. They have built their reputation over thirty years on good quality Scotch beef, but as yet have found no additive-free Scottish supplier.

53.

Stubbing's Really Good Foods
Westgate Nurseries
Market Place
Burnham Market
Norfolk
PE31 8HF
tel: 0328 738337

Opening times Open 9a.m.–5p.m. Mon–Sat (closed for lunch from 1–2p.m.), half-day Wednesday. It is better to phone first to check availability, if travelling a long distance.

Products Beef, lamb, pork and free-range chicken, produced as far as possible on organic principles. All meat is usually frozen in small packs in the normal range of cuts.

Price guide Beef mince £1.90/lb–rump steak £5.50/lb. Pork steaks £2/lb. Lamb shoulder £1.10/lb–loin chops £2.20/lb.

Suppliers do not hold any organic symbols because of the difficulty of being totally organic in that part of Norfolk. They use non-organic straw and non-organic roots as a winter supplement.

The meat is produced from rare breeds, has a good flavour and texture, and is hung for a long time after slaughter.

54.

Harry Wright
Metton Road
Felbrigg
Cromer
Norfolk
tel: 0263 512388

Opening times Please phone to order geese. Lamb from Colin Loveday at Neatishead Meat abattoir 0692 630681.

Products Free-range geese and lamb.

Price guide Check when ordering.

Geese are bought in as day-old goslings at the beginning of April, run out on grass and come in for finishing for

Michaelmas and Christmas. They are hung for two weeks after slaughter, which Mr Wright believes to be essential for flavour. The lamb is grass-fed, with stubble turnips and sugar beet tops in winter but no bin foods, which he believes forces production unnaturally. Lambing takes place in April.

Mr Wright believes in natural, old fashioned methods, and 'wouldn't give a penny' for mass-produced geese, killed, wet plucked and frozen straight away. Both the geese and the lamb are 'well-fleshed with fat on them', and he believes this makes the flavour, and certainly his customers are 'exceptionally well pleased'. He remembers that in the old days the dripping from a goose would feed a family for a fortnight.

55.

Cranes Watering Farm Shop
Rushall Road
Starston
Harleston
Norfolk
IP20 9NE
tel: 0379 852387

N.W. Moore and Sons and S.E. Moore

Opening times   10a.m.–6p.m. Mon–Sat, 10a.m.–12 noon Sun.

Products   Dairy-fed pork (frozen), always available. Additive-free sausages. Corn-fed chicken (frozen, occasionally fresh), usually available. Home-reared lamb, seasonal.

Price guide   Chickens 90p/lb, portions £1/lb. Pork sides 75p/lb, cuts £1.25/lb. Whole lamb £1.10/lb–leg of lamb £2/lb.

Lambs are kept on meadowland. Poultry is kept on deep

litter and fed on proprietary mix and cracked maize. Pigs are kept in groups of ten in pens, with plenty of space to move around and lie down; they are fed mainly skim milk and by-products from the farm creamery plus a little home-grown and home-mixed or proprietary mix ration, containing few if any additives. This produces firm, lean, mild and delicious pork, with crackling which 'crackles without really trying'.

Animals are slaughtered at a local abattoir which the Moores are happy with – they feel that those who criticise abattoir staff should try the job for themselves. The Moores also feel that '*most* farmers treat their animals well, feed them well and do not pump them full of drugs unnecessarily. It's the consumer who wants cheap meat, and who thinks that farmers are money grabbing individuals, who are at fault. Good care costs money, after all.'

56.

Hall View
Church Lane
Claxton
Norwich
Norfolk
NR14 7HY
tel: 050 843 527

Roland and Julia Kaye

<u>Opening times</u> Direct sales to public usually by personal contact.

<u>Products</u> Organic and additive-free lamb, whole, half or joints (pre-packed and frozen). Occasionally beef in same form.

<u>Price guide</u> £1–1.50/lb.

All livestock is grazed mainly on the traditional pastures

of the Norfolk wetland marshes, with home-grown organic hay in winter and some organic supplement from Allen and Page organic foods. Animals are slaughtered at the nearest suitable abattoir which is some thirty miles away.

The sheep are Hebridean which provides a very popular, lean and gamey meat. When crossed with the White Faced Woodland, which has a larger but less flavoursome carcass, the resulting animal combines flavour and moderate size with good growth rate.

57.

Linaria
38 Hall Lane
Wacton
Norwich
Norfolk
NR15 2UH
tel: 0508 31287

Robert and Hilary Maidstone

<u>Opening times</u>   Direct sales to public by prior order with small deposit, rest of payment on collection.

<u>Products</u>   Fresh and frozen, additive-free and whole-grain fed poultry, pork, lamb and occasionally beef.

<u>Price guide</u>   Whole chickens £1.20/lb, guinea fowl £1.50/lb, goose £2/lb. Half pigs £1/lb, individual joints £1.20/lb.

Geese, sheep, cows and goats are all free range. Everything else is deep-litter in small units with natural ventilation, a system arrived at after years of trial and error, which is felt to be best for comfort and lack of problems in livestock production. Deep-litter livestock is fed cut greenstuffs and other wild food. All supplements are of home-mixed straight ground and flaked grains and fishmeal with no binders, anti-oxidants, colourants, or mineral and other 'over-doses' to promote growth and production.

Poultry are slaughtered on the farm and large livestock taken personally to a commercial slaughterhouse with reasonable conditions. In general there is too little choice and therefore too much travelling. Rare breeds such as Dexters and Jacobs are used, so that the carcasses are easily identifiable for the slaughterhouse. As the livestock is slightly older than commercial livestock, the meat has a good flavour and texture and is less liable to fall apart during cooking.

The Maidstones have left the Soil Association Symbol scheme, although they still agree with it in principle. They feel that registration is over-priced and cuts out the small dedicated producers who cannot get the 10–50 per cent premium claimed by others.

58.

Church Farm Shop
Church Farm
Strixton
Near Wellingborough
Northamptonshire
NN9 7PA
tel: 0933 664378

Opening times   Direct sales to public 9a.m.–5p.m. Tues–Sat all through the year. Visitors to the farm are welcome. If unable to get to the farm shop meat is vacuum packed and sent by delivery service.

Products   Organic beef, pork and lamb, different cuts fresh or frozen. Home-cured bacon, sausages, chicken, duck, goose, pheasant, partridge. Church Farm also grows organic vegetables.

Price guide   Beef mince £1.85/lb–fillet steak £7.38/lb. Belly pork £1.48/lb–pork steaks £2.36/lb. Poultry from

£1.35/lb chicken. Breast of lamb 86p/lb–loin chops £3.20/lb. Sausages from £1/lb. Bacon from £2.04/lb.

All stock is looked after to the Soil Association standards and fed on home-grown and home-mixed feedstuffs, which gives the meat a traditional flavour. No fishmeal is used so the pork does not have any fishy flavour. Stock is delivered to local abattoir after a phone call to let them know that the animals are coming. Consequently they go from the field to being killed in the shortest possible time which is beneficial from a humane point of view and the lack of stress is definitely reflected in the flavour and tenderness of the meat. Meat is butchered on the farm and then hung for a considerable amount of time, which also brings out the full flavour and tenderness.

Soil Association Symbol for vegetables and lamb, awaiting full symbol for remainder.

59.

Breckan Rabbits
Sanday
Orkney
KW17 2AZ
tel: 085 75421

William and Elizabeth Sichel

Opening times Farm gate sales all year round, no mail order. Also available at shops on Orkney mainland.

Product Low-fat additive-free farm-bred rabbit, frozen, packs of half a jointed rabbit. Recipe leaflets and book available.

Price guide £1.30/lb.

All rabbits are housed in a pleasant, roomy, well-ventilated, purpose-built unit. The stock are caged in single tier cages of Farm Animal Welfare Council recommended size, provided with a solid resting area. Rabbits are fed on home-mixed concentrate from locally grown grain, and home-grown roughage. All slaughtering is carried out on the premises, so there is no long distance transporting of livestock, and 'welfare of the rabbits is at a premium'. The high roughage diet produces a lean meat, low in fat and cholesterol, and tender, succulent and tasty.

60.

Rose Cottage
Nottwood Lane
Stoke Row
Henley-on-Thames
Oxfordshire
RG9 5PZ
tel: 0491 681821

Mrs Kate Fotherby

<u>Opening times</u>   Direct sales to the public, but please phone first as it is small scale and often sold out. Very seasonal, best to order in advance.

<u>Products</u>   Traditionally reared beef, pork and lamb.

<u>Price guide</u>   Beef – £1.20–£5/lb. Pork – whole and half carcasses 80p/lb. Lamb – whole and half carcasses £1/lb. All cuts frozen unless ordered fresh.

Suckler beef is grass-fed, killed at between two and two and a half years, and the meat hung for two and a half weeks. Some fertiliser is used on grass and hay. Pigs are traditionally reared and bred, the sows kept outside except for farrowing and the porkers kept outside all summer and winter if the weather is suitable. Half their rations are commercial feed, supplemented with garden vegetables, barley meal and excess milk. The lambs are all orphans, fed with milk replacer for six weeks and then grass-fed until seven to twelve months old.

Animals are handled and transported with care on the twenty-minute journey to the local abattoir, after phoning first so that they are slaughtered immediately. This minimises stress and avoids bruising. All meat is mature with good flavour and texture.

61.

Portobello Farm
Shirburn
Watlington
Oxfordshire
tel: 049 161 2372

Mr Richard Parker

Opening times 8a.m.–1p.m., 2p.m.–5.30p.m. Mon–Fri. 10a.m.–1p.m., 3p.m.–5p.m. Sun. No need to order except for Saturday morning collections. Also suppliers to the trade.

Products Game, fresh or frozen. All specialist items supplied in season.

Price guide Venison from £1.50/lb. pheasant £5/brace, partridge £3 each, hare £1.25/lb.

Venison is either wild or park deer, not farmed deer which cannot have the same flavour since it doesn't have a varied diet.

62.

Rannoch Smokery
Kinloch Rannoch
by Pitlochry
Perthshire
PH16 5QD
tel: 08822 344
fax no: 08822 441

Leo and Sarah Barclay

<u>Opening times</u> By mail order from the above address. Also available at delicatessens throughout the UK.

<u>Product</u> Smoked and brined prime cuts of wild venison, vacuum packed. The sealed pack will keep in the refrigerator for up to ninety days, and a ¼lb pack will feed four to six people.

Wild venison is very low in fat, has a completely natural life and diet, and is culled by rifle.

63.

Pimhill
Lea Hall
Harmer Hill
Shrewsbury
Shropshire
SY4 3DY
tel: 0939 290342

Richard and Ginny Mayall

<u>Opening times</u> 8a.m.–5p.m. Mon–Fri, 9a.m.–5p.m. Sat. Easter–end of September: 10a.m.–5p.m. Sun.

<u>Products</u> Pork, sold in half pigs or jointed (fresh or frozen). Old English pork (from wild boar crossbred), sold in joints fresh and frozen. Chicken and duck, fresh

and frozen and beef. All free-range and organically fed.

Price guide Very variable, chicken approx £1.35/lb, duck £1.43/lb, half pig £1/lb, pork shoulder £1.25/lb– pork chops £1.70/lb. Old English pork £3–4/lb.

Free-range poultry. Pigs are brought inside to farrow so that visitors to the farm can enjoy their young. The operation is relatively small scale and therefore great attention is given to details. The Mayalls don't castrate, cut tails or give iron injections. Feedstuffs are home-grown and home-mixed, the majority is organic wheat grown on the farm. By not adding growth promoters the animals are slightly slower growing than conventional livestock, but are healthier as a result and the meat flavour is exceptional.

Animals are slaughtered in a local abattoir without having to wait, causing the minimum amount of stress.

The Mayalls main enterprise on their six-hundred-and-seventy-acre farm is the growing and milling of their famous organic flour. Ginny Mayall started to produce meat in this way because she felt that 'meat in general was bland, and the way in which animals were kept to produce it was unacceptable. This way the animals are happy and the meat is quite different from the conventional. It is full of flavour and of good texture. It must be better for you – the chickens, for instance, select the minerals that they need from the soil and this benefit is passed on to the consumer.' The Mayalls are applying for the Soil Association Symbol for their meat.

64.

Somerset Ducks
Greenway Farm
North Newton
Bridgwater
Somerset
TA7 0DS
tel: 0278 662656

Mrs G. Durman

<u>Opening times</u> Mail order, and from Harrods in London.

<u>Products</u> Fresh ducks, pies, pâtés, sausages and cooked, boned and stuffed duck. No additives in cooked duck products.

<u>Price guide</u> Fresh duck (dressed) 95p/lb. Boned, stuffed and cooked £5.50/lb.

Ducks are kept on deep litter, and water and food is freely available at all times. They are fed on grower's mash from Bowerings of Bridgwater. They are killed at the farm's own licensed slaughterhouse.

65.

Swaddles Green Farm
Hare Lane
Buckland St Mary
Chard
Somerset
TA20 3JR
tel: 046 034 387

Charlotte and Bill Reynolds

<u>Opening times</u> Farm shop open 2p.m.–7p.m. Thurs, Fri, Sat and at other times by arrangement. Phone first to avoid disappointment, especially for large orders.

Next day deliveries nationwide for mail order.

Products   Free-range additive-free beef, pork, lamb, chicken, duck. Christmas geese and turkey. Bacon, ham, sausages, charcuterie, pâté and pies made from own meat from the farm. All meat has no added artificial flavours, colours, preservatives. Bacon is preserved by salt and sugar only, no harmful nitrites/nitrates.

Price guide   Chicken £1/lb. Extra lean beef mince £1.40/lb–sirloin steak £3.60/lb. 100 per cent pure meat sausages £1.60/lb. Smoked back bacon £2/lb. Ham 90p/qtr.

All the poultry range freely all around the farm all year, and are not confined in any respect. Pigs are kept in family groups and farrow untethered in straw sheds. They free range all summer, even the fatteners, but are brought into concrete yards during very wet or cold weather with limited access to the field for digging. Home-grown feedstuffs are used, supplemented with bought-in barley for pigs and especially mixed cereal pellets for poultry containing no antibiotics or high mineral elements for fast growth.

Poultry are slaughtered on the farm, and other livestock taken to a small local farm abattoir where they are slaughtered on arrival.

The meat 'takes longer to mature, and so has better flavour and texture ... the diversity of feedstuffs and high leaf content gained by foraging means that the flavour of the meat is unrecognisable' as compared to factory-farmed meat. Meat produced on the farm is healthy, and there are minimal problems with disease. Some of Swaddles Green Farm pork and poultry, and all lamb, will be Soil Association standard when they have found suppliers of organic grain.

66.

Howtown House
Winsford
Near Minehead
Somerset
tel: 064 385 245

Mr Arthur Oakes

<u>Opening times</u>   Direct sales to the public, and through
Phil Haughton's shop Real Food Supplies in Bristol.

<u>Products</u>   Organic lamb and beef; lamb carcasses are
jointed and bagged ready for deep freeze.

Grass-produced lamb and beef are fed on home-mixed
barley, oats and flaked maize. No proprietary mixes are
used because of possible additives and growth promoters. Sheep receive no medication whatsoever except
herbal and homeopathic remedies.

Cross-bred lambs, from Jacob ewes and Dorset Down
rams, are marketed at six months old, and are always
best roasted. Hereford beef cattle are sold at least eighteen months old. Animals slaughtered at Lloyd Maunders
Ltd, Tiverton, who are good and careful.

Soil Association Symbol.

67.

Gold Label Produce Ltd
Knightley Grange Cottage
Grange Road
Woodseaves
Near Stafford
Staffordshire
ST20 0JU
tel: 078574 495

<u>Opening times</u>   Direct sales to the public; customers

305

are advised to ring orders through in advance. Some local deliveries, and through Datapost. Also at Wholefoods, Paddington Street; Lidgates, Holland Park; Godfrey and Son, Highbury Park; Mr Rav, Lordship Lane; Natural Days Farm; Tolly's Northwood; Cherry Trees Farm, Rickmansworth; Hockeys, Fordingbridge; G. Kent, Mosely, Birmingham.

Products   Chicken, turkey and duck, oven ready or portioned. Pork, whole/half carcass, or jointed. Bacon, smoked or plain, vacuum packed. Venison whole/half carcass or jointed. All available fresh or frozen, no preservatives.

Price guide   Whole chicken £1.30/lb–breasts £3.25/lb. Whole/half pigs 90p/lb, belly pork £1/lb–fillet £1.95/lb. Bacon from £2.75/lb. Whole/half venison £2.20/lb, casserole £2.50/lb–haunch and saddle £3.75/lb. Turkey £1.80/lb (Christmas only at present).

Poultry is free range and kept in small groups in sheds on deep litter of straw. No lighting, additives, growth promoters or routine antibiotics are used. Pigs are kept in small groups bedded on straw, with access to outdoors when ground conditions are suitable. Deer are kept on natural parkland or woodland, with a predominantly grass diet. Feedstuffs are mixed to their own specification, mainly cereal-based with no additives, growth promoters, emulsifiers, medication or animal offal.

Chickens and pigs are slaughtered at a local EC registered plant. Turkeys are killed on the farm. Deer are slaughtered in the field for minimum stress. Chickens are twelve weeks old at slaughter, which ensures a better flavour and texture and makes them easier to carve, with no water loss. They can be hung for a gamier taste. The pork is firm and with guaranteed crackling. Bacon suffers no water loss or shrinkage and has a good flavour, as a result of traditional curing methods, using only saltpetre. Venison meat is lean, but well basted it does not shrink in cooking, and is excellent cold. Turkey has a gamier flavour than the conventional bird, and cooks more quickly, because of the layer of fat under the skin.

Gold Label Produce Ltd prefer to set their own high standards rather than rely on symbols which they feel may be misleading to customers, especially the word 'organic'.

68.

Organic Farmers and Growers Scotland

Organic Farmers and Growers Scotland is a farmer owned marketing co-operative, which supports the UKROFS standards. They are slowly developing into the meat business, and cannot at present reveal details of their plans. However it is more than likely that when their products reach the market, they will be available through retail outlets rather than direct to the customer. The Chairman, Nander Robertson, can be contacted at Glenside Farm, Plean, Stirling, FK7 8BA.

69.

Tablehurst Farm
Forest Row
East Sussex
RH18 5DP
tel: 034 282 3536

Walter J. Rudert

<u>Opening times</u>   Beef available all year round, advance ordering essential.

<u>Products</u>   Demeter beef, reared according to bio-dynamic methods, absolutely additive free, professionally cut and packed to customer's request, half-side minimum.

<u>Price guide</u>   Flat rate economy price, boning out, cutting, packaging inclusive.

A suckler herd of local Sussex cows, established in the 1960s, produces all the stock for beef rearing. The traditional Sussex breed is widely acclaimed for high-quality, well-flavoured beef. Calves are suckled for nine months, grazed in clover-rich pastures during summer, and in winter housed in spacious well-strawed quarters and fed on high-quality hay, silage, grain and root crops, all produced on the farm to Demeter standards. Careful stockmanship, relying mostly on homeopathic remedies, ensures that the stock are free from veterinary contaminants. Animals are taken to a local abattoir for immediate slaughter. 'The Bio-Dynamic farming method ... ensures that the highest quality criteria of farm produce are met.'

Demeter Symbol.

70.

Stairs Farmhouse
High Street
Hartfield
East Sussex
TN7 4AB
tel: 0892 770793

Mrs G. Pring

<u>Opening times</u> Open 10a.m.–6p.m., 10a.m.–1p.m. Sun, closed Tuesday. Best supplies at the end of the week.

<u>Products</u> Additive-free meat from naturally reared, free-range animals. Beef, pork, lamb, kid, chicken, duck, venison, hare, rabbit, pheasant, guinea fowl, veal – fresh and frozen. Joints off bone cut fresh while you wait, joints on bone to order.

<u>Price guide</u> Beef mince £2/lb–sirloin £4.25/lb. Pork joints £1.20/lb–£2.45/lb. Whole chicken £1.60/lb–joints £1.95/lb. Shoulder lamb £1.75/lb–leg £2.95/lb.

Sausages from £1.40/lb. Bacon from £1.75/lb.

Everything is naturally reared, and free-range except in winter when the cattle are kept in barns. Cattle are single-suckled for as long as possible. Feedstuffs are additive-free, mainly hay, silage and sugar beet. Animals taken to a local abattoir personally and slaughtered immediately.

Mrs Pring feels that applying for symbols is a lengthy and expensive business; being small farmers they have to rent land which changes from time to time, so they have less control over it. Their meat is matured longer, using only natural feeds, and hung longer than conventional meat.

71.

Barklye Farm
Swife Lane
Broad Oak
Heathfield
East Sussex
TN21 8UR
tel: 0435 883536

Teresa Haines

<u>Opening times</u> Direct sales to the public, preferably at weekend, better to phone in advance.

<u>Products</u> Organic beef and lamb, fresh or frozen. Whole or half butchered lambs, all cuts to customers' requirements.

<u>Price guide</u> Whole or half lamb £1.25/lb. Stewing steak £2.10/lb–sirloin steak £5/lb.

Barklye is a grassland farm, where the breeding ewes graze for most of the year but come inside for the worst winter months, since the heavy clay becomes very wet.

Stock is fed on home-grown hay, some bought-in Conservation Grade oats and barley from a neighbouring farm. Lambs are grass fed.

Animals are slaughtered at a local abattoir, a mile away, where a good relationship with the supervisor ensures that they are dealt with immediately.

Teresa Haines feels that the symbol is very useful, as consumers are rightly sceptical about additive-free meat – 'it could just mean that the butcher has left out the red colour enhancer.'

Soil Association Symbol.

72.

Boathouse Farm
Isfield
East Sussex
TN22 5TY
tel: 082 575 302

N.H. and M.J. Tebbutt

<u>Opening times</u>   Shop open seven days a week.

<u>Products</u>   Organic beef and lamb, fresh or frozen (lamb available June–September).

<u>Price guide</u>   Beef packs £2.90/lb.

All animals are kept to Soil Association standards. Beef is single-suckled, and all feedstuffs are home grown. The animals are slaughtered in a local abattoir (five miles away) with minimal stress.

Boathouse farm specialises in traditionally produced beef of the highest quality.

Soil Association Symbol.

73.

Beaumont Organic Fresh Food
363 South Coast Road
Peacehaven
East Sussex
tel: 0273 585551

Bob and Pam Beaumont

<u>Opening times</u> Shop open five days a week, 8.30a.m.–5.30p.m. Late night Friday. Also available in Lewes, Hove and Eastbourne, please phone for details.

<u>Products</u> Organic and bio-dynamic meat, fresh or frozen, and many other organic foods.

<u>Price guide</u> Beef mince £2.60/lb–fillet steak £5.40/lb. Bacon £3.20/lb. Pork sausage £2.50/lb. Free-range additive-free chicken £1.65/lb.

All organic meats meet the Soil Association standards and some are produced to Bio-Dynamic standards. The emphasis is on natural lifestyle and careful husbandry. Animals are fed on organic feedstuffs, and no antibiotics or any other chemicals are used.

After eight years' experience of eating and selling organic food, the Beaumonts think that 'the price reflects the quality and the quality reflects on our health. We are what we eat! We have the good fortune to be healthy and serve (with pleasure) a lot of healthy customers, some of whom were not healthy at the outset.' They feel that symbol standards are important, and that 'some farmers don't seem to know what organic means ... and allow customers to believe that additive-free meat is organic.' They suggest financing the standards with an overt tax shown to the customer on the price label, i.e. 24p/lb plus standards levy 1p/lb.

74.

Adsdean Farm
Funtington
Chichester
West Sussex
PO18 9DN
tel: 0243 575212

Mr Dennis Hoare

<u>Opening times</u>   Shop open 10a.m.–5.30p.m. Wed and Fri, 10a.m.–4p.m. Thurs, 9a.m.–4p.m. Sat. Please phone in advance for special orders. Delivery of fresh, vacuum-packed meat by Datapost.

<u>Products</u>   Additive-free beef and pork, bought-in local lambs. Fresh meat cuts, and frozen joints, sides and hind and fore-quarters (frozen in a blast freezer for better keeping).

<u>Price guide</u>   Beef brisket on the bone 68p/lb–fillet steak £6.25/lb. Shin of veal £1.30/lb–escallopes £4.65/lb. Breast of lamb 38p/lb–chump chops £2.66/lb. Ox liver 34p/lb–lamb sweetbreads £1.92/lb. Belly pork 60p/lb – pork fillets £3/lb.

Outdoor herd of pigs, fatteners reared mainly in strawed yards. All pigs and cattle are free of antibiotics, growth promoters or hormones. Feedstuffs are mostly home grown and home mixed.

All animals are slaughtered at Coggan's abattoir, Fareham. Mr Hoare delivers them himself and they are usually killed straight away, without waiting in the lairage.

Adsdean Farm take great pride in all their meat, but particularly the beef, which is of a very high quality and particularly tender.

75.

Malthouse Cottage Farm
Malthouse Lane
Ashington
Pulborough
West Sussex
RH20 3BU
tel: 0903 892456

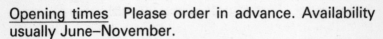

<u>Opening times</u> Please order in advance. Availability usually June–November.

<u>Products</u> Organic lamb and kid, half or whole, butchered as required and bagged.

<u>Price guide</u> £1.30/lb–£1.40/lb. (Market price plus abattoir charge plus butchering charge plus 20 per cent.)

The farm operates an extensive system on organic pasture to Soil Association standards. No regular worming of lambs and kids, and special organic dip is used. Animals are slaughtered at a local abattoir. Grown fast on spring grass, the meat is very tender with an excellent flavour.

Soil Association Symbol.

76.

Camphill Village Trust
Larchfield Community
Stokesley Road
Hemlington
Middlesbrough
Teeside
TS8 9DY
tel: 0642 593566

<u>Opening times</u> Direct sales to the public, but please

313

order first. Also available by order from David Newbould (butcher), Trimdon Avenue, Aklam, Middlesbrough.

Products Free-range, organic and additive-free pork, available half or whole pig, fresh and jointed for the freezer, on and off throughout the year. Whole organic lambs for the freezer. Beef will be available in the future.

Price guide Pork 68p/lb. Lamb 98p/lb.

Pigs are outside most of the year, and in winter are kept in strawed yards (not concrete). Feedstuffs are barley, peas and beans, soya, seaweed, cider vinegar and molasses, at least half of which is home grown. Lambs stay with their mothers until early August. Larchfield uses linseed oil and turpentine as a wormer and a pyrethroid dip. Most of the oats, and all the hay and silage, for the sheep and cattle is home grown.

The slaughterhouse used is relatively small but Larchfield farmers are still not entirely satisfied, feeling that 'it is the make or break of what we are trying to do. Why go to a lot of trouble to raise animals this way to throw it all away by stressing the animal at the end ... economies of scale will always mean ... pushing animals through straight off the wagon.'

Larchfield farms according to bio-dynamic principles, but local customers can see the farm's standards for themselves.

Demeter Symbol.

77.

Henry Doubleday Research Association – HDRA (Sales) Ltd
National Centre for Organic Gardening
Ryton Gardens
Ryton on Dunsmore
Coventry
West Midlands
CV8 3LG
tel: 0203 303517

<u>Products</u>   Frozen organic beef from Kite's Nest Farm, and pork, chicken, bacon and venison from Gold Label Produce Ltd. Other meats are sometimes available.

<u>Price guide</u>   Beef mince £2.70/lb–rump steak £5.84/lb. Pork chops £1.95/lb. Chicken £1.55/lb. Venison steaks £4.50/lb.

The Henry Doubleday Research Association's National Centre for Organic Gardening has a well-stocked shop selling a wide range of organic produce. The best place to see organic gardening in action, it takes several days to absorb everything the gardens have to offer.

78.

Levett's Farm
Clench Common
Marlborough
Wiltshire
tel: 0672 52035

Martin Pitt

<u>Opening times</u>   Direct sales to the public, but please order first. (Visitors to the farm prior to purchase also welcome, but only by appointment. Mr Pitt tries to arrange small groups whenever possible so that the public can see the high welfare standards for themselves.)

315

Products   Organic whole or half lambs, jointed if
requested, fresh or frozen, available from August
onwards until sold out. Also available – organic free-
range boiling fowl and organic sheep's cheese and
milk. Trade enquiries are welcome.

Price guide   Whole/half organic lamb £1.05–£1.30/lb.

All grassland, and some of the arable acreage is organic
to Soil Association standards. The lambs are produced
by a flock of milking ewes crossed with a Texel ram
which gives unusually good conformation, especially in
the leg and shoulder. They are fed home-grown and
home-mixed Soil Association standard feedstuffs. The
hens are free range and fed on additive-free food. Mr Pitt
delivers animals to a small local slaughterhouse, where
they are humanely killed immediately on arrival.

The animals are slightly older than usual, which gives
time for the flavour to develop, and the meat is ultra-
lean. Mr Pitt says that the Soil Association Symbol is
vital – 'organic is the most mis-used and over-used word
in the English language'.

Soil Association Symbol. British Culinary Institute
approved. Supplier to the Q Guild of Butchers.

79.

The Ginger Pig
Broadleaze
Boyton
Warminster
Wiltshire
tel: 0985 50208

Opening times   Please phone first. A very small business, selling locally by personal contact.

Products   Frozen additive-free pork, ham (preservative in the cure), sausages (no preservatives),

cooked casseroles. All from pedigree Tamworth pigs.

Price guide   Pig's liver 80p/lb. Leg of pork £1.50/lb–honey-roast ham £5.50/lb.

Pure-bred Tamworth pigs fed on home-mixed food, and kept extensively. Two pigs per week are sent to a small slaughterhouse.

'Old fashioned' tasty ham and pork with crackling that crackles unaided, and sausages that taste – of pork!

80.

The Real Meat Company Ltd
East Hill Farm
Heytesbury
Warminster
Wiltshire
BA12 0HR
tel: 0985 40436/40060

Richard Guy and Gilly Metherell

Opening times   Direct sales from Real Meat Direct, Deverill Road Trading Estate, Sutton Veny, Warminster, tel: 0985 40501, and the three company shops at 7 Hayes Place, Holloway, Bear Flat, Bath, tel: 0225 335139; 61 Manor Street, Chelsea, tel: 071-823 3509; 3 Nugent Terrace, London NW8, tel: 071-286 3124. A list of other retailers who sell RMC meat is available on request. Also direct delivery of fresh chilled meat anywhere in mainland Britain.

Products   Additive-free beef, pork, lamb, chicken, duck, geese, turkey, ham and bacon from East Hill Farm and other producers. The shops also sell burgers, ice cream, cheese and free-range eggs.

Price guide   (London and Real Meat Direct) Beef mince £2.14/lb–fillet steak £7.89/lb. Belly pork £1.42/lb–tenderloin £4.16/lb. Stewing lamb £1.25/lb–fillet half leg £3.85. Ox liver 45p/lb–lamb's kidney £2.45/lb. Whole chicken £1.79/lb. Bacon hocks £1.05/lb– smoked gammon steaks £3.30/lb. Sausages from £1.84/lb. Home-cooked ham £4.95/lb.

Real Meat Company animals are all free range, except for the pigs which are kept on deep litter. They are fed home-mixed or specially made bought-in feedstuffs, without growth promoters, antibiotics or other additives. All the meat is produced in accordance with the mandates drawn up by Compassion in World Farming. The meat is of a very high quality, and difficult to match in terms of tenderness and succulence. It has won many accolades in the Press, including 'Best Bacon in Britain' from the BBC 'Food and Drink Programme'.

Since they founded The Real Meat Company in 1986, Richard Guy and Gilly Metherell have been successful in bringing good meat to an ever-increasing market. Horrified at the lack of integrity which they encountered when they started in the meat trade, they have built their reputation on the stringent standards which they impose on their thirty or so suppliers, whose farms are checked and double checked in detail. Richard Guy says 'we spend much time and money making sure that everything that we say that we do is done', and the occasional would-be supplier, far from being taken on, have found themselves reported instead to an animal welfare organisation!

81.

Sunny Bank Farm
Stoney Lane
Alvechurch
Near Birmingham
Worcestershire

B48 7DG
tel: 021-445 1106

Mrs D. Senior

<u>Opening times</u>   Open any reasonable time but advisable to phone first.

<u>Products</u>   Pork (half and quarter pigs, joints and chops) and lamb (half or whole lamb), always available frozen, fresh to order. Kid meat to order. Beef, chickens and turkeys occasionally. All additive-free and with no growth promoters.

<u>Price guide</u>   Half or whole pig 65p/lb, smaller quantities £1/lb plus. Half or whole lamb £1/lb. Kid meat £1/lb.

All animals are free-range as far as possible. If yarded, they are loose housed with straw bedding and access to fresh air. Feedstuffs are all home mixed, and as much as possible are home grown. No additives are used apart from simple minerals, as so many people have allergic reactions to copper and so on. Homeopathic remedies are used as far as possible in treatment of illnesses. Humane treatment is always the first priority. Mrs Senior takes her animals to a small abattoir where she is guaranteed to get her own animal back, especially important with liver and kidneys.

   Animals from Sunny Bank Farm grow more slowly, which gives the meat more flavour and a better texture. Customers with allergies find that they can enjoy the meat without adverse reaction.

82.

Kite's Nest Farm
Broadway
Worcestershire
tel: 0386 853320/853621

H.A. Young and family

Opening times   Direct sales to the public, 10.30a.m.–4.30p.m. every day. Please phone first for specific orders, but some cuts are always available. Also available from Garland's Farm Shop, Upper Basildon; Only Natural, Malvern; Brewers Basics, Leominster; National Centre for Organic Gardening, Ryton-on-Dunsmore, Coventry; Carrot Connection, Wapshott, Woking; Willersey Post Office and Stores, Willersey, Worcestershire; Neil Sutton Butchers, Wythall, Birmingham.

Products   Totally organic beef.

Price guide   Beef mince £1.98/lb, sirloin steak £5.34/lb, sausages £1.96/lb, liver £1.52/lb.

Kite's Nest Farm is totally organic, and all food fed to the animals (and humans) has been grown on the farm without chemicals of any sort. The cattle are reared without stress from birth to death, and have several fields at a time to range over and a large, comfortable barn when they ask for shelter. The Youngs take their animals to a local abattoir themselves and stay with them until the moment of death. They are currently investigating the possibility of building their own abattoir.

The Youngs have been at the forefront of the organic movement for many years, and their beef is considered to be the very best. Kite's Nest Farm is justly famous and has featured in countless articles in the press and on television.

Soil Association Symbol.

83.

Goodman's Geese
Walsgrove Farm
Great Witley
Near Worcester

Worcestershire
WR6 6JJ
tel: 0299 896 272

Judy Goodman

<u>Opening times</u> Direct sales to public, between Michaelmas (September 29th) and Christmas (December 25th). Please order at least ten days in advance, or three months before Christmas. Also available from Rackhams, Kendals and Harrods, and butchers shops in West Midlands. Also by overnight delivery.

<u>Products</u> Free-range oven-ready geese and free-range long-legged geese.

<u>Price guide</u> £1.85/lb September–October, £1.95/lb November, £2/lb early December, £2.15/lb Christmas.

Geese are reared inside for the first three to four weeks and then go outside on a free-range grass system, with extra corn feed to fatten them up. Feedstuffs are mixed specifically for Goodman's Geese with no additives, home-produced wheat and barley are also used and home-grown straw. Birds are slaughtered on the farm and hung in a cold room for ten days before sale.

84.

Only Natural
99b Church Street
Malvern
Worcestershire
WR14 2AE
tel: 0684 561772

<u>Opening times</u> Normal shop hours.

<u>Products</u> Organic beef (frozen), wide range of cuts including beefburgers and sausages. Organic pork

(also frozen), sausages, and bacon. Fresh organic chicken to order. All meat sold is produced to Soil Association standards.

Price guide   Chicken £1.75/lb. Beef mince £2.08/lb–sirloin steak £5.30/lb. Pork sausages £1.85/lb, chops £3.30/lb. Bacon around £2.30/lb.

At Only Natural the single most important feature of the meat is that it is produced humanely and non-intensively, but it's also important that it is free of additives, hormones and antibiotics. They feel that the symbol scheme for producers is very useful.

85.

Gibson's Farm Shop
Hopetown House
Burneston
Bedale
North Yorkshire
DL8 2JN
tel: 0845 567252

S.C. and J.H. Gibson

Opening times   Direct sales to the public. Please order in advance if possible.

Products   Home-produced pork, black puddings, sausages and burgers. Also beef, lamb, poultry and game.

Price guide   Prices move with seasonal demands. Chicken livers 68p/lb, extra large chickens 75p/lb. Beef mince £1.44/lb, sirloin steak £4.45/lb. Whole pigs 68p/lb.

Straw grown on the farm is used for bedding, and the pigs enjoy rooting in it. Sows are in crates for three weeks when they farrow, to protect the piglets. The growing pigs are then kept in groups with an outside run. All are fed on home-mixed feedstuffs to formulated rations. Home-grown corn is fed to the pigs. A vet visits every three months, and advises on welfare and treatment of the animals. Animals are taken to a local slaughterhouse five miles away, and great care is taken not to stress them too much.

Gibson's Farm Shop has been operating since the mid-1970s and only sells local produce with guaranteed quality. The Gibsons feel that there is a 'happy medium between the extremes of intensive livestock units and of extensive free-range systems. The modern pig ... is lean and non-hairy and not suited to live outdoors in cold, wet climates or on heavy soils.' They also feel that the quality of meat is in danger of being compromised by the public's demand for lean meat.

86.

Burgate Farm
Harwood Dale
Scarborough
North Yorkshire
YO13 0DS
tel: 0723 870333

Mrs C. Cook

Opening times   All meat must be ordered in advance. Killings take place roughly twice every year, sometimes every three months.

Products   Free-range and additive-free pork sold in half pigs, jointed, bagged and labelled to customers' own requirements ready for the freezer.

Price guide   Approx 15p/lb more than commercial pork, sold for the freezer. January 1989 price – 85p/lb for half a pig.

Free-range pigs, reared more slowly and killed at an older age, have a good flavour and really crunchy crackling. The pigs are a rare breed (Oxford Sandy and Black) and that coupled with an older age at killing means they contain more fat than 'supermarket' pork. All feedstuffs are home grown. Pigs are slaughtered at a small local butcher.

Mrs Cook recommends that her pork, which is solid and dry, is cooked in a very hot oven for perfect crackling and to render out most of the fat. She is a member of Organic Farmers and Growers, but does not always rear the pigs to their standards, as they sometimes need worming for their own good!

87.

Vicarage Farm
Claxton
York
North Yorkshire
tel: 090 486 222

E. and E.G. Bullivant and Daughters

Opening times   Direct sales from the farm, but please phone to order in advance.

Products   Additive- and antibiotic-free beef, lamb, and pork, all frozen. The Bullivants also sell Sunrise Farm Natural Chicken. A limited number of home-cured York hams also available.

Price guide   Beef mince £1.45/lb–fillet steak £4.95/lb. Belly pork 90p/lb–pork fillet £2.65/lb.

Cattle, sheep and pigs are kept by traditional methods which the Bullivants have used for thirty years at Vicarage Farm. Cattle are suckled by their mothers, and are outside on grass in summer and yarded in winter. Breeding cows are kept for many years. Pigs are bought in as weaners, and kept on deep litter of home-grown straw, in large, airy folds and pens. No steroids, antibiotics and growth promoters are used.

The two Bullivant daughters feel that to be totally organic is unrealistic, especially while people continue to want cheap food. However they do feel that some farmers have gone mad with sprays, and in order to guarantee the quality all their feedstuffs are home grown. The animals are fed entirely on grass, cereals, hay and fodder beet from the thirty-acre farm, grown with an absolute minimum of sprays. The pigs also have potatoes, comfrey and weeds. Beef cattle are slaughtered on arrival at a local abattoir, at two and a half years or more, and hung for ten days. The butcher can recognise their animals because they are older and have more fat than most, which means they are guaranteed to get their own animals back!

They feel that the good flavour of their meat is due to the feedstuffs, especially fresh green food, and the age of the beast, in the case of beef. Since one of the daughters has allergies herself, and they supply many others with similar conditions, this gives them a good yardstick for the purity of their product.

88.

Round Green Deer Farm
Worsbrough
Barnsley
South Yorkshire
S75 3DR
tel: 0226 205577

Opening times   Direct sales from farm, open all sociable hours. Phone if travelling a long distance, or for mail order.

Products   Additive-free venison, frozen available all year, fresh available by prior arrangement. All cuts and whole carcasses. Sausages and burgers.

Price guide   Casserole cuts £2.40/lb–steak £5.60/lb.

The deer spend their first winter indoors, fed on hay or silage and calf rearing nuts, and thereafter they graze in the fields. No growth promoters or routine antibiotics are used.

Deer are shot in the field which seems to be the most humane method – the other deer do not even run away.

Farm venison is very lean and has extremely low-fat content. Coming from young animals it is much more tender than the average wild venison.

89.

S & C Meats
259 Shay Lane
Holmfield
Halifax
West Yorkshire
HX2 9AG
tel: 0422 244859

Christopher Argent and Steven Holmes

Opening times   8.30a.m.–5.30p.m. Mon–Fri, half days Thursday and Saturday, closed for lunch each day, 12.30–1.30p.m. Please order organic beef in advance. There is no mail order at present.

Products   Organic beef, fresh or frozen, cut and packaged to customer requirements, supplied in large or small quantities from the Argents' farm in Oxenhope, Keighley.

Price Guide   Subject to market fluctuations. In general organic beef is 10–15 per cent above normal retail price.

The Argents keep a suckler herd with a variety of hardy crossbred cattle on which A I bulls are used – Charolais, Limousin, Angus or Simmental – to suit the predominant breed in each particular cow. The best heifers are retained for breeding. The herd is 'one big family and it shows – a good suckler cow has a long life in animal terms – minimum of ten years if healthy and well cared for.' All feedstuffs are home grown. As no chemicals or artificial fertilisers have been used since the 1930s the hay is of exceptional feeding quality. The farm also has a substantial amount of rough grazing and a combination of the two gives exceptional quality and flavour to the beef.

The Argents have always been satisfied with their local abattoir which is run by a family they know well. Until recently it was in the village, but has been forced by rising costs to move to a unit in a bigger abattoir in nearby Denholme.

S & C Meats believe that good beef depends on the type of animal, traditional feeding and rearing, and quality butchering. They hang their beef in the side and supply to the customer at the best time from the point of slaughter, so that nothing is lost nutritionally.

The Argents say 'We are not extremists. The farmers are not to blame for our present dilemma; they have pursued the course recommended to them by the Ministry, whom they have trusted. But nature has been abused and is retaliating, as it does. The limits of human meddling have been reached.' They do not hold any organic symbols at present but feel that it may be necessary in the future. 'At present we are promoted by satisfied customers and our good name, established over many years.'

ORGANISATIONS

The following are the main voluntary organisations concerned with farm animal welfare, and safe, ecologically sound methods of farming and food production. Their approach varies; some adopt a low profile, preferring to work in a practical way with individuals, while others have a more combative approach, searching out publicity in the media for campaigns to change legislation.

They are all membership based, and always looking for both practical and financial support. They need all the help they can get to put forward the alternatives to mainstream methods, which have millions of pounds' worth of commercial back-up from the multinational agrochemical companies and establishment organisations.

The Bio-Dynamic Agricultural Association
Woodman Lane
Clent
Stourbridge
West Midlands
DY9 9PX
tel: 0562 884933

Bio-dynamics is based on the work of Rudolph Steiner, the philosopher and scientist, whose theories and methods gave organic farming an extra cosmic dimension. A bio-dynamic farmer 'takes into account the whole environment, including the underlying rock structure, the soil, the atmosphere, the natural vegetation and, above all, the cosmic forces acting upon it – and also the social context in which the food is being produced.' The farmer has to study and act upon the 'dynamic' relationship of the interrelated organisms of nature. Bio-dynamic preparations are a special feature – herbal mixes added in small quantities to compost, soil and plants to give added vitality and fertility.

The Bio-Dynamic Agricultural Association exists to educate and help those who want to follow the method on their farms or gardens. It also runs the Demeter Symbol certification scheme for bio-dynamic produce, makes and supplies the preparations, and publishes a twice-yearly newsletter and magazine, the *Star and Furrow*. Membership is an average of £18 per year – those who can afford it are asked to pay more than those who can't.

Chicken's Lib
PO Box 2
Holmfirth
Huddersfield
West Yorkshire
HD7 1QT
tel: 0484 861814/683158

Chicken's Lib has a succinct description of itself – 'a non-violent pressure group dedicated to the total abolition of battery cages and any other systems for poultry keeping which impose severe restrictions on the birds, depriving them of a reasonably natural lifestyle.' By concentrating single-mindedly on perhaps the worst aspect of factory farming, the group has mounted an impressive and effective campaign, undermining the poultry industry's case with a barrage of meticulously researched facts and figures.

In 1989 Clare Druce, a founder member, wrote *Chicken and Egg – Who pays the Price?* (Green Print) which puts a well argued case against intensive systems. One of the keypoints of her argument is that these systems already contravene many existing laws and regulations governing farm animals, and therefore are even now illegal.

Chicken's Lib now has a good chance of fulfilling its

aims, and it continues to need all the support it can get. Membership is £5 which gives you a newsletter and access to all the information leaflets and pamphlets.

Compassion in World Farming
20 Lavant Street
Petersfield
Hampshire
GU32 3EW
tel: 0730 64208/68863

The Athene Trust
3A Charles Street
Petersfield
Hampshire
GU32 3EH
tel: 0730 68070

CIWF – 'the voice of livestock liberation' – probably has the highest public profile of the farm animal welfare groups. An organisation based in the small Hampshire town of Petersfield, it has an active national network of members who are urged to write to MPs, supermarkets and other interested bodies to make their views felt in an effective way.

CIWF has published the ten mandates programme in answer to the 'ridiculous ... farce of existing voluntary welfare codes'. The mandates have been adopted by The Real Meat Company as their minimum welfare standards.

CIWF runs many campaigns. In 1988 it launched a controversial series of adverts in cinemas and mass market magazines against battery egg farming. In 1989 it tried to stop the importation of frogs' legs and *pâté de foie gras*, and prevent the introduction of large-scale facilities for the killing of deer in abattoirs, and it also campaigned for the upgrading of the status of farm animals in the European Community from that of 'agricultural products' to that of 'sentient beings'. CIWF has also written to supermarkets asking for meat which has been ritually slaughtered to be clearly labelled. On a more mundane level it supplies a steady stream of impressive fact sheets, leaflets, posters and videos and its sister organisation The Athene Trust publishes educational material specially prepared for schools and colleges.

All members of CIWF receive a free bi-monthly magazine called *Agscene*, which is extremely informative and interesting. The annual subscription to CIWF costs £10.

The Farm and Food Society (FAFS)
4 Willifield Way
London
NW11 7XT
tel: 081-455 0634

The Farm and Food Society was founded in 1966, to work for 'farming which is humane to animals, wholesome for consumers and fair to farmers'. It has an international membership and an impressive, distinguished list of patrons, both past and present. The FAFS offers an informed perspective on the whole food chain, and is equally concerned about animal and human welfare, agriculture and nutrition. 'Action is aimed at creating a social climate which will enable farming to combine the best traditional methods with wise use of technology; a movement away from industrialised agriculture with its need for large capital investment and high input of oil, fertilisers and pesticides, towards a non-violent system of farming in harmony with the environment, and with as many people as possible involved with the land. This would inevitably improve the quality and safety of food and the living conditions of stock, while providing employment for people at all levels, reducing pollution and conserving an attractive way of life now threatened with extinction.'

Exalted ideals, but well worth supporting. The FAFS

publishes papers and pamphlets and a comprehensive newsletter for members, which brings together reports from the specialist press. Minimum subscription is £4.

The Homeopathic Society for Animal Welfare
Newparc
Llanrhidian
Gower
Glamorgan
SA3 1HA
tel: 0792 390943

The Homeopathic Society for Animal Welfare is an 'association for smallholders and animal enthusiasts' which promotes the homeopathic treatment of animals, and campaigns for the training of homeopathic vets. Through the newsletter the members keep up to date with developments in the professional practice of homeopathy, and exchange their knowledge of remedies which have been successful for their own animals. These anecdotes will be mystifying to those unfamiliar with homeopathy, but if you are already using the remedies for yourself and your family, you will be sure to find the HSAW extremely useful if you decide to get going on your animals.

Subscriptions are £6.

Humane Slaughter Association (HSA)
(Council of Justice to Animals and Humane Slaughter Association)
34 Blanche Lane
South Mimms
Potters Bar
Hertfordshire
EN6 3PA
tel: 0707 59040

The HSA was founded in 1911 and is the only charity which specialises in the welfare of food animals throughout the marketing and slaughter processes. It was instrumental in effecting the change from the traditional methods of pole axe stunning and bleeding of still conscious animals, to the mechanical methods of humane stunning by captive bolt pistol and electric current. It is actively involved in the design and development of more humane equipment and systems, and campaigns against ritual slaughter and the export of live animals.

The HSA tries to work in a practical way with farmers, auctioneers and slaughtermen to improve conditions, and the field officers lecture, demonstrate and give advice to the trade. A slogan on one of its leaflets reads 'Remember we are friends not fanatics'. This approach helps to distance it from the current hostility between farmers and the public.

The HSA has recently established and strengthened links with organic farmers, recognising that they demand high standards of livestock handling. It gives advice regarding on-farm slaughter and recommends suitable abattoirs.

Anyone can join the HSA and the subscription is only £5.

The Irish Organic Farmers' and Growers' Association
Killegland Farm
Ashbourne
County Meath
Eire
tel: 01 350225

The IOFGA is a voluntary organisation which operates its own symbol scheme for producers of organic foods in the Republic of Ireland. The standards cover all aspects of food production and processing, and IOFGA inspectors ensure that these standards are met by members of the scheme. The Association also seeks to provide information to producers and consumers, to encourage research and education, and to aid the marketing and promotion of organic food in Ireland.

A network of local groups encourages communication between members, and the Association also publishes a bi-monthly magazine and a list of symbol holders to help you find suppliers of organic meat in your area.

Everyone is welcome to join the IOFGA, and subscriptions are I£15 for individuals, I£25 for organisations and I£10 for students and unwaged people.

The London Food Commission
88 Old Street
London
EC1V 9AR
tel: 071-253 9513

The London Food Commission is a voluntary organisation providing an independent source of research, information, education and advice on food. Although originally partly funded by the old GLC, with its efforts concentrated on food issues in London, it has now become a national organisation. The emphasis of its work is on the mass market and it is particularly good on background information about the big food businesses. During the food scandals of 1989 staff of the LFC played a major part in keeping the public informed, with frequent appearances and quotes in the media.

The LFC has published many excellent comprehensive books and reports on food issues and co-ordinated many campaigns. It also runs courses for those working in the food business. Four times a year it publishes the excellent *Food Magazine*, which is free to members but also available on subscription for £12.50. Interesting reading for those who want to keep up to date with developments in the food industry.

The McCarrison Society for Nutrition and Health
24 Paddington Street
London
W1M 4DR
tel: 071-935 3924

Sir Robert McCarrison's pioneering work in nutrition in India revealed that 'the greatest single factor in the acquisition and maintenance of good health is perfectly constituted food'. His studies led him to the conclusion that food should be grown on a healthy soil and should be eaten whole and fresh. His book of lectures *Nutrition and Health* was a bible for those who went on to develop the theory and practice of 'wholefoods'.

In 1966 the McCarrison Society was formed by a group of doctors and dentists who wanted to disseminate information about nutrition through conferences and lectures, to fund the publication of books and papers and to encourage and initiate research projects. Although the society has an academic bias and is of particular interest to those professionally involved in nutrition, anyone who supports its aims is welcome to join. The subscription entitles members to special rates for conferences and for the respected quarterly journal *Nutrition and Health*, and a quarterly newsletter which is full of interesting articles.

Subscriptions range from £20 for professionals to £5 for the unwaged.

Parents for Safe Food
Britannia House
1–11 Glenthorne Road
Hammersmith
London
W6 0LF
tel: 081-748 9898

Parents for Safe Food is a pressure group launched in

the summer of 1989 by the actress Pamela Stephenson and other media personalities, who delivered a personal letter expressing their anxieties about food to the Prime Minister. The group was established originally in response to publicity about Alar, a chemical used on apples, which is possibly carcinogenic (encourages the development of cancers). The group intends to continue to campaign for a healthy food and agriculture policy that gives parents and all consumers the choice of safe and wholesome food. It is also aiming to help raise public awareness of the problems caused by unnecessary and unsafe elements in food, and to work in partnership with interested and informed individuals and organisations towards a better quality food supply.

Parents for Safe Food has already published a sample letter in mass market magazines for parents to send to supermarkets, expressing concerns about pesticides and asking pertinent questions. An information pack and a book are also planned, and the group is hoping for a wide membership base.

The Permaculture Association
8 Hunter's Moon
Dartington
Totnes
TQ9 6JT
tel: 0803 867546

Permaculture is a system of design rather than methods. In the growing of food the aim is to create a system which is as sustainable, diverse, conserving and permanent (by using trees and perennial plants) as possible. 'Maximum observation, minimum interference' is the catchphrase; the 'unit' should produce more energy than it consumes, soil should not be lost, nutrients should be cycled and the food needs of a region should be met locally. Permaculture principles are applied at several farms in the directory section of this book, but it works just as well in a small back garden, and anyone can do it.

Further enlightenment can be obtained from the Permaculture Association (Britain), an active network of practitioners who organise courses and disseminate information.

The Rare Breeds Survival Trust
National Agricultural Centre
Stoneleigh
Kenilworth
Warwickshire
CV8 2LG
tel: 0203 696551

Modern commercial agriculture only has need of a narrow range of hybrids and cross-breed animals to suit uniform conditions. This has led to the rapid disappearance of many native breeds and twenty have become extinct this century. In 1973 the Rare Breeds Survival Trust was formed to halt this trend, and its work has been very successful. No breeds have disappeared since it started, and the numbers of many have increased sufficiently for them to be taken off the danger list.

Most of the Trust's work has the ultimate aim of keeping a healthy gene pool available for future animal breeders, so that they can improve stock, and breed for certain characteristics as they are needed. This has particular relevance to more humane methods – if organic and conservation farming are ever to be adopted on a widespread scale, the thriftiness and hardiness of many of the native breeds will be essential to their success.

The Trust still has forty breeds on its books and much scientific research to be done, the finance for which has to come from membership. Subscription is from £12 and entitles you to a monthly copy of *The Ark*, the organisation's informative magazine, and various other facilities of particular interest to those who keep animals, whether on a commercial or hobby basis.

The Royal Society for the Prevention of Cruelty to Animals (RSPCA)
The Causeway
Horsham
West Sussex
RH12 1HG
tel: 0403 64181

The RSPCA is the grandparent of the animal welfare organisations and has been campaigning for better conditions for farm animals since 1824. It is totally opposed to intensive farming methods, but does not take what it describes as an extremist view, being in favour of such techniques as tail docking for lambs to protect against fly strike, and de-horning for animals which are kept in yards. The RSPCA campaigns at the highest levels for changes in legislation, and the inspectors also act at a local level, bringing charges in the civil courts against farmers who break the existing laws which govern the keeping of farm animals.

In the autumn of 1989 it launched a campaign to establish a code of practice on humane rearing and slaughter. It is also seeking the help of the supermarket chains to introduce a symbol, possibly a green tick, for the labelling of products which comply with it.

Membership costs £8 and entitles you to a quarterly magazine, voting rights and campaigning information.

The Soil Association
86 Colston Street
Bristol
BS1 5BB
tel: 0272 290661

The Soil Association was founded in 1946 to 'promote a better understanding of the links between organic agriculture, care of the environment, food quality and human health'. Today it is the major membership organisation in the UK promoting the organic ideal. The SA researches organic issues, publishes the findings, provides expert advice to decision makers in government, and supports commercial farmers and growers by working with their organisations, British Organic Farmers, the Organic Growers Association and Elm Farm Research Centre. Recently it launched the Living Earth campaign to provide information and educational material to the public, encouraging the use of consumer power to effect change in food production.

The most well-known aspect of its work is the Symbol Scheme, which was started in 1973. The coveted Soil Association Symbol is awarded to producers of fresh and manufactured food and agricultural and horticultural products which meet the stringent standards, and there are plans to extend the scheme to include retailers. The Symbol defines organic farm management practice, and offers a quality mark which protects the consumer from fraudulent trading and the farmer from unfair competition.

Subscription is £12 minimum, and entitles members to vote on policy issues and to free copies of the quarterly *Living Earth* magazine, which covers all organic topics.

INDEX

Page numbers in *italics* refer to illustrations.

LIST OF RECIPES